**That's why they call it the American Dream,**

**because you have to be asleep to believe it.**

*— George Carlin*

**The American dream does not come**

**to those who fall asleep.**

*— Richard Nixon*

**In the end, the American dream is not a sprint, or even a marathon, but a relay.**

**Our families don't always cross the finish line in the span of one generation.**

**But each generation passes on to the next the fruits of their labor.**

*—Julian Castro*

**For my extended "family,"**
**whoever that may include...**

**...for after all, we come from one...**

**...regardless that today we may seem many.**
**Our origins we share—our fate, too.**

*Tap Roots Betrayed: How Our Dreams Got Derailed in America*
Volume 3 of the Pentalogy *Oceans of Darkness, Oceans of Light: Our Family's Trials and Treasures in the New World*

Volumes 1, 2 and 3 are available as E-books and available on-line via Amazon.com, etc.

author: Michael Luick-Thrams
with Anthony J. Luick and Gary Luick

published on behalf of the TRACES
Center for History and Culture
ISBN-978-0-9857697-8-9

Contents

**Parts I-IIIa, with the first of three conclusions ("from the *persona*: my disrupted granny") are in Volume I: *Roots of Darkness: Our Dreams and Nightmares in America***

**Parts III b and IV, with the second of three conclusions ("about the *populi*: my disappearing people") are in Volume II: *Chasing Restless Roots: The Dreams that Lured Us Across America***

both by the same author; further information at www.roots.TRACES.org

*unidentified Luick-Jenison cousins, early 1900s*

Their parents, grand- or great-grandparents—our common ancestors—came from all over the world to be part of the largest migration, the greatest project of all time till that time: the creation of America.

My family took part in that great migration, that project of unmatched scope and impact. From 1630 onward, we plowed open a Garden of Eden, then crafted fields into a massive breadbasket. So grafted onto New World soil, we grew with the country—shaping it even as it shaped us, to the point that we cannot think of ourselves as anything but "Americans," products of a distant land our ancestors claimed as their own, then transformed per European visions of "civilization." Up to this very moment, we live inseparable from the legacy of all their efforts. The question, however, remains: "Where from here?"

As I dug through my own family's roots, then compiled my findings into a comprehensive account, it occurred to me again and again, ever stronger, that "The country we have now doesn't remotely resemble the vision our ancestors had of the country they wanted to build when they set sail from Europe. Were they here today, would their incredulity and disappointment be so great, so complete, that they'd rub their eyes, scratch their heads and shrug their shoulders, then wander off?" I fear so.

Unlike our mostly long-dead ancestors, we know what's become of the project they began with such high hopes and driving dreams. By calling and by conviction a social historian, I use family (hi-)stories as case studies to understand the stories of nations, a means by which to induce the macro by reducing the micro to its core particles—à la Herr Herbst's *Geschichtswissenschaft*, or "historical science." In such admittedly subjective, agenda-driven work, I often feel ashamed, even incensed by what seems the massive betrayal of our forebears' most passionate longings and intimate motives. Although at present in Germany most of the time in self-imposed exile, I cannot divorce myself from the land in which the people who bestowed me Life invested the best they had, so ardently and for so long. Still, the perfidy of America's once-seemingly-infinite potential, of the lofty promise implied in the "pursuit of happiness" codified in the nation's declaration of sovereignty, leaves me both depressed and indignant at once.

Of course, it's easy to judge—a person, a group, a nation... one's self: It can be fun, albeit toxic and dangerous. While at times pleasurable, even useful, self-righteousness must be closely watched. Like too much salt in soup or gas in a lamp, we *need* the ability to judge, to differentiate; still, too much kills.

Whatever ails America these days, it didn't simply happen or appear overnight: We are talking about long-term, subliminal dynamics long at work. As most humans grow old, they seem to become who they always were, just more so. Similarly, is the essentially broken country we have today not what America *always* was (excessively individualistic, addicted to wealth or at least comfort, and violent) just *more* so?

Something happened to us along the way, after the point of disembarking from that ship and landing at the spots we now inhabit. What was it? To know, we have to do something at once dangerous but necessary, politically incorrect yet morally imperative. We must dissect our national psyche and check our collective hearts, to look closely at the dreams we and our people have pursued since arriving in the New World. Once we have succeeded in dragging deep, cloaked dynamics into the Light of day, we must find the fortitude to name what we have found, then assign it a value. Only at that point, can we stop wasting time dealing with distractions and set about the real business of getting America back on track.

Having—for most our parts, at least—not built but rather inherited this country from others who sojourned here before us, what we pass on to those who follow us will be our legacy: Future generations will assess us and assign us a value based on the content and quality of that legacy. For some, the plea that we "owe" past generations a national healing and a revival offers a motive swaying enough to make changes in their personal lives. For the remainder, a reminder that the world we now create, together, will be the one which our children will inhabit for decades might move them to act.

*Grampa's cousins, Myrle and Leslie Luick, circa 1911*

---

On one hand, in the Germanic province of *Schwaben* in the early 19th century, the Luicks were fed up. Their young men had to serve a disliked, disagreeable king by fighting unwinnable wars instigated by a little, psychopathic French dictator. And, hunger stalked the land as recurring crop failures or diseases weakened their people. Many were rendered impoverished if not indigent, the recipients of raw charity.

Fiery cavalier Heinrich Luick dreamed of leaving tired old Europe behind and taking his wife, Katherine, and their young children to much-touted "*Amerika*." Though the Luick clan lived for ages mostly in or near Esslingen, they petitioned *Bürgermeister* Lang of Aich repeatedly over a few years for permission to leave. By the time Lang granted it, Heinrich's bottled up anger (per family lore) led him to commit a capital offense: Migrating to North America no longer remained an option; it had become a necessity.

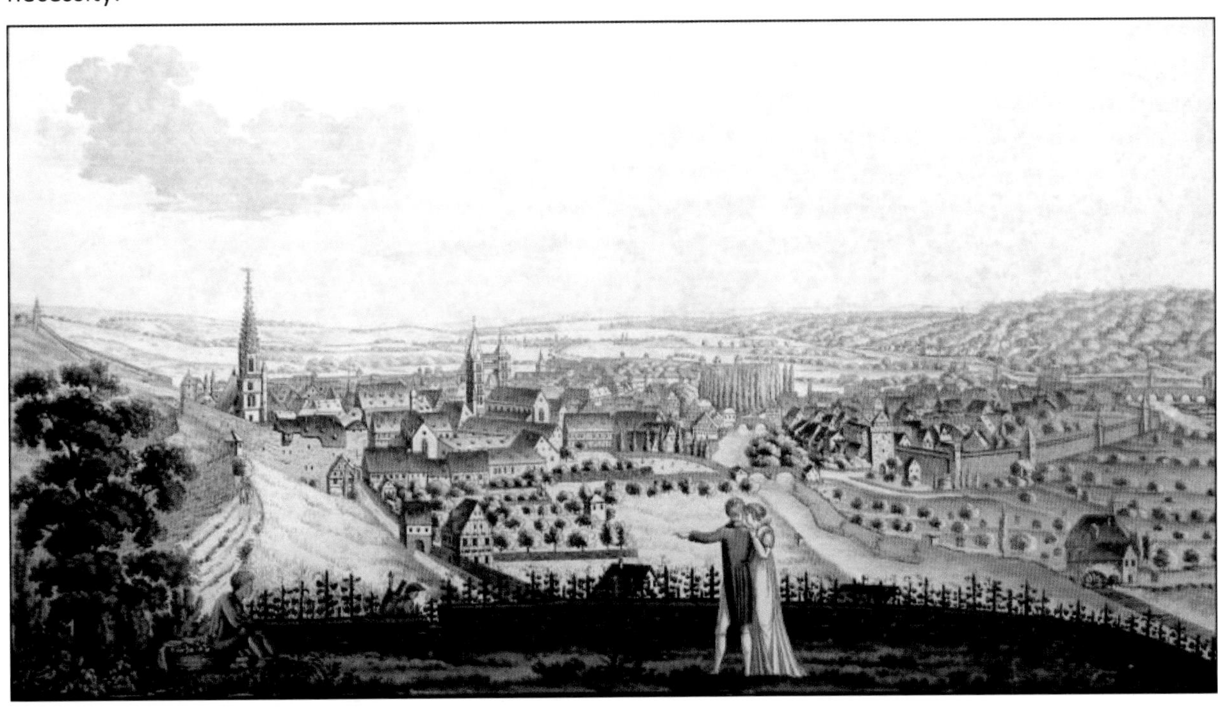

*Esslingen-am-Neckar as seen from the sloping vineyards west of the city, circa 1815*

On the other hand, leaving behind for all time not just family and friends, but everything they had ever known—from their mother tongue to Central Europe's climate, from ancient traditions to laws and norms—did not come easily. In those pre-jet days, the ship's passage to North America constituted a permanent cut with one's native land, indeed with one's very sense of self and sovereignty. (For us moderns, it was akin to boarding a rocket headed for Mars with no thought of ever returning to Earth.)

Still, they went—along with millions of others.

The moment emigrants set foot in the New World, the Old one—for them, at least—ceased to exist. The Luick family—like unending waves of other arriving families—had no choice but to adapt to the country, to the culture that they found here. Once they got settled, they could not be dissuaded from imparting bits of their native culture to their neighbors or at least own children in the adopted country. In Michigan, however, even well sheltered from the most foreign aspects of Anglo-American culture by having bought land in the German-speaking enclave of *Klein Deutschland*—"Little Germany"—near Washtenaw County's Ann Arbor, they could determine their surrounding social landscape only so much.

That changed, however, the moment the Luicks migrated on to Iowa, some twenty years later.

The Buffalo Trail *by German-born American Albert Bierstadt, 1867-68*

When my father's people arrived at Franklin Grove—a stand of stray trees on the banks of the Iowa River—they clung to the purely symbolic safety of some of the few trees then to be found on the open prairie. Otherwise, all they could see in all directions was an ocean of waving prairie grass, with occasional columns of bison or elk crossing the river not far from their cabin's door. This, a world, a cosmos away from the narrow, cobbled streets that lay just outside the Luicks' door back in *Schwaben*.

Given the tabula rasa that was then the frontier in the Upper Midwest, my people and their first neighbors built from scratch the world that was to be, any way they chose to craft it. For that short moment, these former serfs truly lived as masters of their own fates.

Within limits set by the local climate or the evolving availability of building materials, the first settlers of what would become "Belmond, Iowa" were free to form their environment in any of innumerable ways. There was no inevitability in the formula of what America became, only limits of imagination, political will and funding. Still, almost from the start a norm settled upon the fledgling community—and it stuck, till today.

*my grandfather's aunts, Marion (left) and Mattie Luick (right) with unidentified woman, mid-1910s*

It was into that cultural mold that subsequent generations of Luicks, Jenisons and so many others grew up. They took for granted as "normal" the pop-up world their predecessors had hastily erected on the prairie—when, in fact, they were but the second, third or so generation of non-natives to live in the heart of North America. Even I, born in 1962, belong to only the fifth generation of Luicks born in the U.S. My father's father witnessed the cutting of the last prairie hay as a boy, and his grandfather grew up in a log cabin: Yes, we are the successors of the pioneers.

Today, however, it feels as if the pioneering spirit in America has faded to the status of quaint antiquity, its once robust energies dulled by stultifying wall-to-wall comfort and material over-abundance. We, the inheritors of the New Canaan our families established in the New World, grope our way forward, unsure in which direction or why. If this trajectory continues, where will it lead the nation our people worked so hard to forge? What kind of country will our children inherit? What will become of our defining legacies?

Somehow, I expect more. In my gut, I sense we were meant to be more, to do more—to do better.

---

We had met them over lunch. On a roof in Fès, in the heart of arid northern Morocco. On New Year's Eve, 2013. Now, five months later, Christian and I had a date to meet Andreas and Paola for dinner. In her sprawling, warren-like flat in Rome. On the evening of Ascension Day, at the end of May.

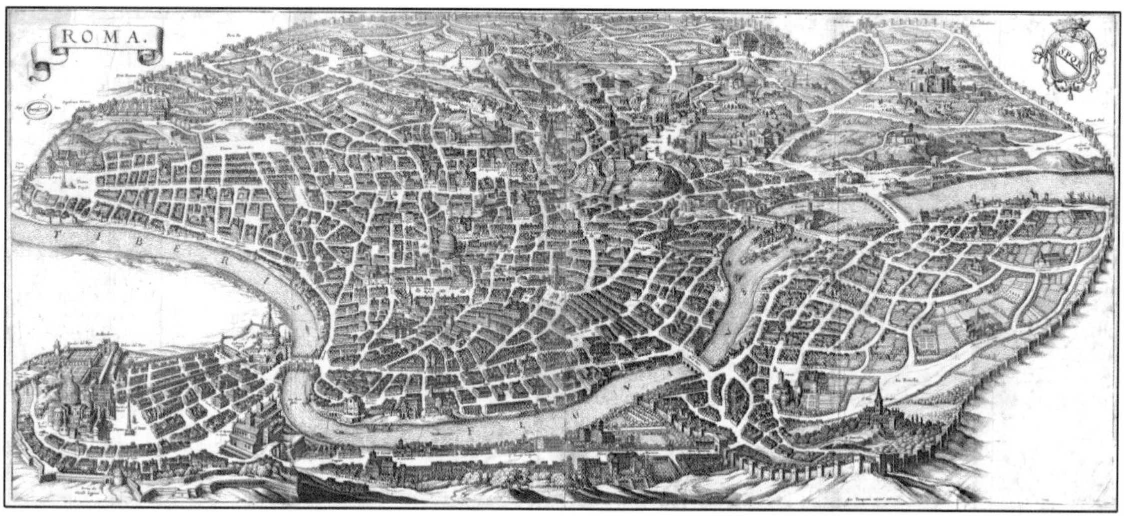


*per source, "Panoramic view or map of Rome, Italy—Geographicus Roma-merian, 1642"*

Andreas had flown into town earlier that afternoon from his life in Nürnberg, where he works for a respected German institute focused on molecular medicine and genetics. Having been partnered with Paola for sixteen years, she has spent stints living with him in San Francisco or, as she calls it, "Nurembergo." He visits his blonde, shapely bombshell a couple times a month; once a year the two take shared vacations of some twenty days—like the one to Morocco, where we met them by chance, dining in the dusty medina, looking out over that ageless, romantic "royal city" in the Maghreb.

Our intense talk started within moments of entering beautiful Paola's chic apartment, appointed as it is with souvenirs of their travels to exotic places, a built-in wall of books in the open-ended living room that flanks the IKEA kitchen, and soft lighting that casts a cozy feeling the second one enters the genetic researcher's private retreat. It began, by raw coincidence, with European-Union politics.

"You Germanas" Paola accused me, as she poured a glass of crisp white wine, "don'ta understanda, that we Southerners, we in Greesa, in Spania anda Italia, we ara diff'renta." Extending me the chilled glass, she added "We can'ta be expected toa be so organizeda, so focuseda likea youa. We ara mora chaotica; we liva mora in the momenta."

"But dear Paola" I rejoined, "I'm *not* a German, so—"

"Buta you thinka likea wona" she interrupted, at which point I recoiled, smiling even as I whispered a soft "*Touché*!"

More measured Andreas jumped in: While Christian and lovely Paola drifted into harmless chat about the delicious, self-baked corn chips smothered in garlic-laced olive oil, topped with halved cherry tomatoes bursting with tangy juice, he and I swapped ideas about cultural influences and genetic adaptation.

"You know" he started, "I lived over eight years in the States—first in Miami, then in the Bay Area, researching molecular medicine. While I lived in your country, I increasingly had the impression that those who went to America and those who remained in Europe were, loosely seen, of two sorts of differing genetic disposition."

"Really?" I baited. "How's that, Andreas?" Not missing a beat, I hinted "Got any more chips?"

"You who became 'Americans' were the restless ones" he offered as he absently handed me another tray of chips, "the ones eager to test and to try and if it didn't work out, not to swim in 'failure' but to get up and to try again, from a different angle."

*Did Belmond's Martin Thoe capture America's soul in miniature?*

"Interesting" I interjected, piling up another plate of those thin, long, oil-basted chips. "It could be—I mean, we Americans certainly like to think we're something special."

"But you *are*" Andreas retorted, "and that's what so fascinated me. I saw in Americans what neuroscientist James Fallon calls the 'warrior gene,' brain characteristics that he, himself, accidentally discovered he has, too. He says they are neurological and genetic correlates of psychopathy, which lead a person to be restless and aggressive, to fight for what they want or think is right. We complacent Europeans—we don't have that acculturated response nearly as much as you who turned your backs on the Old World and set off to build a new one."

"Well, it is true: Ol' Heinrich Luick did sortta check outta Stuttgart awfully quick, then fled to *'Amerika'* after thrashing a cheeky royal. And, most Luick men I know of have been mad bobcats ever since." I shoved a few chips into my open hopper and chewed a bit on the images flying round the room.

"And, you?" Andreas challenged.

"Yeah—and me? *Hum-m-m*, I guess my CV's embodied that of an eternal, ever-ready fighter—but why do you think that is?" I pushed back, feeling both bemused and butter-soft from the white wine.

"In Germany at least, there were two dominant influences—"

"One's gotta be the Thirty Years War, 1618 to 1648" I supposed to Andreas out loud, curtly.

*"The miseries of war; No. 11, 'The Hanging,'" by Jacque Callot, 1632, during the height of the Thirty Years War*

"Why, yes" Andreas smiled, marveling that I wasn't as poorly educated as most Europeans assume most Americans to be, "that's right." Smiling with amazement and slightly nodding his head, he noted "While the borders and allegiances of those more than two hundred Germanic principalities kept rolling back and forth for a couple generations—flipping between Catholics and Lutherans, with endless waves of marauding Danes, Swedes, French, Austrians and others washing across the country—they finally calcified into either Catholic or Protestant regions. Over such a protracted, recurring threat to our collective survival, we Germans learned to adapt to the powers that were, to fit our environment—or be wiped out. At the same time" he continued, after pausing a moment to munch on delicious Paola-baked crunch, "we needed each other to survive—and to survive, we had to carry the weakest with us, to pick them up enough to be able to keep pace, even as we pulled the strongest back a bit, so as to not lose the slower ones. You see this" Andreas asserted, pounding a fist gently several times into a cupped palm, "in the subsequent rise of labor unions and, later, in programs to assure the welfare of all—say, with child and medical care, free universal education, employment protection, old-age pensions and the like. The safety net that emerged is without compare in almost the entire world—and survives today"

"All of this truly is very interesting" I goaded, "but you cited three factors in forming the German—well, if one will, the central European—mind and character: What might the second be?"

"*Neid*" Andreas replied in German, "nothing less than base and naked envy."

"*Ah-h-h*" I stalled, "you got that right—but from where do you think this close and resentful score-keeping between neighbors, even friends or family members comes? It's not really 'American.'"

"We're a tightly-settled land" Andreas explained, "squeezed in between neighbors who have not always indulged us our hard-working ways or the wealth it creates. We always have been land-locked on Europe's tight, central stage, with few natural resources other than that between our ears. Sure, in raw numbers, early on—I'm talking about pre- and early-history—our population density was nothing compared to today, but in those pre-industrial days, it took more space to raise more food and the sources, the supply of consumable goods was much smaller, much harder to generate than now."

"Well, this is all grippingly fascinating, but subjective" I noted. "Still, what's the third factor?"

As we four—having nibbled our way right through the crackling appetizer and already sipped dry two bottles of wine—rose in unison and shifted our conversations to the table, Andreas continued "Oh, that's easy—our stupid habit of pushing out those who don't conform to our conformist culture."

"Oh, you mean like the 'Forty-eighters,' the men who advanced the first democratic German revolution, then fled when it failed, stamped out by a frightened elite?"

"Exactly!" Andreas confirmed, again visibly impressed.

"You know" I pointed out, "many of them regrouped in the Midwest—men like Carl Schurz, who built a new life and political career in Wisconsin. There, he turned to anti-slavery and took up the Republican cause, early on in that party's

*Carl Schurz, after arriving in* "Amerika;" *1850s*

long, ideologically-lopsided career." Andreas nodded intently, obviously interested in the poster-boy biography of a German-American role model. "He became a reform-minded journalist—"

"Is that so?" Andreas interjected.

"—*ja*, and later a weighty U.S. senator for Missouri: the first German-born in American history."

"That sounds like a true Forty-eighter, all right" Andreas affirmed, handing me a small plate of pesto-dressed pasta.

"It'sa bita al dente" Paola warned us as she tucked a blond lock behind her tanned ear.

"Just as I like it" I beamed back, then turned to Andreas and resumed with "Schurz' wife, Margarethe, and her sister, also in self-imposed exile, began the first *Kindergarten* in America in 1856—in German. And, look at our entire educational system—patterned after the Germanic, not British one."

Carl and Margarethe (Meyer) Schurz, 1852

"Well, the Schurzcs are only well-known, historical cases with high profiles, but we did this so many, many times, with less famous folks—the most fatal for Germany being the expulsion of—"

"—the Jews by the Nazis" I again completed Andreas' sentence, though he seemed not to mind.

"Indeed—our most creative minds" he concurred, tapping the glass table with a determined finger. "Throughout German history, the freest thinkers, those with the newest ideas—so talented and so vital—either fled or were extinguished. This" he shook his head listlessly, "we have done again and again—" his voice trailed off, before he blurted out "—but, we Germans, we always nurse our need for stability! On one hand, it's understandable, given the unstable position we've occupied for two thousand years in the middle of a diverse continent—but that closely-guarded stability can suffocate, too."

"And now?" I pressed.

"And now" Andreas sighed, "I fear it's too late. Today mediocrity is more and more the norm in Germany, as the best minds drift elsewhere: scientists, film makers, composers, writers..."

I didn't know with any certainty where "the best minds" were these days, but before I could speculate about possible answers, Paola broke into our very-male mental masturbation session with a loud "Anda nowa"—she smiled at us even as she cast a one-eyed blink towards Christian—"nowa we gotta eata." Andreas and I self-consciously tittered as, with gusto, his multi-talented partner served thinly-cut, finely-seasoned roasted meat, then graced new, bigger plates with baked stuffed zucchinis and roasted red peppers. "You Germans ara so seriouso" Paola teased as she returned to her seat. "You gotta enjoya lifa a bita mora!"

"Northern Europeans didn't have it as good as you people down here along the Mediterranean" I noted lightly, "where ripe olives and figs fell onto your plates as you sat outside most of the year, savoring wine and sunshine. In the North, winters were long and cold, the growing season short and too cool for good crops: People had to scurry to harvest as much as they could, as long as they could, for the coming fallow season. They had to work—and to work *hard*. It was 'focus and produce—or die.'"

"I understanda thata" Paola answered, "but things hava changeda: Humans don't havta worka so harda as in the olda daysa. We have machinesa that can worka, despita the climatico."

"Paola" Andreas only half-seriously scolded, "you know as well as the rest of us that human adaptation takes generations to evolve and the resultant behavior lasts for generations, even after the original stimuli have subsided—or even disappeared."

"Yes and no" I countered, handing Christian a second helping of zucchini and peppers. "We also can change quickly, provided we consciously recognize a beneficial motive for doing so. Look at colonial New England" I offered between bites, even as a pinch of parsley clung to the corner of my busy mouth, "where individualistic English settlers arrived but initially starved among the rocks and icy winters. To survive, they formed a religious-based, communal-focused culture that endured for centuries."

*a 19th-century vision of an early Thanksgiving fest, with Native-Americans already on the sideline*

"A 'leveling' one, arising as the Puritans did out of the English reformation" Andreas stopped me long enough to remind me, "in the same era of theological tumult as your Quakers arose—"

Uneasy with his alluding to Quakers in the same breath as Puritans I broke in with "Wait a second, here! The Quakers were 'too radical' for the fundamentally conservative Calvinists—who hung the 'blasphemers' on Boston Common because they wouldn't obey bans on private bible-study and said the spirit speaks directly through people, making clergy basically irrelevant. The Puritans feared us."

"The Puritans who set up shop in New England" Andreas editorialized further, "were rigid religious zealots, who kept stiff, state churches: Massachusetts only disestablished its as late as 1833."

"That's true" I conceded, then barreled on, explaining "but their English compatriots, coming out of the same cultural origins, only a bit later, arrived in the South where flatter, more easily cultivated land and a warmer climate let them maintain the hierarchical, elite-run society they had known back in Britain. Under different conditions, they didn't foster a communal culture but rather a diffused one, based on brutalized forced labor, with little chance of social mobility. And those two opposing streams in American history" I pounded on the table as I drove my point home, "have been competing ever since."

"Vayt a moment, Honey" Christian abruptly protested, clearly perplexed, "you alvays tell of eight millions of Germans...

"Yes, I *speak* of eight millio**n**" I corrected my sweet, East-German-born boyfriend, mid-sentence.

"Ya, you alvays *speak* of eight millions of Germans who migrated to America."

*German immigrants arriving at New York City's early processing center, Castle Garden; 1866*

*"Um-hum."*

"Vell, if Andreas has right, dat da Germans had more group feelink, so could not feel so vell in a place like da South, an' da Pertans—"

"The P**ur**-**i**-tans" I censored Christian quietly.

"—da Peritans vouldn't vant millions of German Luterans oder Catolicks in Neu England, dann..."

"Bunny, that's why—while there were, of course, individual German **im**migrants who found a future in the South—the vast majority settled in the Mid-Atlantic colonies or later the Midwest, which was culturally and politically an extension of, say, Pennsylvania and Upstate New York."

"Oh, I see" easily-placed Christian nodded demurely.

"That's also why all of the truly 'German' American cities were in the Midwest: Milwaukee, Cincinnati, Cleveland, Saint Paul, Saint Louis—even Iowa's little Davenport-Bettendorf, and the like."

As Paola cleared the third-course plates, Andreas ventured "My guess is, the Germans felt drawn to areas most climatically, geographically as well as politically familiar, or at least agreeable, to them."

"That's right" I confirmed, "and as a bloc, they remained adamantly anti-slavery, politically."

"Theya were?" Paola questioned as she placed a fifth course of crisp salad in front of each of us.

"Yes—partly because although they had nobility in almost each of the couple hundred tiny Germanic states, and those local nobles could act arbitrarily, even cruelly. So, tightly-bonded Germanic culture lacked the entrenched class divisions and resulting resentments of, say, the more individualistic and pluralistic English or French: The Germans had to band together in ways unlike other Europeans."

*mid-19th-century Daguerreotype of older New Orleans woman with a young enslaved servant*

"Really?" Paola said under her breath, as if the thought of fair-minded Germans seemed to her a contradiction in terms.

"Yes" Andreas piped in, "despite being conformist, the Germanic mind has long functioned along a certain base fairness and, ultimately, equalitarianism. Sure, both the Nazis and their nemesis, the Communists, misused that drive for social cohesion, but it runs deep, till today."

"Since venn?" Christian complained.

Holding a fork full of stabbed lettuce mid-air in front of his mouth, Andreas asked the rest of us rhetorically "Why did the absolute monarch, Friedrich the Great of Prussia, allow that miller next door to his palatial retreat of Sanssouci to keep the commoner's noisy mill, even though it kept the king awake?"

"Because da man—he reminded da king dat only da High Court in Berlin vas able" Christian stammered as he tried to correctly recall the alluded-to German-history lesson from his long-forgotten school days, "was able to take avay his mill?" Andreas nodded approvingly and, proud of his feat, Christian beamed "Dat vas to say, even da king had to obey da rules."

Setting down his wine glass for a moment, Andreas argued that "This drive to always strengthen 'the community,' to reinforce group cohesion and well-being—even if that meant tolerating the deadly excesses of the Third Reich or the so-called 'German Democratic Republic' the Soviet puppets installed in the east after the war—had its price. Such a solid social contract means 'til today that while even the least able, the most challenged have to be brought along with the rest of the society, the most able, the most motivated are held back. Excellence is met with stifling envy, which discourages innovation or being exceptional—all in the name of equality. 'Whatever you do, don't stick out' we were always told, growing up. 'Don't draw attention to yourself.' Sure" Andreas shrugged, "there's more equality in that, but that also breeds a lot of mediocrity. We are 'safe' from real harm, but where's the nudge to soar?"

*East and West Germans atop the Berlin wall, November 1989*

"It's true, Paola, that with few exceptions" I noted between bites, "the German immigrants were resolute in their opposition to slavery—and many also felt uneasy with the slaughter or wholesale removal of Native Americans—because targeted discrimination offended the German sense of fairness."

"*Hum-m-m*" she hummed behind the squirting cherry tomato she'd just popped into her mouth.

Seeing that our hostess wasn't sold on the image that her Teutonic neighbors to the north could be so "nice," I explained as credibly as I could that "It was the pro-abolitionist votes of newly naturalized German immigrants that helped put that unlikely, unknown candidate from the frontier, gangly and homely Abe Lincoln, into the White House—and you probably know the rest, about how the Civil War—"

"But Lincoln wasa Republicano, no?" she asked, swallowing hard.

"If you can imagine it or not" Andreas played the conflicting images further, "at that time Republicans advocated the end of human bondage and so-called Democrats defended slavery."

Seeing Paola's and Christian's deep disbelief barely budging, I nodded affirmatively.

"Oh, how times *do* change" Andreas quipped, as he instigated collecting the empty salad dishes.

Charging once more before I lost my still-attentive audience, I added "At that time, recently-arrived Germans joined the newly-founded Republican Party in droves, in hopes of ending slavery and somehow holding together the country they now adopted as their own." I paused to admire the chilled-glass tiramisu cups Paola was busy distributing around the table, accompanied by shiny spoons, before noting that "Grateful for campaigning on his behalf, Lincoln appointed our *guter Freund* Carl Schurz minister to Spain—but when he returned a year later, Lincoln made Schurz Brigadier General. Thousands of German-immigrant men fought for the Union—and many of them, of course, died for it, too."

*Carl Schurz posing with a Ute delegation; original caption reads "In 1880, Chief Ouray and other Utes traveled to Washington, D.C. to negotiate a treaty that would result in the removal of the White River and Tabeguache Utes from Colorado to the Uintah Basin in present day Utah. Chief Ouray died at age 47 shortly after this trip. Seated from left to right: Chief Ignacio of the Southern Utes, Carl Schurz, Secretary of the Interior, Chief Ouray and his wife, Chipeta. Standing are Woretsiz and General Charles Adams." Original caption of right photo reads "Spring festival at Carl Schurz Park between East End Avenue and the East River Manhattan's Upper East Side," taken June 1973.*

"Dey did?" Christian asked, astonished at newcomers paying the ultimate sacrifice for a country not their native one.

"Indeed."

"Vy did dey do dat?" he wondered out loud.

"If it helps, think of it this way: It was one of the most visible 'new Americans' of the time, our Carl Schurz again, who coined the usually misquoted admonition 'My country, right or wrong'—which he then went to say 'if right, to be kept right; and if wrong, to be set right.' What he meant was—"

"Stoppa! Michaeli, youra tiramisu is gettinga colda" Paola joked as the others laughed with her. "But tella me wona thinga" she asked: "How dida youra people geta from Germania to Iowa?"

"Oh, that" I smiled, "is a *long* story." Saying nothing more, I could feel all their eyes on me. Caving in, I asked "Where to start?" As I slid half a spoonful of her homemade tiramisu into my already salivating oral abyss, I paused to savor a perfect moment. Noticing that my friends were still awaiting an answer, I began to recount the saga of my German-American family, at home in the heart of America.

---

PART V
Runaways and Pioneers

## Section 9:
## Heinrich (Sr.) & Katherine (Gerstenmaier) Luick

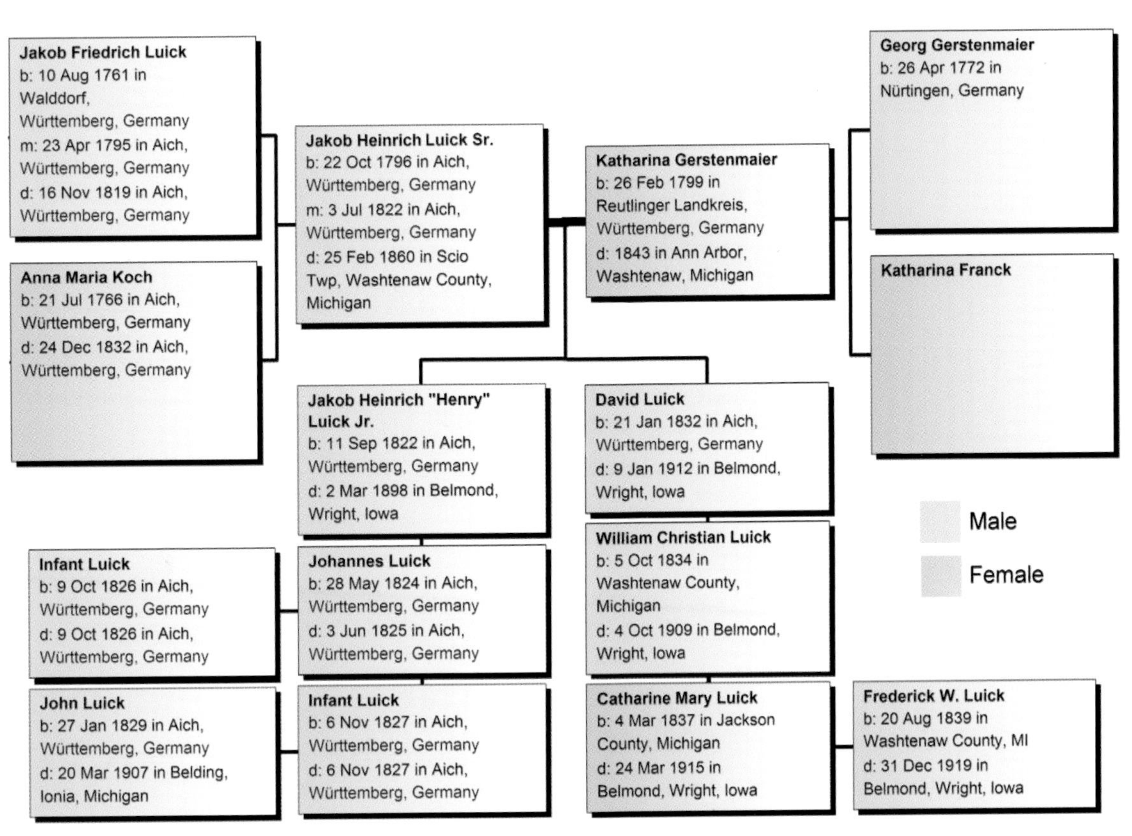
Jakob Friedrich Luick
b: 10 Aug 1761 in Walddorf, Württemberg, Germany
m: 23 Apr 1795 in Aich, Württemberg, Germany
d: 16 Nov 1819 in Aich, Württemberg, Germany
Anna Maria Koch
b: 21 Jul 1766 in Aich, Württemberg, Germany
d: 24 Dec 1832 in Aich, Württemberg, Germany
Jakob Heinrich Luick Sr.
b: 22 Oct 1796 in Aich, Württemberg, Germany
m: 3 Jul 1822 in Aich, Württemberg, Germany
d: 25 Feb 1860 in Scio Twp, Washtenaw County, Michigan
Katharina Gerstenmaier
b: 26 Feb 1799 in Reutlinger Landkreis, Württemberg, Germany
d: 1843 in Ann Arbor, Washtenaw, Michigan
Georg Gerstenmaier
b: 26 Apr 1772 in Nürtingen, Germany
Katharina Franck
Jakob Heinrich "Henry" Luick Jr.
b: 11 Sep 1822 in Aich, Württemberg, Germany
d: 2 Mar 1898 in Belmond, Wright, Iowa
David Luick
b: 21 Jan 1832 in Aich, Württemberg, Germany
d: 9 Jan 1912 in Belmond, Wright, Iowa
Male
Female
Infant Luick
b: 9 Oct 1826 in Aich, Württemberg, Germany
d: 9 Oct 1826 in Aich, Württemberg, Germany
Johannes Luick
b: 28 May 1824 in Aich, Württemberg, Germany
d: 3 Jun 1825 in Aich, Württemberg, Germany
William Christian Luick
b: 5 Oct 1834 in Washtenaw County, Michigan
d: 4 Oct 1909 in Belmond, Wright, Iowa
John Luick
b: 27 Jan 1829 in Aich, Württemberg, Germany
d: 20 Mar 1907 in Belding, Ionia, Michigan
Infant Luick
b: 6 Nov 1827 in Aich, Württemberg, Germany
d: 6 Nov 1827 in Aich, Württemberg, Germany
Catharine Mary Luick
b: 4 Mar 1837 in Jackson County, Michigan
d: 24 Mar 1915 in Belmond, Wright, Iowa
Frederick W. Luick
b: 20 Aug 1839 in Washtenaw County, MI
d: 31 Dec 1919 in Belmond, Wright, Iowa

and

## Henry (Jr.) & Melissa (Overacker) Luick families

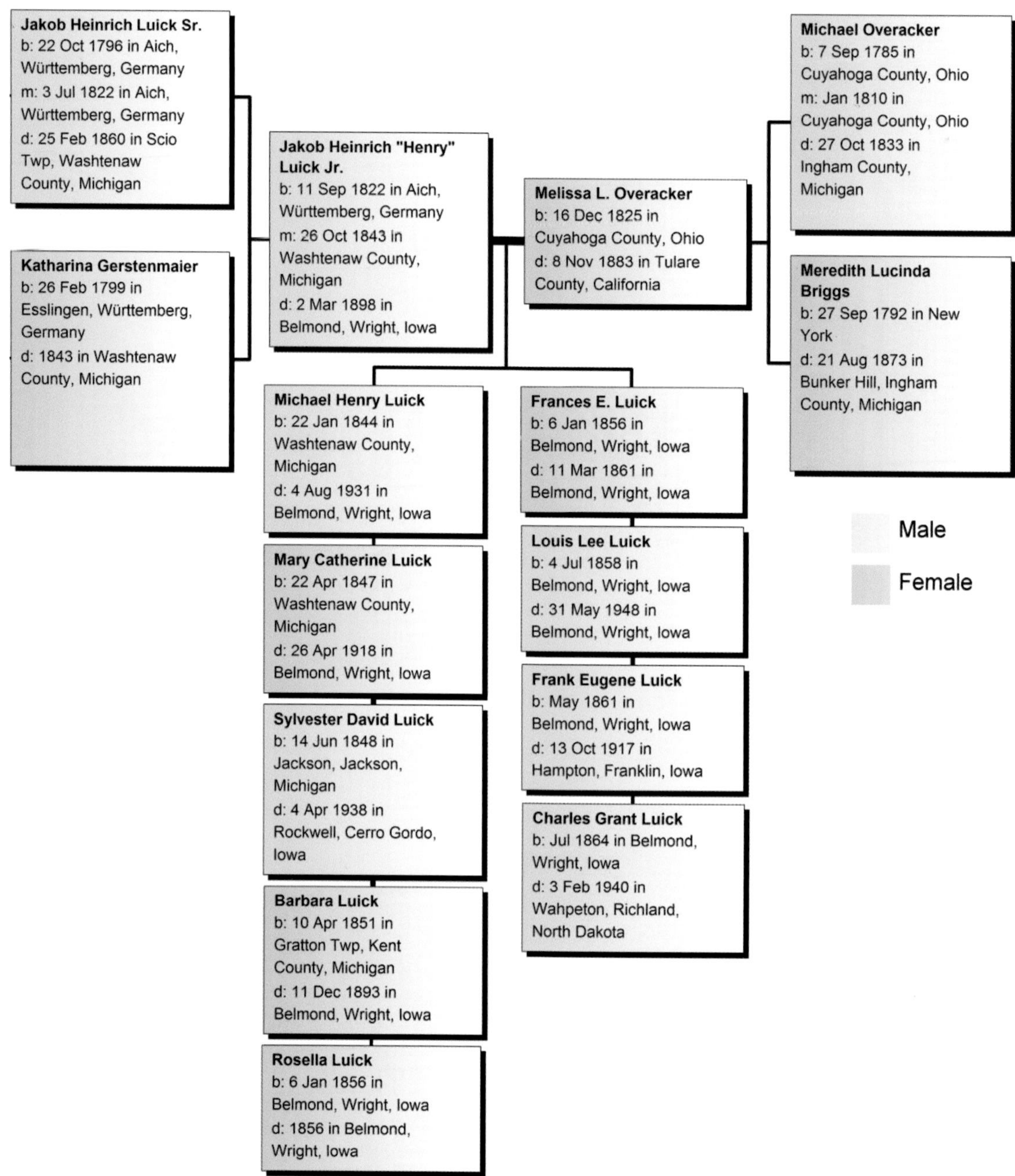

Jakob Heinrich Luick Sr.
b: 22 Oct 1796 in Aich, Württemberg, Germany
m: 3 Jul 1822 in Aich, Württemberg, Germany
d: 25 Feb 1860 in Scio Twp, Washtenaw County, Michigan
Katharina Gerstenmaier
b: 26 Feb 1799 in Esslingen, Württemberg, Germany
d: 1843 in Washtenaw County, Michigan
Jakob Heinrich "Henry" Luick Jr.
b: 11 Sep 1822 in Aich, Württemberg, Germany
m: 26 Oct 1843 in Washtenaw County, Michigan
d: 2 Mar 1898 in Belmond, Wright, Iowa
Melissa L. Overacker
b: 16 Dec 1825 in Cuyahoga County, Ohio
d: 8 Nov 1883 in Tulare County, California
Michael Overacker
b: 7 Sep 1785 in Cuyahoga County, Ohio
m: Jan 1810 in Cuyahoga County, Ohio
d: 27 Oct 1833 in Ingham County, Michigan
Meredith Lucinda Briggs
b: 27 Sep 1792 in New York
d: 21 Aug 1873 in Bunker Hill, Ingham County, Michigan
Michael Henry Luick
b: 22 Jan 1844 in Washtenaw County, Michigan
d: 4 Aug 1931 in Belmond, Wright, Iowa
Mary Catherine Luick
b: 22 Apr 1847 in Washtenaw County, Michigan
d: 26 Apr 1918 in Belmond, Wright, Iowa
Sylvester David Luick
b: 14 Jun 1848 in Jackson, Jackson, Michigan
d: 4 Apr 1938 in Rockwell, Cerro Gordo, Iowa
Barbara Luick
b: 10 Apr 1851 in Gratton Twp, Kent County, Michigan
d: 11 Dec 1893 in Belmond, Wright, Iowa
Rosella Luick
b: 6 Jan 1856 in Belmond, Wright, Iowa
d: 1856 in Belmond, Wright, Iowa
Frances E. Luick
b: 6 Jan 1856 in Belmond, Wright, Iowa
d: 11 Mar 1861 in Belmond, Wright, Iowa
Louis Lee Luick
b: 4 Jul 1858 in Belmond, Wright, Iowa
d: 31 May 1948 in Belmond, Wright, Iowa
Frank Eugene Luick
b: May 1861 in Belmond, Wright, Iowa
d: 13 Oct 1917 in Hampton, Franklin, Iowa
Charles Grant Luick
b: Jul 1864 in Belmond, Wright, Iowa
d: 3 Feb 1940 in Wahpeton, Richland, North Dakota
Male
Female

## Heinrich (Sr.) and Katherine (Gerstenmaier) Luick

| | | |
|---|---|---|
| **born:** | 22 October 1796 | 26 February 1799 |
| **where:** | Aich, Württemberg/Germany | Reutlingen, Württemberg/Germany |
| **married:** | 3 July 1822 | **where:** Aich, Württemberg/Germany |
| **died:** | 25 February 1860 | 1843 |
| **where:** | Scio Township, Washtenaw Co., Michigan/USA | Ann Arbor, Michigan/USA |

## Henry (Jr.) and Melissa (Overacker) Luick

| | | |
|---|---|---|
| **born:** | 11 September 1822 | 16 December 1825 |
| **where:** | Esslingen, Württemberg/Germany | Cuyahoga County, Ohio/USA |
| **married:** | 26 October 1843 | **where:** Washtenaw County, Michigan/USA |
| **died:** | 2 March 1898 | 8 November 1883 |
| **where:** | Belmond, Iowa/USA | Plano, California/USA |

"Am I sick—or even crazy?" I wonder. When I look at this photo of Henry Jacob Luick, I see my father! I dislike that, but I do. I'm jus' lev'lin' with ya here, folks.

Worse, I see something of "that Luick man" that I swear I can spot in the whole damn lineup—my dad's dad, Donald, and his dad, George... yeah, right up to today, to my big brother and my ain't-untainted small Self.

*Jacob Henry Luick, circa 1880—with showy gold chain*

"Is it curable?" I ask myself, meaning both the "mad bobcat" nerve that Henry's later-estranged wife Melissa saw in her erstwhile husband, as well as my nagging, constantly nibbling fears that *this* Luick man does not stack up—that as a gay man, I'm not a "real" Luick male. The doubt disables me.

Were it not for Luick men having always loomed so larger-than-life over me, every day that I've been on the planet, I wouldn't care so much. On one hand, those I most immediately followed left big shoes to fill. On the other, I've been through too much therapy to try to deny that I don't carry the "warrior gene" that both James Fallon and my genetics-researcher friend Andreas tout. I both resent and revere the double-headed monster I carry inside me.

More than any previous chapter, I find wading into this one most daunting. It hits so close to home; it's so intimate yet so elusive, so convoluted and nuanced, so full of moral as well as factual ambiguities and contradictions. Even more than this book's opening chapter, which focused on what it was like, for me, to grow up in my father's house (oh, yeah: Mom was there, too—no?), this one takes on that messy Luick Male Gene—an epic drama that cuts to the core of not only how my family got to be the way it is, but how **I** got to be at all. My Luick Family Story speaks of primal wounds; it starts with a capital crime that set the stage for a saga of aggression and subsequent flight from rage's poisonous fruits, and casts a shadow until today.

Almost everything about the Luicks' odyssey from Swabia to Iowa is "different" from those of the other mortals whose stories this pentalogy retells. This chapter, for one, is really two fused into one, for it is the tale of *two* "Jacob Heinrich Luicks." The fates of both the father (referred to here by the Germanic name to which he was born and later was carved onto his Michigan gravestone) and his oldest son (called here "Henry," as the Junior Luick would have referred to himself for all but about ten of his seventy-six years on the planet) cannot be understood without knowing the other.

SUICIDE.—J. Henry Luick, residing at Scio, one of the old German settlers of this county, committed suicide last Saturday morning by shooting himself with a shot-gun. An inquest was held by Wm. F. Roth, Esq., and a post mortem examination made by Dr. Boxheimer. The verdict of the jury was, that he committed the rash act under a temporary derangement of mind, and when we consider the character of the man and his respectability, we certainly cannot come to any other conclusion ourselves.—*Ann Arbor Local News*, *Feb. 28.*

*A Scio Township, Michigan, gravestone translated from the German, reads: "Here rests Jacob Heinrich Luick, born [on] 22 October 1796, died 25 February 1860;" the lower inscription is illegible. That of his second wife, Dorothea "Dolly" (Herrmann) Schiff, is in German, too. She returned to Michigan after living with her step son's family in Iowa immediately after Heinrich's death—cited in the 1860 mortality schedule as "shot himself—accidental." On 28 February 1860 a* Detroit Free Press *article betrayed the "accidental" nature of the gun shot that killed Heinrich. It read: "SUICIDE—J. Henry Luick, residing at Scio, one of the old German settlers of this county, committed suicide last Saturday morning by shooting himself with a shot-gun. An inquest was held by Wm. F. Roth, Esq., and a post mortem examination made by Dr. Boxheimer. The verdict of the jury was, that he committed the rash act under a temporary derangement of the mind, and when we consider the character of the man and his respectability, we certainly cannot come to any other conclusion ourselves.—*Ann Arbor Local News, *Feb. 28." He was 63 at the time.*

What also strikes attentive readers is that the two men's respective wives seem to have been the last who left enduring signs of having been personages in their own right. Heinrich's wife Katherine, for one, came, reportedly, from nobility. Said to be well-educated in an era when women weren't, her direct descendants accredited her with instilling in them an appreciation for knowledge, refined penmanship, even theology. Heinrich's later daughter-in-law, Henry's self-reliant wife Melissa, grew up swinging as she repeatedly carved out corners of her own in a family of fifteen children—eleven of whom were males who reached at least teenagehood, if not old age—and was descended from generations of warriors dating back through the American Revolution to Nieuw Amsterdam. After Henry... well, you'll see... she didn't miss a beat before picking up her youngest children and returning to Ann Arbor to seek familial comforting and counsel, despite the rigor involved in riding from the Iowa frontier to Southeast Michigan soon after the end of a devastating civil war, accompanied by several young children.

*five generations of amorous Luick men's women: Henry's wives Melissa (Overacker) & Lydia (Lathrop Johnson); Louis' wife Mary (Hunt); George's wives Lorena (Jenison) & Olga (Hansen Christensen); Donald's wife Charlotte (Juhl) & long-term lover, Lynann (Maloy; forename altered upon family's request); Bud's wife, Phyllis (Thrams)*

The other women who subsequent generations of Luick men chose as wives (or long-term lovers) in the New World left few worldly-recognized signs of leadership or other distinction.

- Lydia, the lady-in-black with whom Henry replaced shoulder-to-the-wheel Melissa, seemed content to lounge in the moneyed shadow of the landed inheritor she hitched her wagon to, finely dressed and pearled, but leaving no lasting mark on the world that Tony, Gary or I could find in our extensive research.
- Louis, for example—although said by his grandson, Gary, to be "a ladies man and because of this he didn't receive any of his father's land"—eventually took as his wife docile Mary Louisa Hunt, repeatedly praised for her devotion, but sans mention of her longsuffering her amateur-musician husband's endless absences.
- While the Jacobsen grandchildren described Lorena Ethel Jenison as being "very English—very proper and proud: everything had to be in order, to be correct and just right," she seemed unable to either read the relationship winds that blew her husband of forty years out the door one day, when George simply did not come home from buying groceries, or ever fully recover from that incontestably wicked blow.
- Her daughter-in-law, Charlotte Adelia Juhl, seemed to this grandson to be exceptionally intelligent and entertaining, yet expressly unable to free herself from a philandering, undemonstrative mate.
- Although Donald didn't officially replace Charlotte with his teenage lover, Lynann, he financially supported her—and the baby girl the two created—six years after they met. A perverse, cruel twist of fate, afterwards Lynann took Charlotte's cousin, Worth Juhl, as her protector-partner, making Donald Luick's child a "Juhl."
- And, my own dear mother? As long as I've known her—over half a century now—she's proven to be completely sweet and loving, but consistently timid. Like her mother-, great- and grand-mothers-in-law, she seemed only too happy to let the man of the household constantly call the tune. Such a strategy was typical of power "sharing" for pre-Lib women, but some of us children barely survived dancing to the music made by our heavy-handed, veto-yielding fathers.

Untangling the truth, sorting out facts from the legends behind a pioneer family becomes even more complicated by the nostalgic revisionism typical of the Belmond branch of the Luick clan. Documents suggest that our self-fascination started already in the middle of the 19$^{th}$ century, but I can testify that it survived at least until that fast ride in the Pontiac almost forty years ago, returning to The Lake from that memorable cemetery visit one Memorial Day with my gawking brother, David, and our folks.

As all historians know too well, first-person accounts of an event add a color and emotionality that "dry" third-person ones simply can't, *but* the accuracy of or any shred of objectivity in the recollections of witnesses at times stumbles. A weak ego might embellish in order to puff out one's own lagging sense of self. The reminiscences of the majorly emotionally wounded might become ridiculous exercises of "past-recasting" by individuals wanting to convince either themselves, their audience or both that their families were better than actually experienced and less deranged than secretly feared.

This account of The Luick Family, then, consists primarily of two extremely differing, at times conflicting perspectives. One comes from Heinrich and Katherine's grateful grandson, Albert Lee Luick—my great-great-grandfather Louis' cousin and an early family chronicler who clearly focused on how well "the Luicks" did. The other arises from the journey of a once-broken son of a wounded, wounding Iowa-farmer father, who one day set off into the wider world, seeking a straight answer to a simple question.

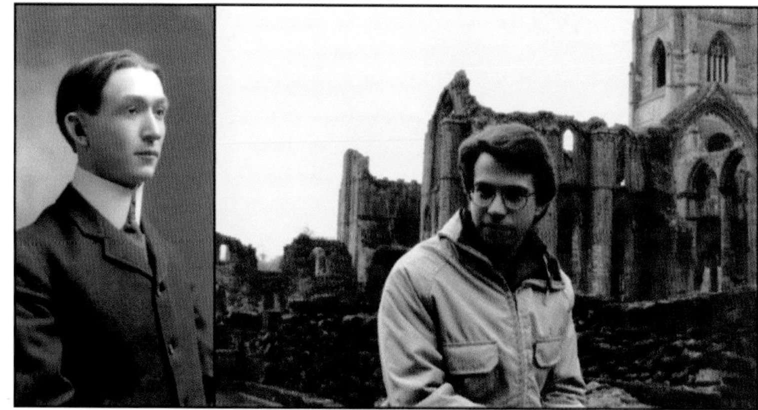

*Albert Lee Luick, circa 1910; author, born "Michael Lee Luick," at the ruins of Fountain's Abbey, North Yorkshire, 1981*

---

## chapter 1: runaways and pioneers

Albert Lee Luick was born 8 June 1877 in Belmond, Iowa, the son of David and Rose Pierce Luick, and nephew of Henry Luick, Junior. He would have been 21 when his Uncle Henry died, 34 when his trapper-pioneer father, David, followed, so knew both men personally. He also knew almost all of the individuals he mentioned in his thorough account of the Luick family, save for his paternal grandparents, Heinrich and Katherine, whose cabin in Michigan he visited in 1887 at the age of ten, and likely Melissa (his mother's paternal aunt), who left for California before Albert's birth and died when he was six.

*Albert Luick's family, with sisters (back row) Ida, Emma, Amelia and Mabel, and parents Sarah (Overacker) and David Luick, circa 1890*

An ambitious and bright boy, the 1910 Federal census shows him as a cashier at the State Bank of Belmond. The Iowa census half a decade later documents that he'd quickly moved up to bank president.

J. C. Butterfield T. H. Kenefick
A. L. Luick Jno. Berg

Belmond Land Co.,
Belmond, - Iowa.
Real Estate Bought and Sold.
Make a Specialty of Iowa, Minnesota & Dakota Lands.
Correspondence Solicited.

*"Lee" Luick served as president of the State Bank of Belmond, working with partners Earl Madsen (left) and John Berg. The men also bought and sold land in four Upper Midwest states—per this ad in a local newspaper of the time. Albert's house reflected his wealth and aspirations.*

By 1930 he'd moved to Minneapolis, where that year's census notes him as a "bond salesman," likely a tough sell in the months soon after the collapse of Wall Street in October 1929. By the time he retired, however, Albert appeared to have thrived, for his narrative is a positive, upbeat extension of his own (at least public) perceptions of his—*ah*, make that "our"—people. Written after Belmond's centennial celebration in 1956 but before his death on 20 February 1962, the few patriotic allusions in his retelling of the Luicks in *"Amerika"* reflect the standing-tall optimism of that now-faded postwar era, when the United States was riding the apex of the "American Century." His heroic, rose-tinted narrative begins:

> At the end of the 18th century, there lived in Stuttgart, Germany, a family by the name of "LUICK". There were three brothers in the family—Jacob, David, and my grandfather, Heinrich, all over six feet tall and very rugged individuals. They were sons of a "Schneidermeister" Luick, noted Master Tailor of Stuttgart. During that period of German history, the country was in great turmoil and all three of these young men were forced into the Germany army; in fact, were in many battles of the Napoleonic wars.

His truly is a lovely start for a romantic tale, full of feeling and action-packed images as it is. Albert's narrative, however, also has a few, well, "problems." But, *ach!*—where to start in qualifying, in trying to relativize a "hobby-historian" grandson's sentimental glorification of shared origins, with a trained-historian great-x4-grandson's exacting *Geschichtswissenschaftler's* scalpel; how "deep" may I cut? Oh, bells—let's just jump in!

For one thing, Albert actually began his account with "At the end of the 19th century," but while I am loathe to alter first-person texts, he clearly meant the late 1700s—when the Luicks had not yet left the candle-lit, half-timbered villages of Württemberg—and *not* the late 1800s, by which time already they strolled along Belmond's gas- or electric-lamp-lit streets on summer eves, listening to Louis Luick treat the up-and-coming prairie townsfolk to his violin's soft serenade.

In the same first sentence (luickly, the poor man is not alive today to watch me weigh his every word!), he speaks of our family coming from "Stuttgart." All known ancestral documents cite the surrounding settlements of Esslingen, Fellbach, Aich, etc., but none suggest our ancestors hailed from Stuttgart per se. Perhaps Albert was trying to do his geography-challenged compatriots a favor by offering relatives and other readers a more easily-identified place-name. The difference, however, is not trifling: a parallel would be to tell the world something of "Des Moines" when one really meant to share something about "Ames" (at a distance from Iowa's capital comparable of that of Esslingen from Württemberg's *Hauptstadt*), but both sets of towns are distinctly different from each other, not to mention the lives their respective inhabitants lead.

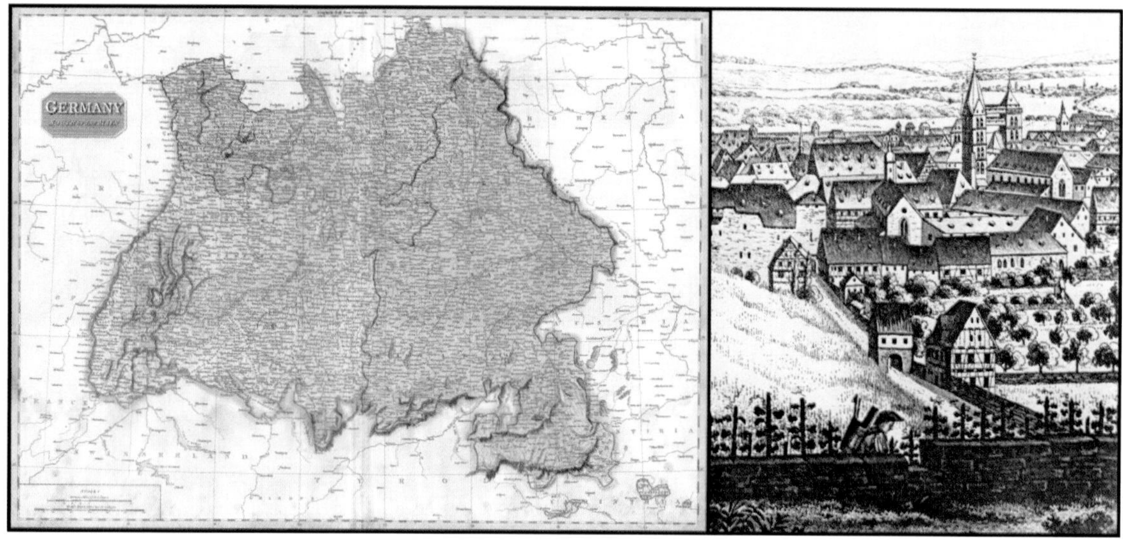


*Esslingen as seen from its western vineyards, circa 1800; map of southern Germanic states, per its source: "...from Frankfort south to Lake Constance and east to Bishop. Includes the provinces of Swabia, Bavaria, & Franconia as well as parts of adjacent France, Switzerland, Austria & Bohemia [...] with political divisions & color coding at the regional level. Identifies cities, towns, castles, important battle sites, castles, swamps, mountains & river ways[.] Two mile scales, in German Miles & British Statute Miles [...] This map comes from American edition of* Pinkerton's Modern Atlas, *published by Thomas Dobson & Co. of Philadelphia in 1818."*

Then, there's the problem of the term "family" and the phrase "brothers in [that] family." While the "patchwork" families so prevalent today in North America, Europe and increasingly elsewhere on the globe more typically result from divorce than death, the phenomenon of cobbled-together "families" is ageless, even if earlier they resulted more from sudden physical demise than gradual emotional disillusionment. Cousin Tony's most-defendable research, as case in point, suggests that "brother Jacob Luick" had been born a "Schuler," but when his soon-thereafter-widowed mother, Anna Maria, married Heinrich's father, Friedrich, in 1787, the latter let the boy take his mother's new family name, too—the epitome of pre-modern patchwork.

As for the three "brothers" being "all over six feet tall and very rugged individuals," I'd be surprised! First of all, while possible, such across-the-board bodily vitality at that time would have been improbable. Such super-human traits fed the Luicks' larger-than-life legend, yet at the time of their births Europe generally, Württemberg specifically had suffered recurring bouts of bad harvests and widespread malnutrition. Second, as with other migrants, anywhere, then and today, human beings tend to go where they have been told life is better than where they began it—and they tend to go in groups, either as singles or with family members in tow. Terry Stollsteimer and Dale Herter—both descended from the same wave of *Schwaben* ("Swabians" in English) from Württemberg that carried the Luicks to Southeast Michigan—have conducted scientific surveys of the Germanic peoples who settled around Ann Arbor. In their studied view,

> Swabians tended to be of short stature, often stout, and dark-haired, in contrast to the taller, usually more slender and fair-haired northern and central Germans. [And, they] spoke a dialect of the German language that is distinctive to this day.

Descended from wandering tribes referred to as "Suebi" by Roman colonial officers as well as travelers, who both studied and feared them, the Swabians are an ancient people, at home in a rolling landscape occupied by human beings for tens of thousands of years. The world's oldest surviving human-made figurative art—per latest carbon-dating techniques—came to light in caves near Ulm, just east of the Schwäbische Alb: it dates back an inconceivable 40,000 years.

*16th-century tailor shop; Württemberg's coat of arms, 1817 to 1922 (top) and Esslingen's (below); "Sveviae," 1572*

Worst of all his text's "problems," while I compliment Albert on ferreting out that Heinrich's father, Friedrich, was a *Schneidermeister* ("master tailor"), I shudder at what at first seems a gross departure from historical fact. Granted, we know that Jacob was listed as being a "soldier" in the early 1800s, but the "Napoleonic Wars" had their roots in the French Revolution of 1789, then raged from 1803 until finally ending in 1815 with the little French sociopath's defeat at the Battle of Waterloo. Perhaps, given the nearly universal conscription in Central Europe in effect at the time, all "three Luick brothers" did find themselves in Württemberg's royal army just before Napoleon's downfall (in 1814 Heinrich would have been the prime cannon-fodder age of 18) and after the shooting stopped at least some of them remained in His Highness' employ.

*German cartoon (1813) titled* Aufstieg und Niederfall Napoleons *("Napoleon's Rise and Fall"); portrait of France's future dictator, age 23, as Lieutenant-Colonel of a battalion of Corsican Republican volunteers*

Then again, perhaps not. In his narrative, however, Albert swears that at the point the Luicks "fled" in 1832, Heinrich was "a minor officer of the King's Horses, a cavalry division."

---

In any event, Dear Reader, lest we get irretrievably lost amidst the clopping of horse hooves or choke in the smoke of endless armed conflict, let us review here how warfare dictated the well-being (read: the survival—or not) of European commoners in recent centuries past. For starters, even if surprising to most laypeople, Western historians plant the beginning of our Modern Era firmly in 1648, with the signing of the Treaties of *Westfalen* ("Westphalia" in English), which formally ended a disastrous Thirty-Years War that had resulted in the death of at least three million Europeans and the wholesale destruction of much of what's now known as "Germany." And, that post-war "peace" laid the foundation of European power structures lasting centuries. While a harbinger of the horrific "modern wars" to come, let's first look for clues even earlier:

While those of us who grew up in the Americas (both North and South) or Oceania might find the idea of fluid borders inconceivable—spared as we've been by having had virtually no lasting warfare between other nations take place on our soils—until 1950 Old-World history followed an unbroken chronology of shifting peoples and identities. When I briefly swapped the Iowa prairies for the Yorkshire Dales, for example, I was shocked to learn that in the so-called Middle Ages Yorkshire and neighboring Lancashire to the west had waged a prolonged and bloody War of the Roses, two "counties" dueling for regional dominance vis-à-vis London. Later, holidaying in the South of France, I discovered—in a similar vein—that the later "French" regions of, for example, Brittany, Lorraine or Provence originally were under other rule and only after struggles over political (and thus economic) supremacy did they become part of *la Grand Nation*. And, where did I spend—for Christian's tastes, "too much"—time during our recent long-weekend romp round Rome? Deep in the bowels of the vast Vittorio Emmanuel memorial, learning about the forced fusion of previously competing states into one "Italian" one, as late as 1871!

*cartoon depicting European power dynamics of the mid-19th century: The proponents of failed revolutions are being cast off—to* "Amerika."

If that date seems familiarly momentous, it's because it should: It was in the same year that Chancellor Otto von Bismarck served up a purely "Prussian" king the final of a series of victories over Denmark (remember the hungry, hopeless Juhls?), Austria and then France. As of that day, the Hohenzollern family (originally from Swabia) ruled over a "Germany" which had never before existed. Like "Britain," "France" and "Italy," that hardworking, earnest-but-cozy land between the North Sea and the Northern Alps that we call "Germany" is no more than a recent, melded-together invention. As implausible as it sounds, at the not-so-ancient age of 52, I've witnessed—often literally—more than a third of "Germany's" swiftly-changing history.

———

## chapter 2: contact is made

I'm not the only Luick, however, to see first-hand much of the 20th-century story of modern "Germany" unfold. Many others in our extended family have witnessed much more of it—and much closer—than I ever could... or would want to.

Actually, what I learned came about as a result of my Skipton friend Biffy's idea. On the way to visit her sister Maggie and the expat-Brit's Italian-doctor lover in Padua over Easter break at Ermysted's, I was to "stop off in Esslingen and introduce [my]self to [my] long-lost German relatives" exactly a century-and-a-half after my family left the one-time *Reichstadt*, or semi-autonomous city. What my carrot-topped chum in back in Craven didn't expect was that it would be *they* who would do most of the "introducing."

Karl Luick was a big man. I first spied him waiting for me at Stuttgart's cavernous *Hauptbahnhof* at the head of a platform swirling with travelers, anxiously trying to identify the "*amerikanischen Cousin*" he only

*Karl Luick and Labrador, "Arco," on bridge over the Neckar, April 1982: Note the towers and ramparts of the remains of Esslingen's hilltop castle.*

a short time before did not know he had. I immediately thought of those towering Luick boys, "over six feet stall and very rugged," standing across from my Dad, Grampa Luick and Grampa George, none of whom were over 5'10" or anything even close to being blond.

As we drove in his well-polished Opel over the *Autobahn* to Esslingen, Karl tried to explain in broken, nearly-forgotten school-boy English (I spoke not a word of German then) how we were related despite a separation of 150 years. I only smiled stiffly and nodded agreeably. When we soon reached the solid, multi-generational Luick *Haus*, I felt relieved by the reprieve from strained, one-on-one communication.

Karl's diminutive, black-haired wife, Ruth, greeted me at the door and, after a bowl of delicious Swabian lentil-sausage soup, asked if I'd like to rest. I'd only traveled that morning via a non-tiring train trip from Luxembourg—having visited overnight my school mate, Matthew Simon's Anglican-pastor parents—yet I grabbed the chance to regroup. I'd never navigated being on my own in a country where I didn't speak the language. That Ruth spoke even less English than her square-shouldered, raspy-voiced husband quickly exhausted me physically and my inner ability to muddle through murky cultural waters.

As my flawless, thoughtful hosts closed the door to Karl's study-cum-guest-pad and my eyes adjusted to the dimmed room, however, I softly shrieked when I spied in the corner a large, framed picture of a German officer dressed in full Nazi-officer regalia. Directly opposite it, on the adjoining wall, with a matching frame and bulky matting, hung a yellowed letter with clunky typing and, at the top, an eagle-with-swastika seal. Unable to easily read it for lack of light, I leaned to within a nose length, then, making out the signature to be that of "A. Hitler," I froze. *"Oh, god,"* I freaked, *"the Luicks are all old Nazis!"* At that moment, unable to cope with one of my first cases of debilitating culture shock, I laid down on the sofa-bed and quietly cried myself into an unsettled sleep.

*1926 dust jacket to Adolf Hitler's political treatise,*
My Struggle: The National Socialist Movement

When I eventually awoke from an unwanted nap born of emotional escape, a young man with spikey hair and a silly moustache was sitting in the Luicks' smoky living room. A dental technician just off work, Karl and Ruth's young son, Jochen, had stopped by his parental home to translate. After the obligatory courtesies, me being me, I had to ask *"Ah-h-h,* about those two framed items hanging in the guestroom—"

*"Ja"* Karl interrupted, "dose belongt *zu meinem Vater*."

"And...?" I awkwardly fished.

"Ve are not prout of vhat happened" my host conveyed to me, at times with Jochen's help, at times in the sing-songy, lispy local dialect of the Swabians, "but *es ist* part of our *Familias'* history. *Mein Vater*" Karl explained in heavy tones, with wringing hands, "had been professional *Soldat in der Weimarer Republik. Wenn die Nazis kammen*, he yust changed da uniforms."

"And you?" I rudely pushed.

*"Und ich*?" Karl echoed, sitting back into the over-stuffed armchair and looking towards the wall next to the door to the kitchen. "Me?" he repeated in English, "I servt my countree."

"I wondered about that" I goaded, nodding my head in the direction of a war-booty Orthodox icon, the dark oil painting of Mother Mary and baby Jesus, hanging in a heavy frame between the bookshelves and tiled *Ofen* that had commanded Karl's lost gaze.

With a helpless shrug, Karl asked quietly "Vhat do you do vhen your country goes vrong?"

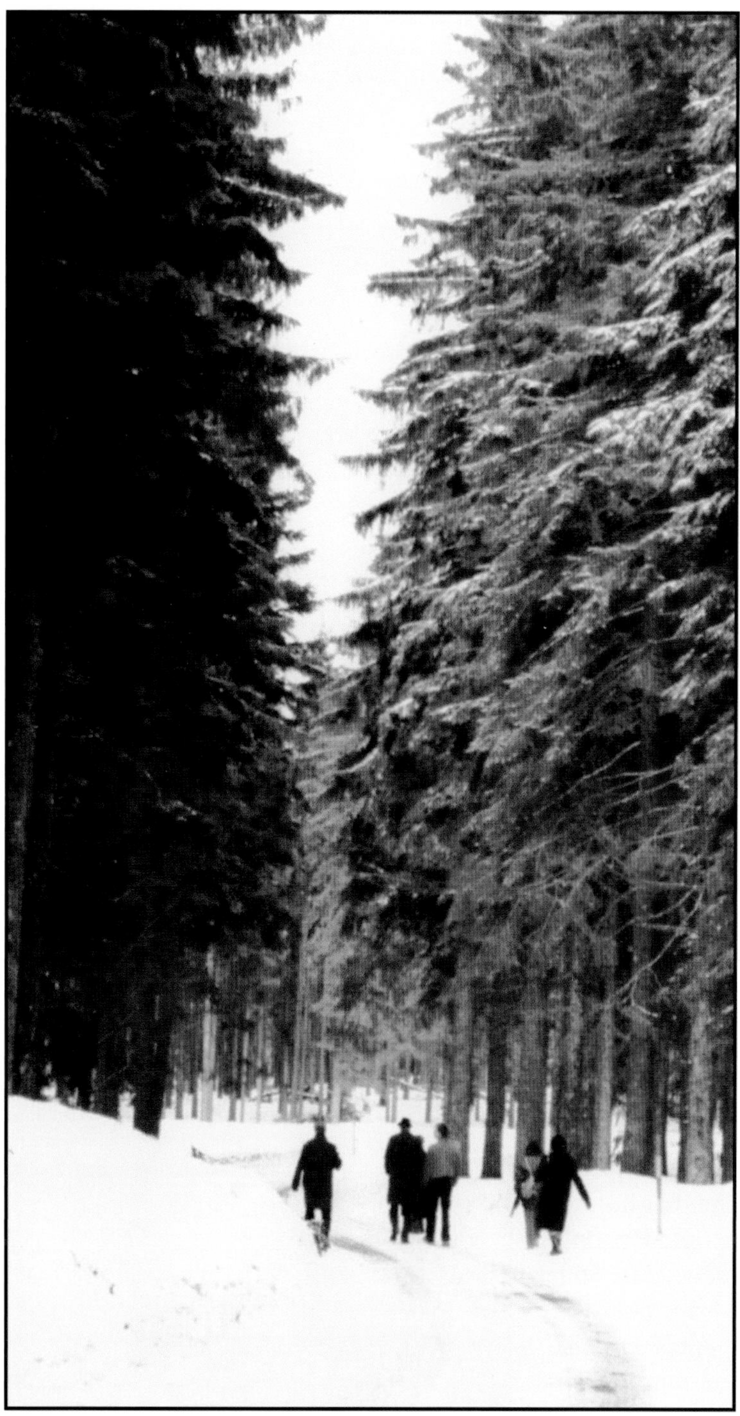

*Karl, Ruth, Jochen, Iris and her parents hiking in the*
Schwarzwald, *the Black Forest, at Easter time 1982*

---

## chapter 3: disillusioned soldiers defect

But, hey: wait! What about the rest of our review of the effects of Europe's wars on its peoples?

*Württemberg cavalry members approaching Esslingen from the south side of the Neckar River, 1820*

The Old-French word for "soldier" comes from the Latin "*solidus*" or coin, from the premise that combatting men are "working" men: Rather than fighting gratis for ideals, forces-for-hire "earn" their "wage" through ransacking and raping their way through occupied territory. Conscription armies—like those deemed necessary to defeat (or, as with the miscalculating Swabian royals, back) the likes of Monsieur Bonaparte—consisting of "subjects" forced to fight for "god and country" per monetary remuneration. They were seen in a light other than that of the flames of greed and base carnage that burned in the throats of conscripted troops' more mercenary predecessors. Still, in "modern wars" civilians paid the steepest prices for elites' armed squabbles over property or patronage as armies passed their ways. The relatively tangential souvenir-hunting of "civilized" post-Enlightenment Europe, however, paled in comparison to the wholesale, unleashed harvesting of booty undertaken in the time of the endless, all-consuming wars of before, say, 1650.

*German parlor scene, circa 1830, with political maps on wall and man in formal military dress*

So, if, as alluded to in written records, at least Jacob was listed as a *"Soldat,"* and if, as Albert recalled, Heinrich, too, curried "the King's Horses," any Luick brothers in Württemberg's armed forces in 1832 served as quasi professional soldiers rather than as the opportunistic scavengers of yore. In theory, their fellow Swabs could have esteemed rather than despised the men. Thus, those connected to crown, church, court of law or school enjoyed higher social status, if not more worldly wealth.

In practice, however, career soldiers felt under constant pressure from above. True, they served, but they also swore—about the chronically low or late pay, lousy food and louse-infested beds, inadequate or antiquated equipment... the classic complaints of soldiers for over two millennia. Their mounting, long-carried frustration might ignite at even the slightest provocation, and singe all those around them—even the privileged and power-yielding, just as:

> My grandfather, Heinrich, became a minor officer of the King's Horses, a cavalry division. One day early in 1832 a nobleman of high rank took exception to the way the horses were being cared for. An argument ensued and my grandfather proceeded to give this arrogant nobleman a good thrashing. Heinrich's action was a capital offense, punishable by death, so grandfather was forced to flee the country and succeeded in getting into the Netherlands.
>
> The three brothers had talked of going to America, where friends had reported of the wonderful opportunities available. They thought that this was the time for them to make the move. The two brothers, Jacob and David, gathered up their families and, with Heinrich's family, proceeded to the Netherlands. There they met Heinrich and engaged passage on a sailing vessel bound for New York—a very hard voyage that took over two months of sailing.

Again, disinterested documents suggest a more complicated sequence of events than sketched in Albert's fanciful narrative. While out of personal experience I can imagine without a milligram of effort a hot-headed, horse-loving Luick male giving an "arrogant" challenger an impromptu "good thrashing," the "early one day" motif of Albert's allegory accurately mirrors neither the desperate tenor of the times nor the long-deliberated departure of the young-male Luick set.

For one thing, for much of the first half of the 19th-century rural Württemberg—especially the Alb, the Ozark-like plateau that runs most of the length of Swabia, from the southwest to the northeast of the then-kingdom—reeled under one wave of hunger after the next. Crop failures, inauspicious climatic conditions, un- or at least under-employment taxed the commoners' nerves even as the grasping king taxed their coin purses. Seeing little chance to advance, the most ambitious, risk-ready Swabs considered striking the set and setting up anew in the New World. Not only the decision, but the process, however, was in no way a "one day" affair.

Was Albert's compelling tale just that—a tall one—or was there indeed a precipitating, violent incident that provided a last nudge in a gradual push for the Luicks to take the nearest exit? In any case, on 13 April 1833 the *Bürgermeister*, the mayor of Aich, finally signed the requisite permission for the Heinrich and Katherine (pronounced "Katerina") Luick family to remove themselves the Royal Realm of Württemberg; earlier applications for official allowance to leave, however, had been considered already five years earlier. Albert's story could reflect historical events: Heinrich's "capital offense" may have only accelerated an existing, years-long process of departure.

*As the first (left) and the last of five pages (right) of the permit show, the old-German script is exceptionally hard to decipher, even for Germans today.*
*As the translation into English below attests, in forsaking their status as subjects of the kingdom of Württemberg, the Luicks had to swear to leave no outstanding bills behind, and to not attack their former homeland. And they had to leave a deposit in case of later, unforeseen costs.*

Die eingeschlafene Strickerin *("The Sleeping Knitter") by Wilhelm Schumann, 1838*

Aich
transcript
from

the mayor's office, dated 6 April 1833.

Jakob Heinrich Luik, citizen and carpenter from here [i.e. from Aich] and his wife Catharina, nee Gerstenmaier from Offenhaußen, appear before the mayor's office and declare that they are determined to emigrate with their three children to North America this spring.

The husband promises that he will not serve [militarily] within a period of a year against king and fatherland and that he will fully discharge his debts and other obligations before his emigration. This, as well as the renunciation of his rights to public support as a citizen and subject is certified by

Jacob Heinrich Luik
Catharina Luikin

The attested local citizen Johannes Rauscher, David's son, is liable as a guarantor for any and every claim that within a period of a year might be filed against J. Heinrich Luik.

**Resolved:**

The Königliches Oberamt [Royal Superior Office] Nürtingen is to be informed of the Luik family's intentions by means of this record extract.

The correctness of this extract is notarized 6 April 1833

Mayor's office and council members,

**Lang**
**Martin Rauscher**
**Johannes Rauscher**
**Jakob Stiefel**
**Joh. Michael Buckgerdt**
**Ludwig Neudeck**
**Jakob Hanscher**

Jakob Heinrich Luik, carpenter from here, who has the intention of emigrating to North America with his wife and three children, is hereby officially sworn that he takes with him debt-free assets of 1200 guilders.

Aich, 13 April 1833

Mayor and town councillors, **Lang** etc.

That the Luicks sought stamped written permission to emigrate—although documented fact—does mirror a wider context. As Islamic countries still do and Jewish culture traditionally did, in those days Christian conscience dictated that the well-being of "the least of these" be genuinely considered and effectively supported. Since the Middle Ages already, as individual families proved time and again unable to carry the least-able or most-ill-fated among them despite their best efforts, local churches and town councils offered their neediest parishioners or *Bürger* additional, official care. This institutionalized system of assuring social cohesion, however, had a price—among others, the full autonomy of those so guaranteed a minimum material existence.

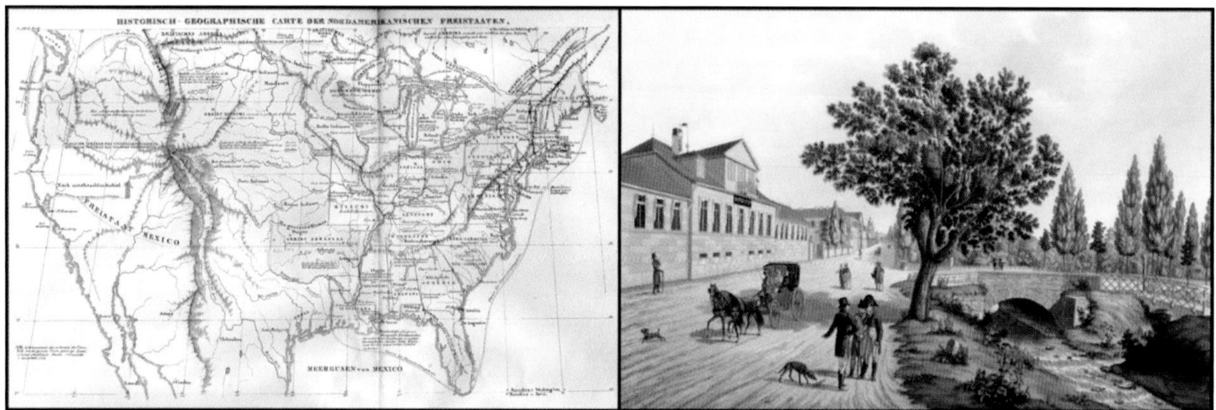


*German map of* Amerika *(1829); picture (1810) of road from Stuttgart to today's "Bad Cannstatt"*

In the Middle Ages, unmarried daughters could be pushed off into convents, and unemployed or unemployable young men sent off on crusades (from which most would never return) in order to cull local welfare rolls. In contrast, in the early 19th century the Old World's poor were simply shipped off to the New—to a point. As is still the case in some industrializing countries, the well-trained or those of military-service age were coveted by their own government, which blocked the wished departure until doing so no longer served the state. In the late-feudal Europe of pre-industrial days, rulers would send their lackeys galloping after peasants who'd high-tailed it in the night for the next port with sea-worthy ships. It was after Friedrich the Great's minions shoved such poor people back to their posts in rural Prussia that the hope-dashed, man-handled would-be emigrants named their homes-by-default back in Brandenburg "Boston" and "Philadelphia."

Around the time that the Luicks weighed forever forsaking the *Heimat*, their homeland in *Mitteleuropa*, villages like Winterbach in the Rems Valley—as one example—offered communal bake- and washhouses in order not only to lessen pressure on local fuel supplies, but to stoke big fires in free-standing stone buildings as a means to lower the chances of devastating house fires that could easily spread and claim much of the town. Other villages distributed free food stuffs; in some, local noble families paid for at least a select number of boys' basic schooling. Still, failing to fully respond to poor people's plights, even the most communal-minded communities in Württemberg were swiftly losing some of the more moxie-blessed specimens in their local gene pool.

But, "the Netherlands?" *Really?* If at least some of the Luicks departed from Le Havre, France, *why* first a rendezvous in the Netherlands? Yes, two centuries earlier the so-called Pilgrims, a fundamentalist splinter group of already-dowdy English Puritans, had lived for a time in Leiden before setting sail for Virginia (they thought—but got blown off course and settled for frozen "New England" instead). And, for some time that tiny, flat country enjoyed the reputation of being a bastion of tolerance, a safe haven for free thinkers—but according to Dale and Terry,

> German emigrants in the early 1800's typically began their journey by river barge or ox-drawn cart, leaving their home villages and traveling through France to Le Havre, through Belgium to Antwerp, or through Holland to Amsterdam in order to board schooners bound for America.

*"View of Stuttgart" as seen from the village of Degerloch, 1850*

Whether wanted by the law or not, at least some of the Luick men—like millions of others from the Germanic states and, later, German-occupied southern Denmark or German-Mennonite-settled Czarist Russia—were so desperate to escape conscription that they would have done almost anything to be forever free of compulsory military servitude. Risking losing their lives at sea or their souls in dog-eat-dog *"Amerika"* seemed like better options than what, a century later, the grandchildren of their fellow Germans who remained behind would call an "inner emigration."

---

**chapter 4: artists take flight**

On the evening of my arrival in Esslingen in early April 1982, Karl suddenly appeared in front of me and proclaimed proudly *"Und* now ve vill eat *Abendessen* vid da udder Familia Luick." Ruth already stood in the door with the couple's amber-eyed, sand-colored Labrador Retriever "Arco" and my jacket, which I could not remember having handed her. "Ve vill valk now to da *Dicker Turm*" Karl beamed, to a restaurant in Esslingen's trademark "Fat Tower" that squats high above the Medieval city, atop cascading vineyard terraces and a maze of narrow footpaths.

When we finally had scaled the steep steps to the Fat Tower that dates from 1525, a delegation of relatives was awaiting us. This included quiet 74-year-old Eugen Luick and his lively French-teaching daughter, Margrit; Jochen's sweet and friendly elementary-school-teacher wife, Iris, and their friends, Roland Dietrich with his striking, shapely wife from the gated-community Ecuadorian elite, Cecilia. That whole meal, of which I literally was at the center, I scarcely heard a word out of Eugen. I was surprised, then, when, as the party later slowly disbanded, he invited me to visit him "on-the-job" the next morning. I would be even more surprised when I discovered that of all of my new German Luick relatives, in some ways he had the most to say.

*Ruth (Luidhardt), Eugen, Michael, Jochen, Karl & Iris (Glaser) Luick, April 1982*

Also enjoying the Easter break from school, chatty, red-haired Margrit met me at Karl and Ruth's early the next morning to take me to see her father—as she put it—"in action." Indeed, when we arrived at his open-air worksite, we found him high up on scaffolding in front of the *Altes Rathaus*, Esslingen's Renaissance-façaded city hall, the bulk of which dates from 1420. "*Guten Morgen*" he greeted us cordially, holding a palette of slick, bright colors and wearing a white, ironed-and-crisply-folded painter's smock that betrayed not a spot of stray paint. I found his restoration work around the gold-gilded, zodiac-decorated astronomical clock fascinating. Even more spellbinding, however, was what *Malermeister* Eugen showed me from the "master painter's" unusual youth during a much-deserved break for *Kaffee und Kuchen*.

*Elisabeth, Margrit & Eugen Luick, 1982: He restored the Altes Rathaus ("Old City Hall"), the red building.*

In his early twenties, as Germany's political and moral center could no longer hold, Eugen and three fellow-painter friends plotted a temporary escape from their country's turbulent times. When the four art students proposed taking a trip to study classic art, their instructor mocked them, as "Grand tours are only for the rich." Not to be dissuaded, they organized their own bare-budget outing to the near East—per bicycle and ferry, sleeping in hostels, tents, under the stars or anywhere else their meager stipends would allow.

As supporters of political radicals on both the right and left came to fisticuffs in the rancorous, blood-stained streets of Germany, Eugen and his adventure-hungry pals peddled over the Alps; they rode down the length of the Italian "boot" via boat, then went to the Mideast and back via Greece. Having set off on 2 December 1932, spending Christmas in Jerusalem and then returning to Swabia on 18 March 1933, the four young adventurers left what had known as the *Weimarer Republik* and returned to a newly-proclaimed Third Reich. Rather than stay and observe the unfolding crisis, they had taken a study tour. While against the Nazi agenda—among other reasons, due to his family's religious convictions—Eugen, like too many millions of other moderate Germans, chose to hide behind a veil of silence rather than speak out against their country's spiraling collective madness.

Eugen sat next to me as I turned page after compelling page of his musty photo album from that trip and marveled over the images he'd captured with his camera of a world now long gone: camels plodding through Old Jerusalem's dusty labyrinth of tapered streets, Muslim traders wearing flowing caftans and Cairo clerks donning fezzes... glimpses into a time and an innocence now lost for all time. Wandering, wide-eyed Mike Luick from Ashlawn Farm felt amazed. I found especially inspiring the frozen, faded images of the four sturdy, knickerbockers-wearing young men atop Giza's massive pyramids, on the stone-strewn Acropolis and later being punted about Venice's Grand Canal in a bobbing gondola—all places and experiences I'd one day retrace.

*Eugen Luick (with zippered sweater) and three art-school buddies, about to bike via Jerusalem to Egypt*

"Still waters run deep" exists as a saying in German, too—and I soon found that calm Eugen possessed a depth that surpassed what most might have guessed at first glance. After returning from what for most would have been "the" experience of a lifetime, Eugen's biography became even more dramatic, for after Hitler—never attracting a majority of votes but rather leveraging power through cynical coalitions—took power, Eugen's carefree days would disappear forever.

In stark contrast to Karl—who proved to be kind to me and open about his or his family's burdened past "anyway"—creative Eugen clearly had anti-Nazi credentials. Coming from a devotedly pious family belonging to the Evangelische Landeskirche in Württemberg, Eugen's wife's aunt somehow walked away from all but one brush with the police, which landed her in prison for a few days. Adamant as she was to not mindlessly mimic those around her and offer a reflexive *Hitlergruss*—the stiff-armed *"Sieg Heil"* salutation characteristic of life in the lock-step Third Reich—she'd rush into a shop or hide in a doorway if she saw uniformed figures coming or some situation calling for *"Sieg Heil!"* Intrigued by the anthroposophy peddled by Rudolf Steiner, Eugen and his subdued wife, Elizabeth, were more interested in the affairs of the

*Michael Luick-Thrams narrating TRACES exhibit shown at the Deutsch-Amerikanisches Institut Tübingen, 2012*

sacred rather than those of the secular world—yet another reason for their deep-seated allergy to Nazi ideas.

Returning to Germany a decade hence to earn a doctoral degree in modern-European history, with a focus on the Third Reich and its scorched-earth aftermath, I would encounter case after case of artists, writers, composers or directors, filmmakers, social workers, academics, theologians and tens of thousands of others who, unable or unwilling to join those fleeing Fascism to live in exile abroad, attempted to survive their country's dive into barbarism by withdrawing from the "New Germany's" public life, going into what became known as an *innere Emigration*, an "internal emigration." Although critical of Nazism or antithetically opposed to Hitler's ghastly goals, such sad souls accommodated an evil regime in hopes of outliving what many assumed would be *der Führer*'s crash-and-burn career. Virtually none, however, would come away from a dozen years of collective insanity and sanctioned bestiality unscathed; many would pay for it with what had been accomplished careers, if not their lives.

———

## chapter 5: leaving "*Europa*" behind

Eugen Luick rode a bike to get to the Mideast, but Heinrich Luick rode *The France* to reach the Midwest. Carrying mostly cargo but not many passengers, the ship departed Le Havre in May 1833. After a short stop in England to take on or leave freight, it arrived in New York on the 12th of July, at which time Heinrich and Katherine's family may have disembarked in those pre-Ellis-Island, pre-Castle-Clinton days on South Street, on the east side of Manhattan's busy tip.

*the French port of Le Havre, circa 1830; the ship* France*, which brought the Luicks from Europe to America*

Indications are that Heinrich's six-year-younger brother, David, and his family took a different ship. It also seems that Jacob [Schuler] Luick had preceded his half-brothers to the New World by as much as a year and taken up brief residence in Buffalo—that boomtown at the end of the Erie Canal that had opened only eight years earlier but already was transforming both New York city and state. The three brothers met at the last stop in the Empire State, where two spent that winter preparing to proceed to a promised land they had been told about, with the poetic name of Ann Arbor.

According to swooning Albert,

> Grandfather had wooed and won my grandmother, Katherine Gerstenmaier, a member of one of the royal families of Germany, against the wishes of her family. But they loved each other very dearly and were very happy with their three children: Henry, Jr., a boy of ten; John, four years old; and my father, David, a baby of only a few weeks.

*Hum-m-m…* Detour here:

Shakespeare's Juliet asks

> "What's in a name? That which we call a rose
>
> By any other name would smell as sweet."

Problem is, even "simple" name-related mistakes just stink. I know: I'm an accuracy-addicted historian-writer. Two real examples of the distressing, indelible dangers of "minor" errors:

In 1979 one of my favorite peers in the niche field of WWII-era German-POW research, who I esteem and respect greatly, published "the bible" of German POWs in America. At the very top of his list of the more than 500 base or branch camps in the U.S. during World War II, however, he erroneously mistyped the first entry as "Camp Algo**m**a, Idaho" when, in truth, it should have been "Camp Algo**n**a, Iowa"—an irreparable mistake that, in his otherwise meticulous tome, has been held as incontestable gospel now by a couple generations of researchers. Having interviewed dozens of both one-time German prisoners as well as American staff who'd been at its base camp, published books about the 20-site Camp Algona "empire" spread over four Upper-Midwest states, spoken hundreds of times on four continents about the topic and curated comprehensive exhibits about it, to this day I have supposed scholars swear that either "There *was* no 'Camp Algo*n*a' in Iowa!" or "Oh, you mean 'Camp Algo*m*a, in Idaho…"

*map of Camp Algona POW-camp system, circa 1945; German POWs working in northern Minnesota, 1944*

Similarly, I knew my mother's paternal uncle, Willard, and two aunts, Florence and Lois; I also loved and, too-briefly, knew their brother, Mom's dad, Grandpa Thrams. Despite being certain, empirically and documentably, that that sweet, wise man did, indeed, once exist, somehow, somewhere, some unknown Thrams relatives put in the internet the "complete" biographical data for all of Christ and Lydia Thrams' children… *except* for that of Elmer Alvin. It is painful, truly, to see this faulty entry, repeatedly—as if my beloved maternal grandfather never was.

*my maternal grandfather, Elmer Thrams, who lived outside Mason City his whole life but traveled much*

Well, somehow, somewhere, some unknown Luick-related hobby-historian sent into the world that Heinrich Luick's wife's maiden name was "Gestenmayer"—as Albert Lee Luick also wrote it, erroneously, in his family chronicle. Well, it wasn't. Google it, though, and—as of today, 10 June 2014—and you'll get 662 results, even as that (in this case) nonpartisan search engine asks in the upper-left corner of the screen, in screaming red letters, "Don't you mean 'Gerstenmaier' you total idiot?!" Oh, you'll also find "Gestenmeyer" or "Gaastenmayer" and, even better (or "worse"), a misspelled first name for the poor-if-noble-born woman, since there is *no* "Catherine" with a "C" in contemporary German. While "*Geste*" in German does exist, it means "gesture;" as "*Gerste*" means "barley" and "*Maier/Meyer/Mayer*" mean "farmer" or "large landholder," doesn't "barley farmer" make more sense as a way to distinguish one family from others, as opposed to "gesture landholder?"

If such name-spelling "bloopers" seem "inconsequential," think again. This researcher was unable for thirty-five years to locate the falsely-cited village in *Pommern* ("Pommerania") from where the Thramses hailed for the lack of a single, paltry missing vowel! And, when it comes to human beings... well, one can only shake one's weary head! Whole families, whole generations have been lost—or (re-)found—based on one dolt's omission or mistake... *ARGH!*

Well, you'll see what I mean, soon—but, for now, back to our story.

---

## chapter 6: arriving in "*Amerika*"

When the Luicks sailed into New York Harbor in spring 1833, the city they found there scarcely resembled the largest town back in *Schwaben*, Stuttgart. North of today's Downtown much of the island consisted of woods, farms and a few scattered villages. The swelling port city itself, however, already comprised what today constitutes a "global city," and boasted a New World vitality and diversity that hardly a city in the Germanic Old World could match—or even imagine.

*view of the tip of Manhattan from Brooklyn, 1824*

With over two-hundred thousand inhabitants in 1830, New York had four times the population Stuttgart had at the time. More than its size, however, what marked Manhattan from the sleepy Swabian capital was its mushrooming role as a center of transportation. And, its can-do spirit.

By 1833 steamboats had plied New York Harbor for over a quarter century, and the turnpike to Albany that opened in 1815 established the city as a hub for would-be emigrants to Michigan Territory via Buffalo. Ten years later, the new Erie Canal accelerated that movement—one that would carry the Luicks to the Great American Frontier they'd heard so much about back home.

Dwarflike in comparison, not even in the Middle Ages had Stuttgart been an important trading center—unlike Nürnberg, Strassburg, Hamburg or other renowned German market towns of old. Especially after the Erie Canal linked the Atlantic to the Great Lakes, New York hummed with trade with the entire world. The Luicks saw there foods and goods unknown to them back in Württemberg. Exotic smells, bright colors, strange sounds awaited them. (Did they, like Mike Luick would do 140 years later, walk the streets of New York with eyes the size of silver dollars?)

Besides a previously unimaginable wealth of wares, with fantastic sorts of things to eat or wear, listen to or stare at, in Knickerbocker New York the Luicks also found myriad sorts of people. Most noticeably, people with darker skin. Having freed its last slaves not yet six years earlier, on the Fourth of July 1827, some twenty thousand African Americans (almost a tenth of the city's 1830 population) called the city home. With the Dutch West India Company having brought the first slaves—exactly eleven, from its slave station in Angola—to the then-lagging colony of Nieuw Amsterdam in 1626, humans with skin of darker hues were forced to clear forests, lay roads or carry out other heavy work. Two hundred years later, at the time the Luicks' short stay, "blacks" typically toiled at low-paying wages, often in jobs that non-blacks avoided.

Besides people of color, New York teemed with people of characteristics unlike those the Luicks had ever seen. Seamen speaking dozens of languages, traders from ports around the globe, top-hatted bankers from Europe's leading counting houses, immigrants from countless lands were just a few of the many crowded into the narrow, stone-paved streets of lower Manhattan.

*scenes of New York in the 1830s: the harbor under full moon and Saint Thomas Church by night fall, 1837*

Even as migrants just passing through, the Luicks got at least a glimpse of the city's cultural vitality, too. Only a short distance from where they also might have disembarked, sat round Castle Garden. Opened on 3 July 1824 as a center for public entertainment, at various times it housed a fashionable promenade, *Biergarten* and restaurant, exhibition hall, opera and theater—at first all open-air, but later roofed to expand its already extensive leisure-time repertoire even more. Later converted into a pre-Ellis-Island immigrant-processing station, in the 1830s Castle Garden still pulsated with artistic events of various venues, adding to Lower Manhattan's rich vibrancy.

*interior of Castle Garden, 1827;* Junk Keying *docked in New York, 1847, with Castle Garden exterior on left*

Besides the visual or aural, New York's cultural scene at the time of my German ancestors' arrival shone brightly with some of the liveliest literary arts, too. Even if they could not read works published in a language likely none of them could yet speak let alone read, later on their new, American neighbors knew of some of the young country's early writers, whose words not only found ever-wider readership but informed or shaped the opinions and values of a nation.

Perhaps then of personal interest to the Luicks given their destination, author Washington Irving had returned in 1832 from a seventeen-year residency in Europe. Soon after his return to New York City, he published *A Tour on the Prairies*, about his expedition to the "Far West" with the U.S. Army. Unknown to them, the Luicks had at least two other ties to Irving: For one, he had traveled widely in Germanic lands the previous decade, including to Dresden, where I'm writing this account of their journey. For another, when the immigrants continued their trek to the frontier and proceeded up the Hudson, they passed directly in front of the "neglected cottage" that Irving would buy two years hence, name "Sunnyside" and transform into a riverfront estate near the village of Tarrytown, north of his beloved Gotham.

As the Luicks left New York and made their way north along the Hudson, they encountered a landscape not unlike that along the Rhein. Lined by big-shouldered hills and large woods, where the land had been cleared the riverside scenery seemed pastoral, broken at times by smallish settlements and occasional ferry landings. Such were their first views of nature in their new homeland. In the Central Europe that they and their people had known for at least a thousand years, nothing could compare with the flora or fauna to be found everywhere and easily in *den Vereinigten Staaten von Amerika*, the United States of America, where wilderness still reined over most of a vast continent and where in some parts ancient peoples largely still roamed free—for the time being.

*New York from Weehawken, New Jersey, 1834; Washington Irving, 1809*

What must it have felt like for my tired yet excited Swabian ancestors, crawling up one of the deepest, longest river valleys on America's Atlantic coast, after weeks at sea laced with uncertainty, now slowly riding into a future offering huge potential but no promises? With two adult brothers heading the party, with their spouses and various children in tow, the extensive Luick family must have seemed like a small, strange-sounding tribe in the midst of all those Yankees on board with them. At least two worlds were colliding there in that moment—a lingual one and a cultural one, an Old World verses the New.

*stretch of the Hudson sailed by the Luicks—at West Point, shown in 1831*

Still, convinced the seemingly unending journey remained worth their waning reserves, the Luicks pushed on, until they reached New York's state capital city, Albany. There, they changed modes of transportation—the open question being, to which?

The Erie Canal began in Albany but geography inconvenient to canal construction provided such hurdles that an enterprising English geologist built a competing sixteen-mile-long (26-km) railway in thirteen

*the Hudson below Albany, where the Luicks changed modes of transit*

months. Cutting travel time between Albany and Schenectady from an entire day per canal boat to less than one hour by a train, it consisted of stagecoach bodies mounted on iron wheels, set on rails "anchored" not with wooden ties but spiked down to stone paving.

*George William Featherstonhaugh, 1856; a replica built in 1893 of the* De Witt Clinton *he designed 60 years earlier*

Its builder, George William Featherstonhaugh—who once surveyed in the Louisiana Purchase and served as the first U.S. government geologist—launched the United States' first regularly-scheduled rail line on 24 September 1831. An engine named for New York's presiding governor, the "DeWitt Clinton," pulled a fuel wagon—first intended to carry coal, but later switched to wood—followed by cars accommodating passengers sitting inside or on outdoor rumble seats.

An early rider, Ebenezer Mattoon Chamberlain, noted in his journal entry of 28 June 1832:

> Among the astonishing inventions of man, surely that of the locomotive steam engine hath no secondary rank. By this matchless exercise of skill, we fly with a smooth and even course along once impassible barriers, the valleys are filled, the mountains laid low, and distances seems annihilated.
>
> I took my seat as near as possible to the car containing the engine, in order to examine more minutely the operation of this, to me, novel and stupendous specimen of human skill. Having thus, as if by some invisible agency flown the distance of 16 miles in 40 minutes, at Schenectady I took passage on the Hudson and Erie Canal for Buffalo...

*boat on the Eric Canal near Pittsford, crossing Upstate New York, 1837*

—as did the newly arrived Luicks, too.

When they reached their final destination, the collection of road-weary travelers that Heinrich Luick headed landed in a typical frontier town. At some point *every* non-native community in what became the United States went through at least one phase where either boom or bust was possible. In Buffalo's case, its early years were marked by boom—and its latter by the opposite.

Originally founded in 1789 as a trading post near where Buffalo Creek met Lake Erie, it remained small and insignificant for decades—not helped by the British, who burned it to the ground during the War of 1812. As late as 1820 the town had just under twenty-one-hundred inhabitants. After the Eric Canal opened in fall 1825, with Buffalo as its western terminus, however, the city's population more than quadrupled, reaching almost eighty-seven hundred by 1830. The surge led to the city incorporating the year before the Luicks arrived. And, it attracted people unlike the Luicks knew or likely had ever seen: A village director published five years before their arrival in Buffalo listed 59 "names of coloured" heads of families. The growing African-American church would later provide a protective place for Abolitionists to meet.

The Swabians had not come to encounter other kinds of people or learn about their particular trials, but rather to spend the winter—reportedly lodging in brother Jakob's home. Their frosty stay in booming Buffalo, then, consisted solely of a chance to recover from the long journey from the lower Neckar Valley to Upstate New York, as well as prepare for the life the Luicks envisioned, further west, but had not yet begun, in earnest, to build.

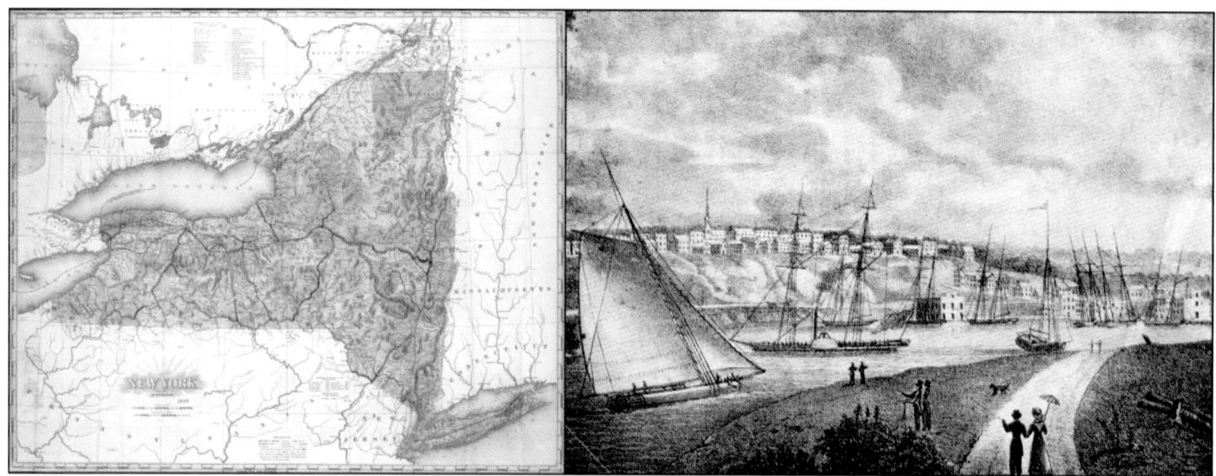


*"Empire State" map showing main water arteries; Buffalo's riverside and Terrace as they looked in 1825*

But then, staying in Buffalo was never the Luick brothers' plan. According to Albert Lee Luick,

> Arriving in New York, Jacob and his family decided to sojourn in western New York state near Niagara Falls... later to migrate to Milwaukee, Wis., as early pioneers there[.] David and Heinrich, with their families, proceeded on to Detroit, a Northwestern Territory fort. Michigan was not admitted as a state until 1837.

When Heinrich and his brother David Luick gathered up their young families, left Buffalo and trekked on to Michigan Territory in spring 1834—presumably via boat over Lake Erie—they entered an endless expanse of land that only a generation before had been almost exclusively thick forest. The pre-Motown Detroit they found as they disembarked was a frontier town in swift transition. Built after 1670 as first a mission, then a fur-trading post by the French along *le détroit du Lac Érie*, the "Strait of Lake Erie" linking two Great Lakes, the settlement had been in uncontested American possession just over two decades, having been recaptured from the British at the end of the War of 1812.

*1807 plan for the post-fire city; as the settlement appeared from Windmill Point on the Detroit River, 1838*

*"Michigan" once stretched over the current states of Wisconsin, Iowa, Minnesota and parts of both Dakotas*

Having been almost completely leveled by a great fire in summer 1805, by 1834 Detroit had mushroomed as the territorial capital of the farthest reaches of an Old Northwest now swelling with settlers. The post-fire plat mimicked that of Washington, DC's fanlike layout, mirroring the ambitious dreams of the Yankee speculators who fed both its profit-spurred and profit-spurring growth.

One family in a growing multitude of newcomers looking for a viable future, if not new fortune,

> the Luicks secured work in helping to build the first railroad in that section, from Detroit to Ann Arbor, a very crude affair. The rails were of hard wood with strips of iron on top to carry the small wood-burning engine and cars.

*1890s depiction of Erie & Kalamazoo Railroad's first locomotive, 1837*

In Ann Arbor, the Luicks

> found there was Government land to be had near Ann Arbor, which they secured. The land had to be cleared of trees and stones before it could be cultivated. The land was very productive.

Detroit was booming, its first semblances of industrializing an early train. In contrast, when Heinrich and his brother David—for whom Albert's father, Heinrich Sr.'s third of five sons to survive to manhood, was named—arrived in Ann Arbor, it was little more than a clearing in the big woods. Thirty years earlier the French had established the first settlement in what became Washtenaw County, at the crossing of several Native-American trails along the banks of the Huron River. It was almost twenty years before two American settlers staked the site of "Annarbor," named after their wives' forenames and nearby Burr Oak trees. As late as 1824, the future county possessed six French-built houses near today's town of Ypsilanti, plus the two American families' cabins among knotty oaks. In 1830 one writer remarked that the two town sites "had become considerable, and many openings could be seen in the forest."

It was those random "openings in the forest" that soon would attract so many Swabs to the woodlands of Southeast Michigan. The Native Americans had created the clearings through setting managed forest fires. Thus they created what the waterway-clinging French—not allowing for the treeless, comparatively endless mid-continental grasslands yet to be settled—called in their mother tongue "*prairie*," or "meadows."

In his Luick-family epic, Albert Lee deemed the land around Ann Arbor "very productive," but was it? Not exactly. Dale Herter (who grew up in Southeast Michigan in a German-American farm family while I was doing the same but in North Central Iowa) attests, along with his collaborator Terry Stollsteimer, to this:

*original title: "Hauling at Thomas Foster's; In the pineries" of Michigan*

> In 1818 the U.S. Congress sent a field party to Michigan Territory to survey its potential for use as soldier's bounty land [given for their service to the country, but when the survey party saw] the low, swampy land in what is now Monroe and Lenawee Counties [to the immediate south of Washtenaw County, they] deemed Michigan worthless for agricultural purposes! After that, much of the westward expansion of European settlers proceeded south of Michigan into Ohio, Indiana, and westward to Illinois.

Despite the ambivalent prognoses already available to pioneers, the land-hungry masses came anyway—including the hard-up, manhandled Swabs yearning to be free. But, they didn't come without encouragement. Still affected by the lingering legacy of Medieval feudalism, life in rural, pre-industrial Europe in the first half of the 19th century reflected the nearest noble's whims regarding land usage. While the division of land varied greatly—at times with radically different traditions prevailing in adjoining principalities—in *Schwaben* instead of the oldest son inheriting an intact farm, each child received an equal portion of a property upon their parents' deaths. Over time, the often miniscule pieces of farmable land constituted little more than large kitchen gardens or modest orchards, with a few grape trellises on the side.

Used to such cramped conditions, for space-starved Swabs even less-than-perfect, often wet woodland like that typical of Southeast Michigan seemed a substantial improvement over what they'd turned their backs on back in the *Heimat*. It would be individual Swabs such as Johann Heinrich Mann, venturing ever westward in search of better soil, who would excite the hopes of thousands of their Old World *Landsleute*. According to Mann's son, Emanuel, his father was

> traveling [in late fall of 1829] from Pennsylvania, where he had recently settled, to Michigan to look for better farmland, and met Daniel Allmendinger along the way. Allmendinger was a fellow immigrant from the Stuttgart area, and had already purchased land in Lodi Township that same year. He convinced Mr. Mann and his friend, Peter Schilling, to also settle in Washtenaw County.

The *History of Washtenaw County*—perhaps presumptuously titled, given it was written in 1881—documented the details:

> On his return to Pennsylvania, he [J.H. Mann] wrote a letter to his brother-in-law, Emanuel Josenhans, in Stuttgart, giving a very favorable account of what he saw of the new Territory and the route by which it could be reached by immigrants from Germany, from New York via Erie Canal and Lake Erie. Mr. Josenhans circulated the letter amongst the peasantry in the neighborhood of Stuttgart. The consequence was that numerous immigration was started for Michigan by a class of small farmers and mechanics who had very limited means.

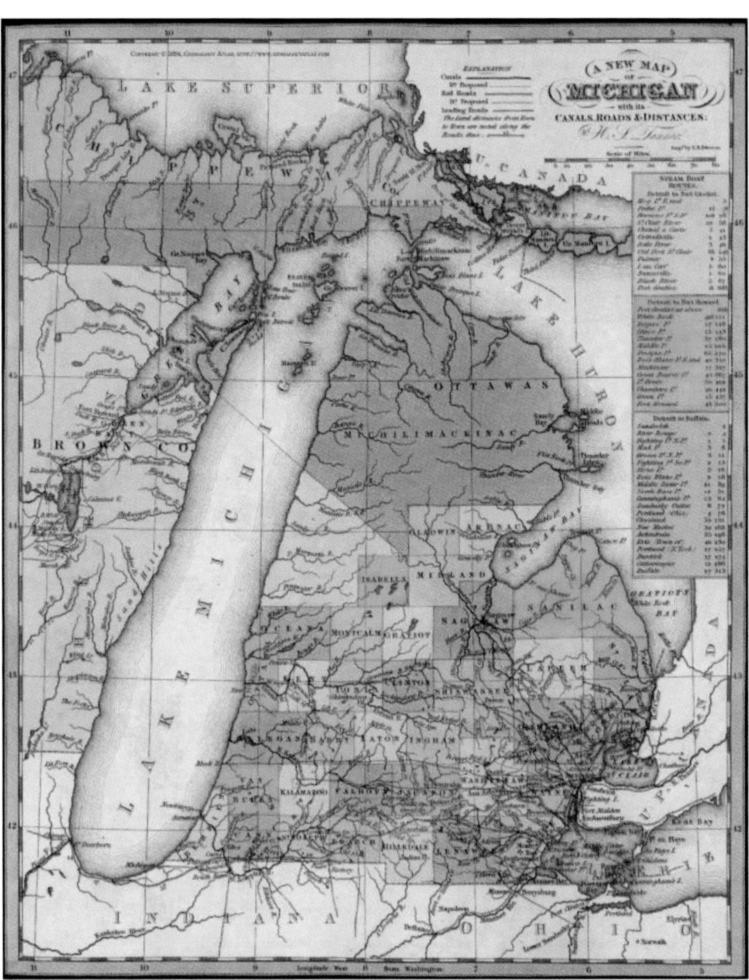

*"Michigan" in 1836 included today's "Wisconsin"*

Based on their extensive research, Terry and Dale estimate in their *History of the German Settlers in Washtenaw County* that although they came from virtually every Germanic state,

> fully three-fourths of the German immigrants to Washtenaw County were Swabians from the kingdom of Württemberg (and some from neighboring Baden) in southwestern Germany. During the early to mid-1800's, this region had been ravaged by the Napoleonic wars and was economically depressed due to high taxation, religious quarrels, the arbitrary rules of local landlords and dukes, as well as a series of failed harvests. Emigration was often the easiest solution to a tough situation and represented hope for future generations.

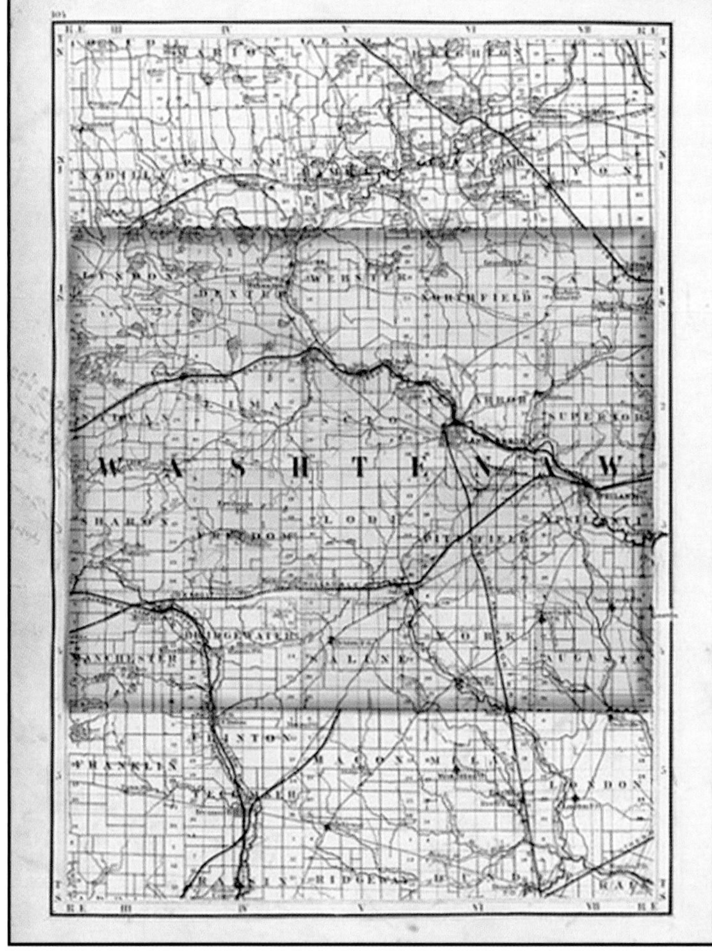


*Washtenaw County, Michigan, in 1873*

---

**chapter 7: midwifing the Midwest**

Feeling forced to leave a land where their people had lived for over a thousand years, they sought to sink new roots, fast. So, soon after their arrival in Ann Arbor, the Luicks set about forging sturdy new homes out of the forest. Based on his tour of the old Luick homestead in 1887, in Albert's assessment

> They were skilled craftsmen and built substantial log cabins for their families. The original log cabin built by my grandfather was still standing and was in excellent condition when, as a boy of ten, I visited the old farm with my mother and father, together with my Aunt Catherine and Uncle Adrian Elder, with their young son George. I remember my grandmother's old spinning wheel in the loft with her old loom. I am reminded that she spun the yarn for her family's mittens, socks and sweaters and wove the cloth for their clothing. I have always marveled as I think of the initiative and ability of these early pioneers to provide as well as they did for their families. At the time of our visit, we saw near the log cabin my grandfather's old wine cellar with its rows of kegs—I suppose containing wine of rare vintage. This cellar was built of stone, under the hill below the vineyard.

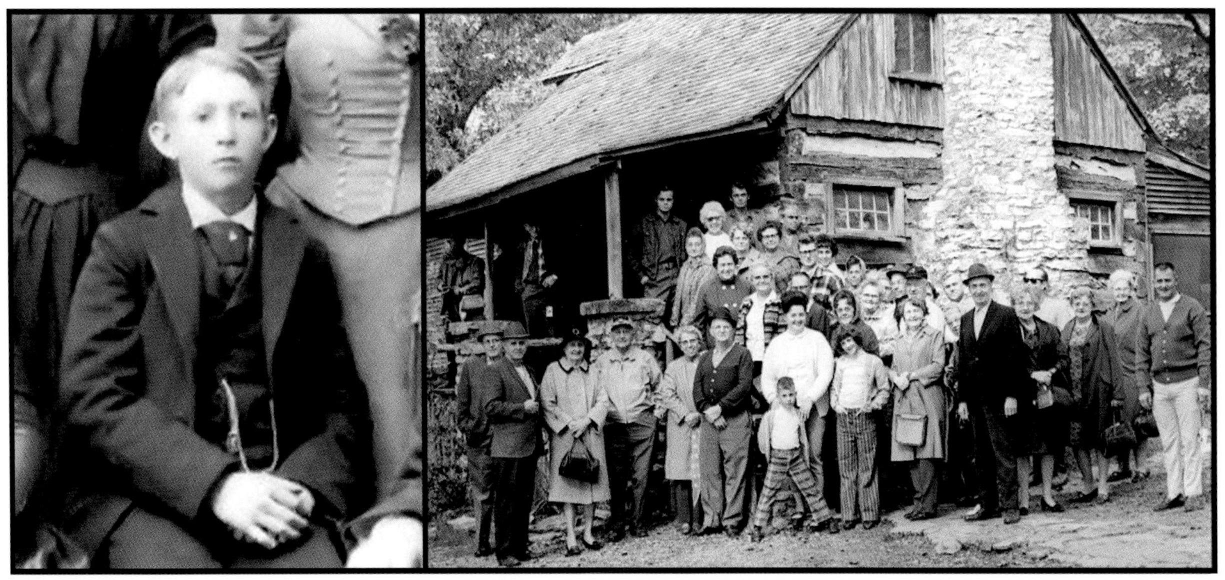

*Albert Lee Luick, about age ten; Mattie (Luick) Farmer in center of group touring cabin, with white buttons*

While a sturdy home might have seemed to provide a safe place to bring new, "American" lives into the world, even the thickest walls, however, couldn't shield the newcomers from ageless trials such as disease and premature demise. In his next paragraph, Albert goes on to relate:

> Katherine and Heinrich had three additional children, all born in this log cabin. They were William and Catherine—later Mrs. Adrian Elder—and Frederick. My father used to tell me about his parents. His father was a very rugged, hard-working man who provided well for his family. His mother was a very beautiful blonde woman, well-educated for that day and an excellent pensman. He recalled that many people came to her to write their letters and calling cards. With her education and the poor school facilities, she was able to impart considerable school to her children. However, her untimely death in 1843 left the family with great sadness. Frederick, the youngest, was a very small boy of four. Katherine had instilled in these brothers and their sister great love and affection for each other that was to endure through the years in their close association and helpfulness to each other.

Fortunately for the forty-six-year-old widower, Heinrich Luick did not have to care for his young, half-orphaned children in isolation. He had a fast-growing German community to help him.

———

As also the case a generation later in North Central Iowa, the initial settlement of Southeast Michigan followed patterns that replicated themselves thousands of times across the American Heartland of the 19th century, already as of spring 1788. It was then that the U.S. Government initiated selling public parts of the land of the Territory Northwest of the River Ohio—more commonly known as the Northwest Territory, the area recently ceded by the British they had held for 50 years west of Pennsylvania and north of the Ohio River, reaching west to the Mississippi and as far north as still-British-held Canada—to encourage rapid westward expansion of the young United States.

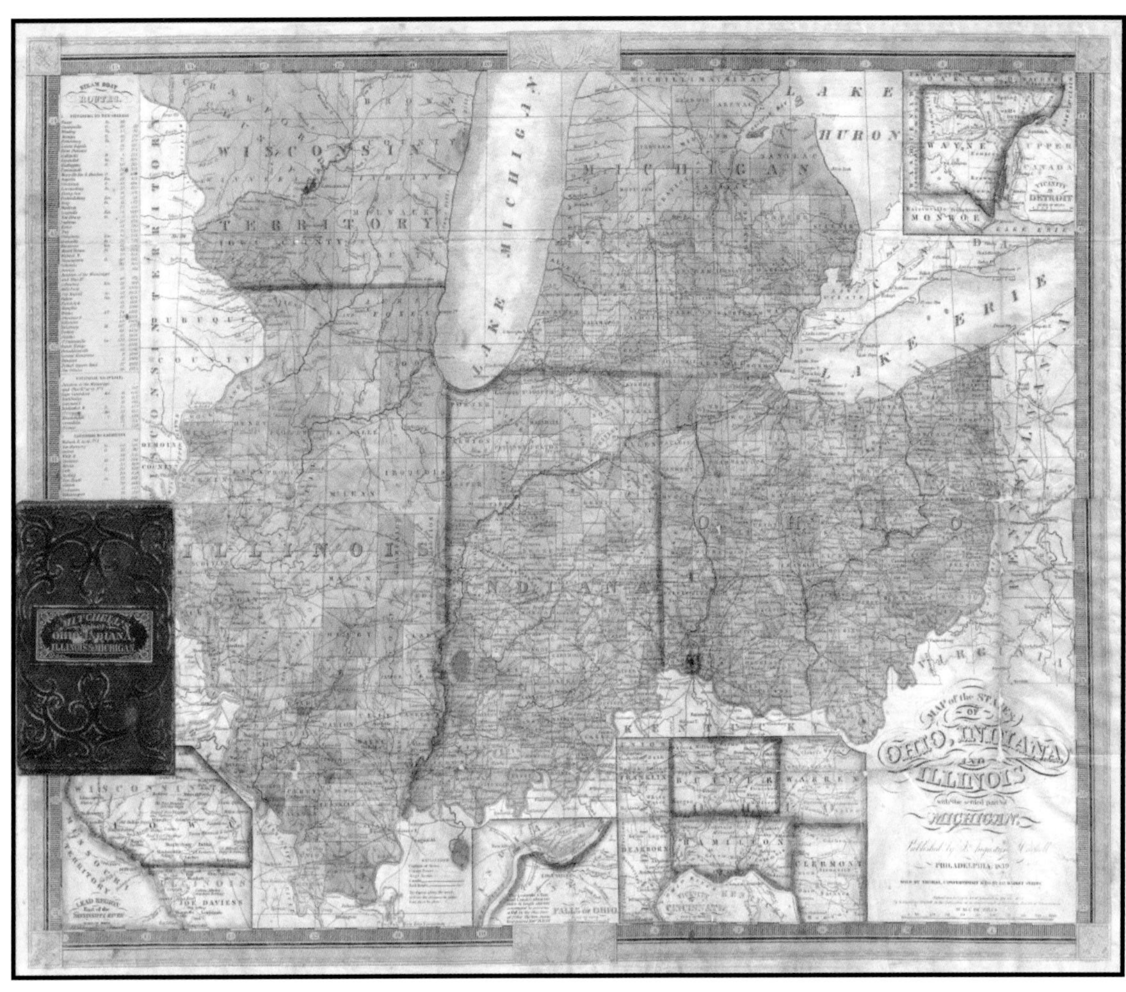


*the Old Northwest [Territories], consisting of today's Ohio, Indiana, Illinois, Michigan and Wisconsin, 1838*

Indeed, the documentable birth of the Midwest, both as cultural concept and per se, took place on Monday, 7 April 1788 with the arrival of the so-called First Forty-Eight (or also "Founders of Ohio") in Marietta. All men (and mostly U.S. Army officers or veterans of the recent revolution), they had been specially vetted and, out of long lists of candidates, selected to initiate the new republic's thrust into the northwest—as well as to push out of the lingering vestiges of Mother England's recent rule. (Perhaps out of a lopsided sense of propriety, the U.S. Government let the first, lone female pioneer, Mary Owen, join the men only three months later. It seems no African Americans were included in the party, either.)

Comparable to contemporary procedures to choose, say, Navy Seal teams or space explorers set to start a Mars mission, the individuals approved by two of the Ohio Company of Associates' co-founders, Rufus Putnam and Manasseh Cutler, were to exemplify "high character and bravery, but also [be] men with proven skills necessary to build a settlement in the wilderness." Not yet chosen to be president of the United States, former Commander-in-Chief of the Continental Army that had fought for independence, George Washington, said of these pioneers "I know many of the settlers personally, and there never were men better calculated to promote the welfare of such a community." During a visit to the country for which he had fought to create, General Lafayette of France commented in May 1825 that the former officers among them were "the bravest of the brave. Better men never lived." With even more ballyhoo, in 1852 the Ohio Historical Society president said of the First Forty-Eight:

So various and eventful lives as theirs have scarcely ever fallen to the lot of man. They were born under a monarchy,—fought the battle of Independence,—assisted in the baptism of a great republic,—then moved into a wilderness,—and laid the foundations of a State,—itself almost equaling an empire. These men not only lived in remarkable times, but were themselves remarkable men. Energetic, industrious, persevering, honest, bold, and free — they were limited in their achievements only by the limits of possibility. Successful alike in field and forest,—they have, at length, gone to their rest,—leaving names which are a part of the fame and the history of their country.

*arrival at confluence of Ohio and Muskingum Rivers on 7 April 1788; Rufus Putnam (1737-1824) in 1796*

In observance of the centennial of Mariette's founding (named after Marie Antoinette, the later-beheaded French queen and, earlier, a Revolutionary-War ally of the young U.S.), in 1888 Massachusetts Senator George Hoar orated "It was an illustrious band; they were men of exceptional character, talents and attainments; they were the best of New England culture; they were Revolutionary heroes."

While Hoar's tribute in its totality bordered on blather, it alluded to at least two enduring truths that had permanent influence on the American character. First, that those who would set the tone and tenor at the core of the emerging new country were mostly New England Yankees and individuals from the Mid-Atlantic states—thus assuring, for example, that slavery would have no future north of the Ohio River or most of America west of the Mississippi, and, per the adopted Articles of Compact, prohibiting primogeniture as well as discrimination on the basis of religion. Second, Hoar accurately assessed that the men chosen to cast the soul of Middle America were forging institutionalized "revolution."

Dismissed in the jet age by unimaginative and uninspired, cocktail-sipping coastal inhabitants as "fly-over land," what that endless chessboard of farms and cookie-cutter towns streaming by below the plane windows embodies, is, in truth, the idea that an "enlightened," democratic society can be scientifically structured. While doing unimaginable damage to rivers and entire watersheds, dividing hill tops from their slopes, and depriving drivers from reaching their destinations over the shortest, most direct distance, the quadrant, measured distribution of land as of that first Federal sale at Marietta reflected several pillars of the Age of Enlightenment.

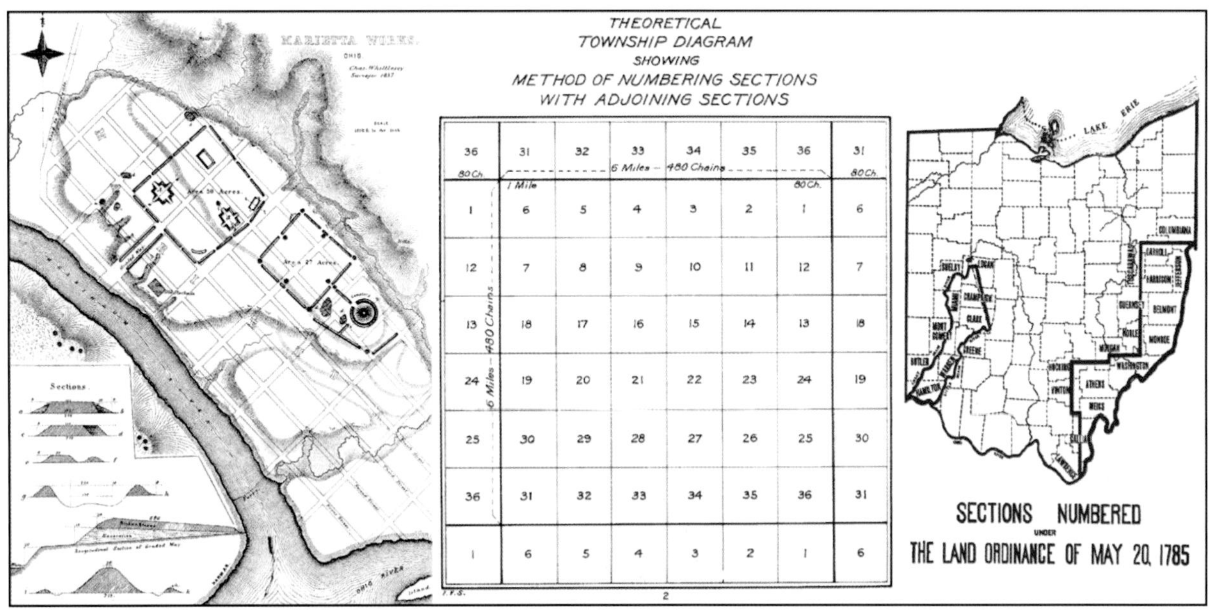


*maps showing "ideal" land division of a town (Marietta), township and counties in newly-formed Ohio*

A polymath who spoke five languages and espoused science-based "progress" in such creative fields as invention and architecture, Thomas Jefferson had studied the English empirics as a young man. Later, as Foreign Minister, he lived in France for the four years leading up to its own revolution and traveled much of Europe. A deist and active member of the American Philosophical Society, who defended ideas advanced by Quaker-raised Thomas Paine in that man's best-selling broadside, *The Age of Reason*, Jefferson had coined the then-radical concept that "all men are created equal," penned the Declaration of Independence and founded the University of Virginia. Along with much of the Northwest Ordinance of 1787, he established the formula of angular townships and counties that would replace the chaotic, confusing hodge-podge of crisscrossing colonial property lines and borders that had come before.

*Thomas Jefferson (Rembrandt Peale, 1800) & Thomas Paine (Auguste Millière, after George Romney, 1792)*

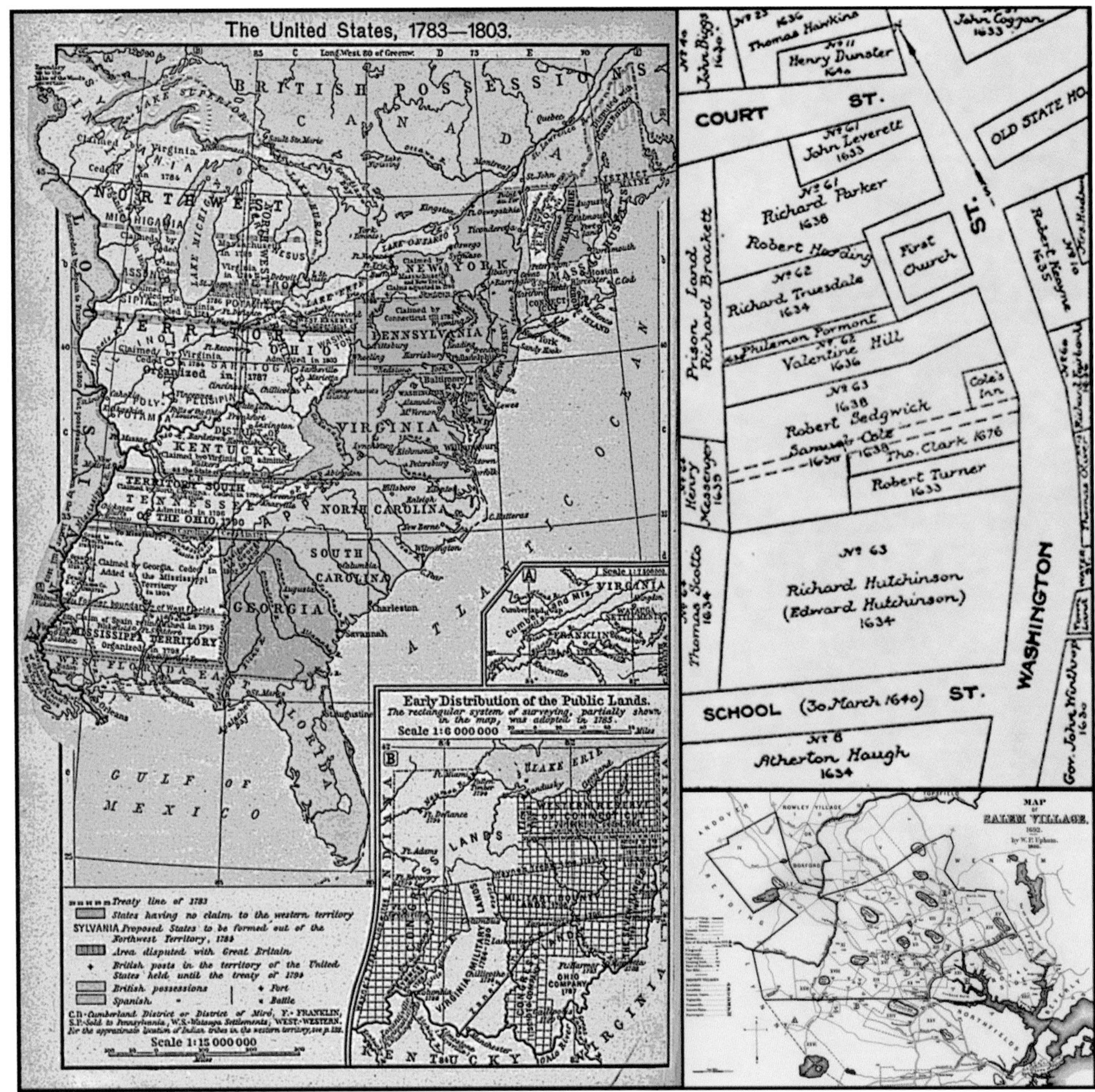


*the U.S., circa 1800; insert contrasts new land-division model with that of colonial Boston (right images)*

Poised to purchase gigantic Louisiana, but already standing at the threshold of an enormous expansion to the shore-hugging start of what soon would become a continental power, Jefferson and his supporters oversaw first the surveying, then the platting of the Northwest Territory. Immediately a hallmark of the no-nonsense Midwest, the math genius from Monticello drafted a system meant to facilitate the quick and efficient sale of land, which he intended, in turn, to facilitate the spread of a yeoman-driven agriculture that, in his vision, would hold in check in perpetuity the urban-based tyranny of moneyed elites.

Thoughtful Tom's revolutionary formula for setting up "model communities" in the newest reaches of the Anglo New World also allowed amble public space vital to the democratic process: It allocated central squares for courthouses or parks, with other land set aside for schools, libraries, post offices, fairgrounds, county farms or other communal needs. For over a century and a half, Jefferson's template for a free society prevailed—and provided a tangible foundation for ideals of freedom.

Among other illogical or inherently unjust Old-World systems of land distribution, Jefferson's attempt to forever codify democratic values in the form of methodically farmed, four-cornered parcels stood in stark contrast to that which the squeezed-out Swabs pouring into the newly opened American West had left behind. Attracted by the allure of cheap, virgin soil, they came by the tens of thousands, even though they usually spoke not a word of the language of their would-be "liberators," of those not just hawking but actually retailing the American ideal of land-owning, equalitarian citizenship—an alleged, inextinguishable ticket to freedom from the fear of tyrants' arbitrary terror or entrenched, wholesale injustice.

*an ad touting "the state 'Michigan' United States of North America;" plans for an Ann Arbor building*

As merely two out of the tens of millions born to the subsequent generations sustained by the fruits of our ancestors' most impassioned strivings and sweat-soaked sacrifices, grateful German-descended Dale Herter and Terry Stollsteimer remind us that

> Theirs is an American immigration story that has many parallels in other parts of the United States, one in which immigrants arrived in a strange land speaking a different language, and therefore tended to form a cohesive community bound by a common language and customs. We often resist thinking of our own ancestors as poor, foreign-tongued immigrants, similar to those immigrants of today, who also tend to stay together in separate communities[.]These were our ancestors too, at one time.

---

## chapter 8: in "*klein Deutschland*"

As in countless other communities, immigrants arriving in Southeast Michigan directly from Europe found themselves in an existing dominant culture. As across the Midwest and, later, much of the West generally, the first non-native peoples to control what became "American" territories consisted mostly of Yankee or other old-stock settlers looking as much to make a fast buck as to turn a lasting furrow. While some did stay at their original destination upon leaving New England or the Mid-Atlantic, most moved on, selling the homes or shops they'd established at a handsome profit. In the process of opening up new lands under the blinding banner of Manifest Destiny, English-speaking pioneers bestowed most of erstwhile frontier America its place names. And, they chartered many of the first institutions (schools, churches, banks, etc.) as well as set leading cultural, social and civic norms for the future residents of most communities. It was mostly their lead that those who followed would emulate.

The ethnically diverse groups that came later either voluntarily fit or were coerced into existing frameworks. Among the largest of the non-Anglo groups—in much of the Midwest forming up to sixty percent of some localities' ethnic origins—were those with Germanic roots. Like the Danes of western Nebraska or Iowa, Czechs of eastern Iowa and Nebraska... and so many other examples in so many other towns across America, the Germans, too, formed lingually and culturally homogenous communities in myriad places—such as among the Burr Oaks of Southeast Michigan's Washtenaw County.

*while Conestoga wagons wait outside, migrants dance at an inn; 1812*

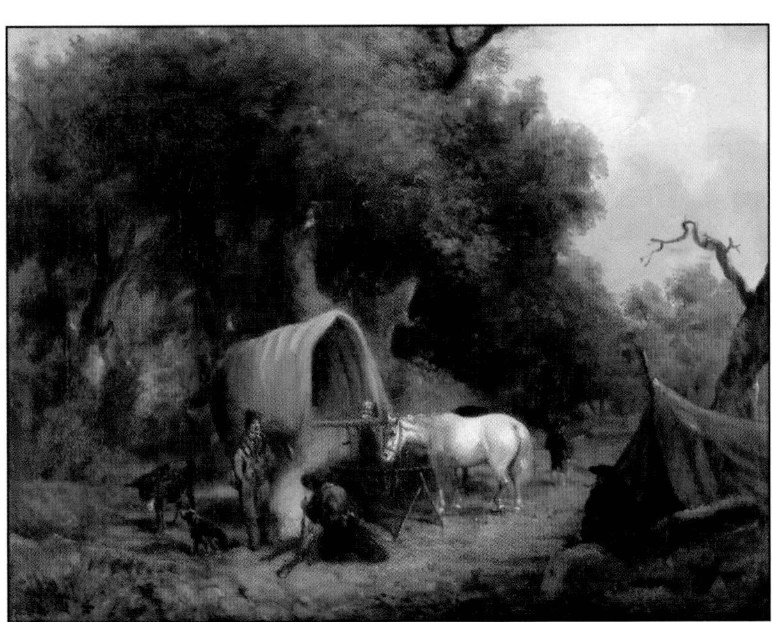

*Pioneers set up camp under a thick canopy of virgin-forest trees.*

While the winters were harsher and the summers hotter as well as stickier, the climate and landscape German immigrants found in the Big Woods of Michigan resembled the Central Europe they had known all their lives. Coming in such overwhelming numbers as they did, by coincidence more than design, the Swabians soon found they had built a *"klein Deutschland,"* a "little Germany" in the midst of the American Heartland. As Terry and Dale have documented,

> Since German was spoken as the childhood language by [many Washtenaw County] farmers well up to 1915, they tended to purchase farms near one another rather than spread too far afield. In the heart of [that] settlement area, almost all of the farmers in Freedom and Lodi townships held German surnames, and the adjoining townships were often occupied at a level of 50% or more. Masked in this illustration are the farms in which a daughter of German immigrants may have married an American of non-German descent, thus cloaking additional German influence.

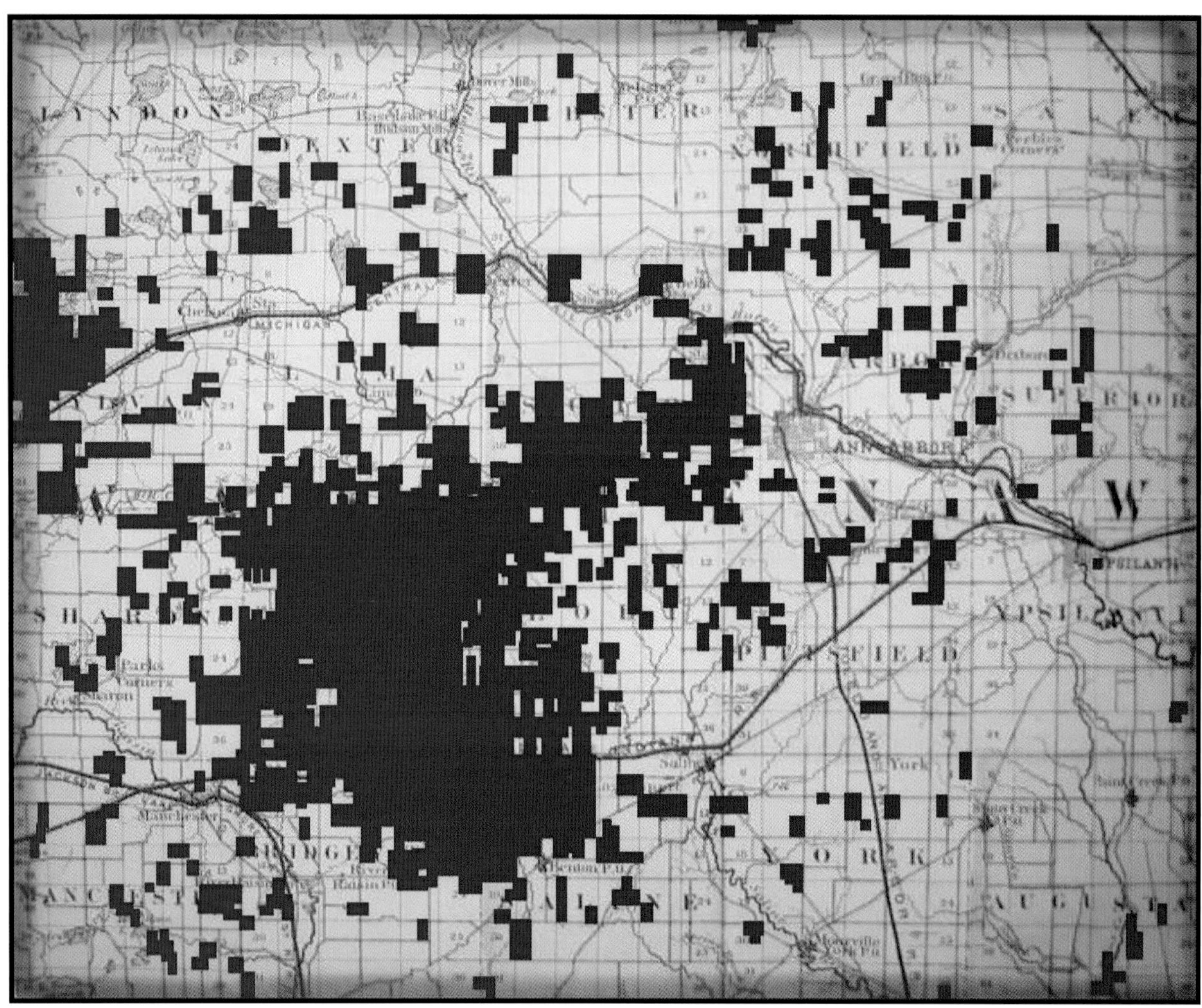


*Terry Stollsteimer and Dale Herter's map of German-owned farms in Washtenaw County in 1874*

Even forming an ethnic majority, in a closely-knit enclave of culturally-connected speakers of the same Teutonic tongue, however, did not assure German immigrants an effortless entry into their new lives in a new land.

> As faced by many pioneers in America in the 1800's, life in Washtenaw County at the time was neither pleasant nor easy. Families cut down trees and hewed logs to build cabins, with only the help of hand tools and their oxen and horses. Sawmills were soon established along flowing rivers, which helped the pioneers produce lumber for framing windows, walls, and roof rafters. Windows were generally kept to a minimum to avoid the high cost of the window panes and to minimize heat loss in the winter. [The] German immigrants complained of the heat during the summer and the cold in the winter, both of which were slightly more extreme than what they were used to in the old country. Fields had to be carved out of the forest, and the stumps pulled before any farming could be done. Early years on a homestead often meant little food and a general lack of luxuries, such as beer or wine, something they had become used to after living near the long-established grain fields and vineyards of southern Germany. [...] Homesteaders were also forced to keep guard over their livestock from marauding packs of wolves. As late as 1834 wolves were still present in the county, as attested by the loss of 20 sheep from a night's marauding by a wolf pack in Freedom Township [immediately southwest of the Luicks' farm].

A common pitfall of benefitting from common language, however, can be suffering from the suffocating cultural conformity that often accompanies two or more souls sharing a mother tongue. Soon wrapped in a snug cocoon of smug group think, German enclaves proved to be seemingly self-contained. According to the University of Michigan Department of History lecturer Jonathan Marwil,

*Wolves posed a danger—both real and imagined.*

> the various immigrant groups were more or less absorbed into the Ann Arbor community within a few years. Not so the Germans. They learned English but kept their native tongue and made sure their children learned it. They joined local groups and entered politics, but they prayed in their own churches, gathered in their own service organizations, formed their own band, and established their own volunteer fire company, which drew the admiration of their Yankee neighbors. Assimilated and much respected for their industry and public spirit, they nonetheless retained for decades a separate identity as well.

In such a myopic-but-enjoyable environment, Dale and Terry recall

> Ties to the homeland in Germany remained strong among the first generation of immigrants. Some even sent their sons back to Germany for an education, and the classic German fables and songs were taught to the children to remind them of their roots. [...] German could be regularly heard on the streets of the town and many public speeches and lectures were also given in German. [...] Sons of German immigrants tended to marry daughters of German immigrants, so that many families in Washtenaw County today can still count themselves as being of full German heritage after five or six generations, attesting to both the size and cohesiveness of this group of settlers. The language was maintained as well, at least for a time. Fluent German speakers persisted in the area at least into the 1980's, fully 150 years after the first group of German immigrants had arrived.

As too often happens, however, the success built by one group often breeds envy and its dark-faced companion, resentment, in another. Written in the early 1880s by The Pioneer Society, the first known recorded history of Washtenaw County viewed the local, omnipresent German community—by then well into its second if not third generation in Southeast Michigan—with begrudged respect or even restrained awe. According to Terry and Dale, the area's Germans

> were best known for their industrious habits and cohesiveness. [The Pioneer Society authors] necessarily wrote [their account] from a mostly Yankee viewpoint. In reading it, one can see that they alternated from opinions that the Germans were somewhat unwanted invaders, to one of admiration for their spirit and industriousness.

*Albert Lee Luick on steps, next to wife, showing sugar-plant, 1920; Belmond high school class, 1907*

What exactly did the unwilling Anglo admirers say in 1881 about their Central-European-born neighbors at the time of the Swabian settlers' first years, a half-century earlier, in Washtenaw County's German-dominated Lodi Township?

> About this time, the Germans established a settlement in Freedom [Township], which adjoins us on the west, which has spread in several directions and now it covers several townships. Three-quarters of the soil in Lodi Township is to-day in German hands. They have not retarded, but accelerated, the improvement of the soil. Industry and frugality are their cardinal virtues. Their strong hands have subdued and made productive the most forbidden and barren places.

---

## chapter 9: heading West—again

Life on the Michigan frontier offered the likes of poor Swabians a rich new start, but it too often also was marked by brutal, premature death—for the Luicks, only a decade after they arrived in *"Amerika"* by that of Katherine, Heinrich's reportedly noble-born wife. With her sudden passing in 1843, a rapid series of events set into motion that would radically change the family's fate in the New World. For one, left to raise six children, Heinrich soon remarried, taking—per Tony Luick's research—as his second wife:

> Dorothea ("Dolly") Herrmann, born 8 Jan 1819 in Oeschelbronn, Württemberg. She married Georg David Schief on 26 Nov 1837, born 9 Jul 1814 in Oeschelbronn. They immigrated via London to America aboard the *Margaret Evans*, arriving in New York on 20 Jul 1846. The couple had 6 children, 4 of whom died within 1 year of birth. Two surviving daughters accompanied them on the journey. Georg died in 1847, likely in Michigan, and Dolly married Jacob Heinrich "Henry" Luick in 1848. The couple had 5 children of their own, all surviving to adulthood. Henry died in Feb 1860 ("shot himself accidentally"), and Dolly was widowed with 3 young children at home. The 1860 US census shows that Dolly owned $3,000 in real estate and $500 in personal property to provide her support. She never remarried and died 12 May 1878.

Only three years older than her eldest new stepson (Henry Junior), "Dolly" suddenly found herself raising seven children in their teens or younger: Johann (19), David (16), Wilhelm (14), Katherine (nine) and Friedrich (seven)—all of whom would be known as adults by their English names—plus the surviving daughters of her previous marriage, Eva and Christine. By the time of Dolly's marriage to his family's patriarch, Heinrich and Katherine's oldest son, 26-year-old Henry Junior, was already well on his own.

*children of Heinrich & Katherine (Gerstenmaier) Luick: William (standing), Catherine (Luick) Elder, David; (sitting) John, Henry & Frederick: 1890s. The photo was taken during John's visit to Iowa from Michigan.*

Henry Luick, Jr., the eldest of the family, was ten years old when they left Germany; but he had received considerable education and after coming to America he became a civil engineer or surveyor. About 1846 he joined a surveying gang to help make the Government survey for northern Iowa. The legend goes that while camped on the Iowa River on the north side of what was known as Franklin Grove, they found that a trapper—a Mr. Beebe—had built a very good log cabin. This trapper wanted to move west, so Henry, who liked the country very much, made a deal for the log house and all the land he could see from a big walnut tree near-by. Henry knew, of course, he would have to file for the land, but he wanted that log cabin.

As noted by German-immigrant descendants Dale Herter and Terry Stollsteimer, "the low, swampy land" of Southeast Michigan was "deemed worthless for agricultural purposes" by U.S. survey parties as early as 1818. Thus, even before Washtenaw County had been fully settled, the children of its first settlers already looked elsewhere for richer, cheaper land. They found it in places further south, like in Ohio and Indiana, and further west, like in Illinois and Iowa. One of the second-generation, opportunity-hungry Americans among them was young Henry Luick.

*typical Iowa log cabin, like the Luicks would have had at Franklin Grove*

Mostly treeless, thick-loamed North Central Iowa, though, offered those pushing westward a fundamentally different environment than that of wooded, scrubby-soiled Southeast Michigan. During Henry's initial tour not yet a state (that would come at year's end, on 28 December 1846), Iowa offered an open prairie, an empty palette of possibilities compared to the swiftly-filling jumble of peoples and problems back in Washtenaw County. With the state's 1846 total population of 80,000 mostly clinging to the "safe" southeast corner of the emerging state's territory (larger than England and Northern Ireland combined), northwestern Iowa's prairieland seemed virtually uninhabited—save for the last, understandably resentful and resisting Native Americans yet to be pushed out, poisoned with firewater and infested blankets, or simply murdered.

Having just stumbled into the area as part of a surveying crew, adventurous Henry was hooked:

> After completing his work on the survey Henry returned to his family at Ann Arbor. He was married to Melissa Overacker, whose ancestors were of early Colonial stock dating back to Nieuw Amsterdam, the early Dutch settlement on Manhattan Island. They had several children, but Henry was determined to take his family to that log cabin in Iowa.

As their first baby, Michael Henry, was born on 22 January 1844, less than three months after they married, it might have been love or, as likely, something less romantic that initially brought Henry Jacob Luick and Melissa Lucinda Overacker together. When then-21-year-old Henry married the 17-year-old girl on 26 October 1843—the same year as the sudden death of the young surveyor's refined mother—he unwittingly married into a family of fighters.

When she was born on 16 December 1825 in Cuyahoga County, Ohio, Melissa's family had been seeking its fortune on the frontier there for at least forty years—within two years of Britain ceding the region to the young United States at the end of the Revolutionary War and before it officially became the Northwest Territory. Born in fall 1785, her father, Michael Anthony Overacker, also had been born in the area given the Algonquian name for "crooked river" and later deemed "Cuyahoga County," yet at the time of Melissa's birth four decades later "Cleveland" was but an unincorporated village on the edge of a marshy swamp. The whole county huddled around it had less than ten thousand residents. Once a "Western Reserve" claimed by faraway Connecticut, the northeast corner of later "Ohio" appealed to the colonial-stock Overackers, who had long been chasing and fighting for their American Dream.

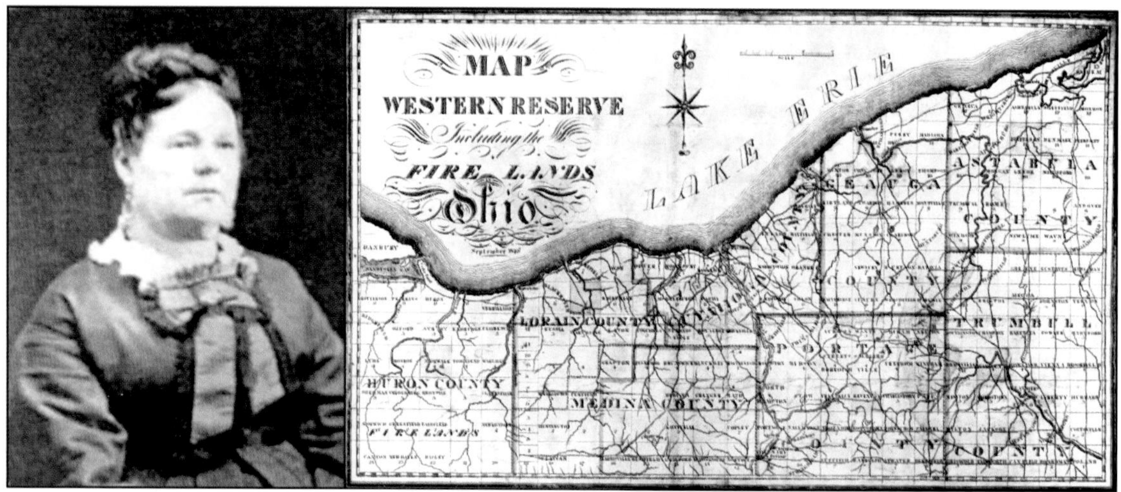


*Melissa's mother, Meredith Lucinda (Briggs) Overacker, circa 1870; map of the Western Reserve, 1826*

The extended, prolific Overacker clan had been in the New World for over two hundred years by the time Melissa married a relatively recent arrival. Born "Heinrich," her new groom had entered the young United States as a nine-year-old-boy via New York, a city that featured so prominently in his future wife's family's American saga. Later renamed "Henry," Junior came to *Amerika* as the elder Luick—his father Heinrich Sr. back in ill-fortuned Swabia—hastily fled military service. Over decades, Melissa's male ancestors, in contrast, had repeatedly sought it out.

Her paternal great-grandfather, Johann Michael Overacker, an immigrant from the *Pfalz*—the German Palatinate on the Rhein—had fled persecution back in Europe. Arriving in the American colonies by 1740, when he married Anna Barbara Stover in Upstate New York (he was about twenty, she eighteen), he later joined the Revolutionary-era Committee of Correspondence in Albany. His son, Melissa's grandfather Adam, served the rebellion as an eager teenage soldier.

*Michael Van der Cook's gravestone, circa 1786; veterans memorabilia*

At the same time, Adam's father-in-law, Melissa's maternal great-grandfather Michael Van der Cook, also served on the Committee, as well as helped coordinate financing the fight in the South. And, he and his wife, Cornelia (Van Ness) Van der Cook, sent all of their five sons to fight the Red Coats. Whatever fed Michael's impulse to risk all—even his sons' lives—it laid deep.

Michael's unusual gravestone—although now almost illegible after decades of environmental degradation—offers many telling details, as well as credible clues. As one modern Michigan researcher belonging to his long lineage—consulting that and other sources—later documented:

> Michael Van der Cook was born 10 November, 1715 in Horseneck, New Jersey [and] married 11 February, 1742 Cornelia Van Ness, daughter of Simon Van Ness and Hester Delamater, at Passaic, Passaic Co., New Jersey. He established himself as a miller; by 1745 the gristmill at Montville, Morris Co., New Jersey, was widely known as "Michael Cook's Mill."

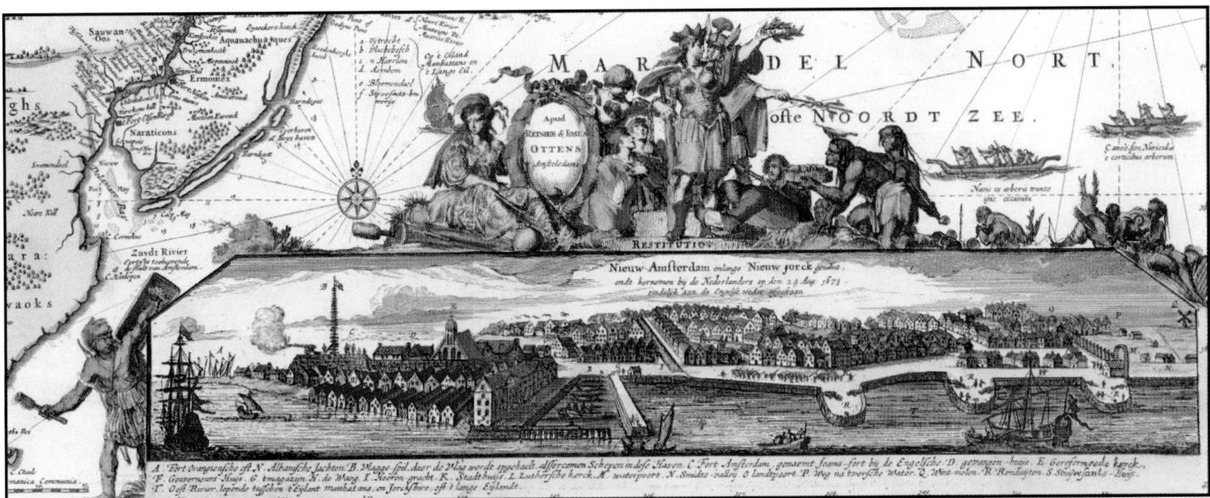


*inscription reads: "New Amsterdam, recently called Nieuw Jorck ["New York"], and now retaken by the Netherlanders 24 Aug. 1673." Per image source: "On the seventh state of this map (issued by R & J Ottens around 1725) there's been added: at last handed over to the English again." This detail is from a larger map.*

Although she said "it has never been proven," the miller's genealogically-minded descendent discovered

> there is some speculation that Michael Van der Cook emigrated from New Jersey because he either lost his land or was required to pay for it twice. When the English took over from the Dutch [in 1664], land ownership became an issue. The English appointed two proprietors who were empowered by the crown to sell land and issue lawful titles to the same. Many of the early settlers in NJ had in fact purchased land from the local Indians. The proprietors either confiscated this property or demanded payment. This eventually became such a heated issue that it touched off a series of incidents called The Horseneck Riots. It is thought that not only did Michael Van der Cook and his family leave NJ on account of this, but that his strong support of the American Revolution may have grown out of his lingering animosity toward the British because of this earlier loss.

By moving up the Hudson River Valley, however, Dutch-descended Michael Van der Cook only jumped from a simmering, English-cast pot into a raging, empire-fanned fire. Per Linda Wilbur Homer's narrative, he became known as the

> "oldest of this place"... the first white settler in that area, having moved his family to his newly purchased 3300 acre patent of land in upper Albany County, New York in May 1762. Michael purchased two additional tracts in 1764, with all three portions of "Cook's Patent" totaling 6,200 acres. There, he re-established his grist-milling business on Deep Kill, the creek that still runs through the area. He also founded Cooksborough, Albany County, [now part of] Pittstown, Rensselaer County. All of the ten known children of Michael and Cornelia (Van Ness) Van der Cook (except, perhaps, Cornelia, their youngest, baptized in NY on September 13, 1761, two months after her birth) were born in New Jersey.

*Hudson River near Albany, the Van der Cook family's adopted home*

As colonial-era records are relatively few and typically sketchy, most of the information known about the Vander Cooks after their removal from New Jersey to Upstate New York comes from the exceptionally extensive biography engraved on Michael's gravestone. Excerpts include:

Here lyeth
the remains of
MICHAEL V.D. COOK
died 2 November 1786
Schaghticoke, Rensselaer
County, New York
The above sage was a firm friend to the liberties
of this country in 1776 by which he lost the
better part of his prosperity and in July 1777
he had his home Rob'd and his life threatened
by some of the British King's Robers, while his
sons and the rest of the military were gone to
the Northward to oppose Burgoyne as also by
the depreciation of the then currency; all of
which he bore with Christian Fortitude.


Shortly after the end of the Americans' revolt against England, Michael Van der Cook's son-in-law, Adam Overacker, took his own young family to the Old Northwest, to what would become Cuyahoga County, Ohio. There, they lived in territory recently forfeited by defeated England. On 7 September 1785, Adam and his wife, Cornelia (Vandercook) Overacker, gave birth to—among seven other children—to Michael Anthony Overacker, Melissa's future military-man father.

Less than thirty years after the British crown had lost its vast lands north of the Ohio, it contested the area again—only to be routed once more in the War of 1812. The last was a war against "Mother England" at least presumably supported by the Overackers, but documentably fought by the larger Vandercook family, including Cornelia's mother's people, the Van Nesses.

Those families boasted long connections to today's Manhattan—erstwhile Nieuw Amsterdam—where the Van Nesses and other, one-time Dutch subjects had long chaffed under British rule.

*Johannes Vingboons'* Gezicht op ["View of"] Nieuw Amsterdam*, 1664—the year England seized the city*

Long and fiercely coveted for being naturally nearly perfectly navigable, today's New York Harbor soon attracted the attention of several vying naval powers. The Dutch, however, were the first Europeans to establish a durable presence at "Nieuw Nederland," from its founding in 1624 until the British attacked, defeated, then annexed the colony in September 1664. While historians disagree how successfully the place functioned as a trading post, most agree that it left lasting influences not only on later "New York" but also "American" society—above all in terms of multiculturalism, freedom of conscience and a moxie for making money.

Originally, the Dutch-sponsored English explorer Henry Hudson attempted to locate an alleged "Northwest Passage." Discovering the harbor to be a sheltered, mostly ice-free artery leading to seemingly inexhaustible supplies of lucrative beaver pelts—then the latest fashion in Europe due to the large water rodent's fur being water repellant—any prospects of a seaway to the Pacific paled in comparison to the mountains of money that could be made trading pelts.

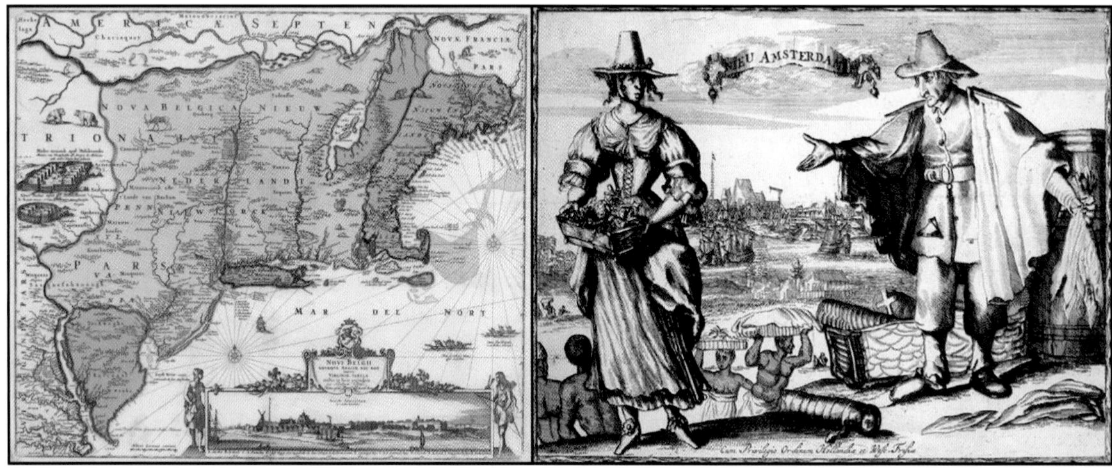


*1656 map of Dutch colony also known as "Novum Belgium;" 2nd oldest image of Nieuw Amsterdam, 1642*

In such an economic climate of unfettered bonanza, the embryonic settlement became a New World Babel even before it had an official name. A Portuguese-African mulatto trader, Juan Rodriguez, comprised its first recorded resident—later followed by Jewish refugees from Brazil, African slaves brought by scrupleless seamen, English émigrés and waves of Dutch settlers... including the Van der Cooks, Van Nesses and thousands more, with ultimately millions of descendants over endless centuries.

———

## chapter 10: off to Iowa

When Dutch-descended Melissa Overacker married the ambitious German-immigrant boy, Henry Luick, two restless families' fates became forever intertwined. While Melissa remained in Michigan and took care of the first of what would be their seven children who survived to adulthood, young-surveyor Henry stomped around the Iowa prairie.

At the time of Henry's 1846 charting trip to Iowa, the young territory was in great flux. As the Indian Question had been settled with the removal of the last "red savages," the earlier "reserves" dedicated to them "in perpetuity" were now set to open to settlement. And, waiting "whites" could hardly wait.

Ten years earlier, as a 28-year-old topographer with the United States Dragoons under direction of Daniel Boone's son "Captain Nathan," Albert Miller Lea had surveyed southern Minnesota and northern Iowa. In his *Notes on Wisconsin Territory. The Iowa District, or Black Hawk Purchase. By Lieut. Albert M. Lea, with Accurate Map of the District*, he extolled the river basin that Henry would find so appealing:

> From the extent and beauty of the Iowa River, which runs centrally through it and gives character to most of it [the name "Iowa"] has been given to the District itself. The general appearance of the country is one of great beauty. It may be represented as one grand rolling prairie, along one side of which flows the mightiest river of the world, and through which numerous navigable streams pursue their devious ways toward the ocean. In every part of the District beautiful rivers and creeks are found, whose transparent waters are perpetually renewed by springs from which they flow. Many of the streams are connected with lakes, and nearly all are skirted by woods, often several miles in width, affording shelter from heat or cold to the wild animals of the prairies.

*an inter-river region map of 1718 with future "Iowa" indicated in white; Albert Lea; map of Iowa's native cessions*

Documentably the first to use the ancient name for the future state, at a time when only a few thousand non-natives resided in what would become "Iowa," Albert Lea felt confident in declaring:

> The character of the population settling in this beautiful country is such as is rarely found in our new territories. With very few exceptions there is not a more orderly, industrious, energetic population west of the Alleghenies than is found in this Iowa District. For intelligence they are not surpassed as a body by any equal number of citizens of any country of the world.

The young man from Tennessee—who had graduated fifth of 33 cadets in the United States Military Academy's Class of 1831—also speculated on the region's future political and economic fortunes:

> This District being north of Missouri is forever free from the institution of slavery, by compact made upon the admission of that State into the Union. What would not Missouri now have been if she had never admitted slavery within her borders? The Mississippi River is, and must continue to be, the main avenue of trade for this country, but there is a reasonable prospect of having a more direct and speedy communication with the markets of the East. New York is now pushing her railroad from the Hudson to Lake Erie; it will then connect with one that is projected around the southern shore of that lake to cross Ohio, Indiana and Illinois, touching the foot of Lake Michigan in its route to the Mississippi River. This will place the center of the Iowa District within sixty hours of the city of New York. It is only a question of time when the business of this region will support such a road.

Unaware at the time of his prophesizing in the mid-1830s about Iowa's future prosperities of his own future miseries in the mid-1860s as a Confederate officer destined to find his dying Union-Navy-officer son in a captured ship off the Texas coast, still-optimistic Lea wrote:

> Some of the most beautiful country of the world is lying immediately west of this District. The Indians are now moving over to the Des Moines [River], finding the country [along local rivers, including the Iowa] no longer stocked with game, they are ready to sell. The pressure of settlers along the border has already created a demand for its purchase. The western boundary will soon be extended, and it is hazarding little to say that this district will have a population that will entitle it to admission among the States of the Union by the time the census of 1840 shall have been completed. Taking this District all in all, for convenience of navigation, water, fuel and timber, richness of soil, beauty of landscape and climate, it surpasses any portion of the United States with which I am acquainted.

Albert Lea wasn't the only early surveyor to recognize Iowa's potential; his later colleague, Henry Luick, did, as well. Hard to imagine as it is today, "that log cabin in Iowa" which according to Albert Lee Luick his uncle Henry had once so desired, actually was no small or insignificant resource. Recorded as "a respectable residence, 18 [feet, or about 5.5 meters] x 26' [7.9 meters] with a wing 14' [4.2 meters] x 14'," in the middle of a immense grassland with scarcely any trees, this existing home waiting for the Luick family to arrive from "out East" made going West all the more thinkable. Further, the same source claimed "In addition to a rough log hut" John Beebe, the trapper from whom Henry bought the cabin,

> contemplated a two-story house and had construction completed as high as a man's shoulders. Mr. Beebe sold his "claim" and improvements to the land seekers for $50. The newcomers completed the wing of the house in the fall of 1854, but the main part was left standing two years, awaiting a sufficient force of men to lift the heavy timbers.

Although lured by the prospect of moving into a ready-made cabin,

> it was 1853, however, before Henry was able to carry out his plan. He induced my father, David Luick, who was then not quite 21 years old, to join him in this undertaking. They loaded their covered wagons with such supplies as they thought necessary, and in the spring of 1853 started on the 700-mile journey into the western wilderness of Iowa, by way of Chicago-then a small city on the bank of Lake Michigan. My father said they could have had all the good land they wanted near Chicago at a few dollars an acre, but Henry was determined to go on to the log cabin in Iowa.

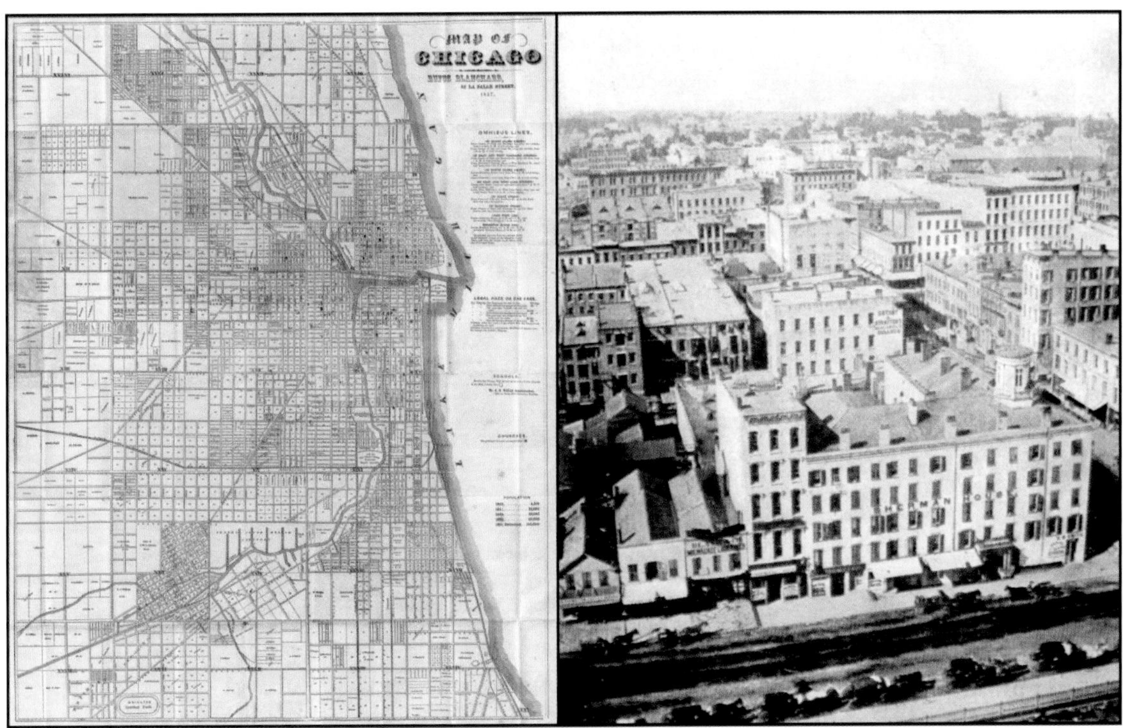


*1857 map of Chicago; looking out over Randolph Street from the Cook County courthouse, 1858*

Had the two Luick brothers stayed in Chicago, as the younger David suggested, the fates hundreds of thousands of their descendants, over generations, would have been completely different. With a population of just under 30,000 souls in 1850, the Windy City's future already then was promising: By 1860 it would grow to just over 112,000; within two decades of the Luick brothers' stay there it would soar to just under three-hundred thousand.

*mechanically raising a block of brick buildings on Lake Street for engineering & technical reasons; 1857*

By the start of the Civil War, a dozen railway lines would connect Chicago to the East, the rising West and even the innovation-resisting South. When Henry convinced his kid brother, David, to push on that spring of 1853, however,

> There were no railroads west of Chicago and only a trail to follow. They proceeded with their caravan to the Mississippi River, where at the lead mining town of Galena, Ill., they were able to secure a ferry across the Mississippi to Dubuque.

*view of Dubuque, Iowa, in 1845, as seen from the banks of the Mississippi River in Illinois*

> After resting there a few days and replenishing their supplies, they started west for some 200 miles on the final journey to the log cabin on the Iowa River, which was to be their future home in the wilderness of north central Iowa.

"Iowa"—with three-fourths of its letters singingly consisting of vowels, the very word rolls off the tongue with melodic ease, even though for most mortals on the planet today it means little in itself. That relative meaninglessness, however, wasn't always so.

When I was in fifth grade Mrs. Salisbury—whose towering, mid-Seventies hairdo was an updated version of what had been a "beehive" a decade or so earlier in the middle-aged woman's visibly manifold fashion career—read aloud to our class from Herb Hake's *Iowa Inside Out*. Hake, a cartoonist by passion, became a radio-cum-television personality by coincidence, having been told during World War II to take over the Iowa State Teachers College's [today: UNI's] radio programming (done until then by now-departing students) or look for another job. He approached our Hawkeye State's history with a folksy casualness that even this twelve-year-old noticed. One of the "truths" Herb peddled to us unsuspecting Iowa school kids during our weekly, curriculum-prescribed "Iowa history" class was that the word "Iowa" came from the Ioway language and meant "beautiful land" or "this is the place." For some forty years, I oriented my intellectual universe on that premise, having chosen to take... Herb Hake's... fake... as gospel.

As with so much of the agenda-driven acculturation we force-feed our undiscerning youth in school rooms and church basements across the nation, being much-repeated, however, doesn't make it true. Current, academic research on the name's lingual origins does, indeed, assign the source of my native state's moniker to Native Americans—as is the source of twenty-seven of the U.S. states' fifty names. According to one credible explanation "Iowa" was the French transcription of *Ayuway*, the name used by the Illini and Meskwaki tribes when referring to the Ioway. *Ayuway*, in turn, is said to be an alteration of the Dakota name for members of the same tribe, the *Ayuxba* (AH-you-khbah) or "sleepy ones."

Whatever the true genesis of its name, even after so many years of living so many other places, doing so many "un-Iowan" things, to me Iowa has always felt like home. And, I'm not alone. Although the Luicks had whiled away a winter in booming Buffalo, sojourned in swelling Detroit, crossed well-connected Chicago—even spent a decade and a half seeking their Mother Lode in the Golden State—they always returned to Iowa. This inexplicable phenomenon, for once, isn't just a quirk of the Luick clan: although my mother's people spent years in Missouri, Dakota Territory—even two decades in Oregon—they, too, always returned to "the beautiful land."

The White Cloud, Head Chief of the Iowas *(1844) and* Buffalo Bull's Back Fat *(1832), both by George Catlin*

---

**chapter 11: the early years**

At the time that Henry and Melissa Overacker Luick trekked to Iowa,

> they had four children—Michael, Mary, Sylvester and Barbara. Louis, Frank and Charles were born after they settled in the log cabin, and all took part in the building of this community. It is hard to describe what a hard, rugged trip this must have been for this family. There were no roads or bridges. There were many sloughs, and at points the black, wet soil of northern Iowa was nearly impassable.

The ten-thousand-year-old prairie might not have willingly made itself "passable" for intruders' wagons, but it did happily offer newcomers visual compensation for their travails as well as spiritual inspiration for the journey to come. Rare among pioneers' accounts of their treks across the unspoiled heartland of North America, John Rowen's narrative represents a lone voice. The sole critical account I've ever encountered in all my research of the westward movement across a vast continent, it nakedly names the environmental degradation Euro-American settlement brought to the Great Plains, as well as other biospheres. That he delivered it half a century before any identifiable, large-scale grassroots environmental consciousness had arisen among the American public generally makes it not only rare, but almost unimaginable.

Rowen's retelling—almost sixty years later—of his family's migration to the prairies of North Central Iowa appeared in the *Belmond Independent* as a serial guest column between 4 September 1912 and 15 January 1913. It began:

*19th-century sketch of ox-drawn covered wagon train in Iowa*

> I arrived in Wright County in the spring of 1855, a boy of 17, having assisted in driving my father's teams and stock from [the family's farm in Eastern Iowa] and I enjoyed every hour of the journey. At the time there was wild prairie land the whole distance on which to feed our stock. We rested either in our wagons or under them. The wagons were called prairie schooners (wagons with covers for shelter from sunshine or storm) and my recollections of living in the wagons are extremely pleasant.

The Rowen party consisted of John, his three brothers and their parents—Irish natives Robert and Elizabeth (McMullen) Rowen—accompanied by Ohioans Edwin and his wife, Emily (Kent) Ballou, along with Horace Riley. Soon upon leaving their homes the nine emigrants quickly found that

> there were no roads, not even trails, and every man made his own road, but when a wagon was stalled we hitched on several teams of cattle and pulled it out.

Despite the exhausting routine the migrants had to endure just to move forward, John Rowen could not help but notice the endless beauty all around the wagon train. Decades later he stated

> How well I remember my sensations as I looked out on the broad expanse of the seemingly boundless prairies, clothed in their virgin beauty. The great stretches of undulating prairie looked like a sea of billowy green, here and there made lovelier still by thousands of prairie flowers which have since disappeared. At times the vastness, the quietude, and the loveliness of it all flung over the mind and soul a feeling of awe, and in those moments one felt that they were in touch with the Divine.

*John Rowen, before 1915: Wildflowers again thrive in Iowa, on scattered parcels of restored prairie.*

"But" the now aged and reflective John went on to say,

> all was doomed to pass away, for civilized man had arrived, and his ruthless, utilitarian hand was to do its work, and the primitive loveliness of the prairies was to be forever destroyed. To the task of writing the history of the pioneers in nature's defacement, the destruction of one of the grandest, loveliest sights human eyes ever beheld, the writer will now proceed.
>
> The frontiersmen began the defacement by girdling trees so that corn and vegetables might be planted. The loveliness of every grove was ruined by vandals and pioneers. My father purchased two claims from an old frontiersman named Ford, paying $250. The improvements consisted of a log cabin and 10 acres of land ready for cultivation. The splendid oak timber surrounding the cabin had been girdled and killed. Bill Murdock, another squatter, had done the same thing on his claim. Many of the finest walnut, oak, and butternut trees were sawed into lumber, made into shingles or split into rails for fences. The worst offenders were the timber thieves, who slashed the best timber on the land owned by non-resident speculators, worked it up into lumber and shingles and sold it anywhere they could find a market.

John Rowen might have been the most unapologetic critic of the newcomers' effects on the local environment, but he wasn't the only one. Even Elizabeth Nieuwen, the daughter of early settlers, observed in her otherwise boosterish account of Belmond-area settlement:

> For over half a century Franklin Grove was the pleasure ground for the Belmond Community and here were held picnics, reunions, Fourth of July celebrations, and old time camp meetings. Since World War I, many of the hard wood trees have been taken out and sawn into lumber and I'm sorry to say that the Grove is not as much of a beauty spot as it was in years past. Then the generation of today, with its modern transportation, goes further afield to hunt and fish and on jaunts for pleasure.

Just as the Luicks had "bought out" the squatter John Beebe so Henry could secure the trapper-built cabin for his later-arriving family, John's father struck a deal with the man who claimed the right to occupy the land the Rowens wanted. Squatters, though, weren't really farmers: Most never intended to cultivate or even graze the land, long-term. Instead, like speculators without capital, they considered their very presence enough to assert possession of pieces of property.

When the Rowens finally reached their destination in North Central Iowa, spent from a long and laborious trek from "out East," instead of settling in, they had to settle up. They found the Ford and Murdock families occupying what was called "Horse Grove." John later summated dryly that

> the Fords slumber quietly on the banks of the Blue Earth River in Minnesota, martyrs to their work in blazing the way for civilization, and the Murdocks were known no more after leaving [North Central Iowa.] Ford was a good example of the squatting pioneer, the man who goes ahead of civilization, and marks the way for the permanent settler. He was an expert with the broad ax and hewed the timbers for the State House in Iowa City.
>
> Father Rowen found his tracks all the way up from Iowa City to [Wright County,] Ford having made 10 claims along the way. When the Ford family left here they moved to the Minnesota wild, taking a claim far up on the Blue Earth River, where they were barbarously murdered by the Sioux Indians at the time of the Sioux revolt.

*$19^{th}$-century image of "Old Capitol" in Iowa City, now University of Iowa*

As for the other family squatting on the land that the Rowens wished to make their own,

> Bill Murdock was a typical frontiersman, a dead shot, always with his nerve in command, whole-hearted, a good drinker, kind to his family and neighbors, only working when he had to, and generous to a fault.

Still, massaging land away from the stiff, grasping clutches of such hardscrabble people wasn't easy—nor cheap.

> Father had bought the land which Mr. Murdock claimed and Father had heard that Murdock was going to shoot him on sight, but my father was not a man to be frightened, and when he arrived he sent for Bill and explained the circumstances and asked what he thought his interest worth. On being told $100, Father paid the gold over and Bill had probably more money than he had ever before possessed.

In 19th-century America, land meant food—and survival. Beyond directly providing for one's family most basic needs, it also meant wealth—and potentially a lot of it. While usually poorly educated, generally unambitious people might serially squat on a chain of places until they'd accumulated a few gold coins, more educated and moneyed types played land games, too, until they'd amassed a mountain of them—but more shrewdly and often with a slick smile. Such a man seemed to be Henry Luick—and so did his enterprising cohorts, including Archer Dumond of Ohio and later Indiana, Illinois-native Dr. Lewis Cutler and other leading figures of what became known as the "Iowa River faction." John Rowen's father and mother hosted the spectacle.

*19th-century photo of the Iowa River*

In virtually every county in America at least one "county seat war" if not repeated political skirmishes erupted over where a given county's regional government—the seat of local power—would ultimately sit. Wright County differed from thousands of other counties across the United States not in the least in this regard—and my great-x3-grandfather Henry Jacob Luick called his men to battle even as he helped fan the flames. As John Rowen recalled,

> Never was there a more interesting convention [to secure the local placement of a county seat] in Wright County than the first one held in August 1855 on the Iowa River. The convention was not a party affair, but was an attempt to organize the eastern part of the county, looking forward to securing the county seat. The struggle was between the Boone and Iowa River [factions of would-be-community boosters] and upon the part of the Belmonders to secure the county seat. The affair was engineered by four persons: Dr. Cutler, Henry Luick, Mr. Dumond and Mr. Brooks.
>
> Dr. Cutler was the real head of the movement, a man of more than ordinary intellectual power, but [a man cited elsewhere as "F.O."] Brooks was a very good second and the scheme they organized was a good one for the end they had in view. There were about 13 families at what was then known as "Horse Grove" and there were quite a number of voters among them. Cutler's scheme was to hold the convention at Horse Grove, midway between Franklin Grove [as future "Belmond" was known at that time] and Otis Grove [today "Dows"] and while giving all the important offices to Franklin Grove, fling a few sops in the line of township offices to Horse Grove and Otis Grove.
>
> Well, the day came and brought with it a large delegation from Franklin Grove, including Cutler, Brooks, the Luicks, the Overackers, and the Dumonds. The convention was held under a big oak tree which stood

near where the bridge crosses the creek on the Rowen farm. The convention was called to order in a flamboyant speech by Mr. Brooks and Dr. Cutler was given the honor of the chair. After organization was accomplished, a free dinner was served by my parents in our cabin at the top of the hill; the men taking turns at dinner, and I can see the ever-ready Brooks, as if it were yesterday, coming to the door and jollying the men at the table, telling them to go slow, that there was a big crowd of hungry men outside; and there was, but in a matter of that kind my mother was in her glory, and her good Irish heart and hand were alert and open.

A harbinger of local power dynamics to come, the cleverest heads present made sure to divide political posts painstakingly—as far as possible, in-family. They knew the calculated, managed division of local resources and power would result in lasting, tangible rewards for entire familial groupings, with advantages for all. In short: Early community leaders took care of their own.

*Kate (standing), George, Charles, (sitting) Adrian & Katherine (Luick) Elder, circa 1890; Frederick Luick house in Belmond, about 1900; Edith (standing), Chester, (sitting) Alice (Packard), Harold & Fred Luick, about 1887*

Archer Dumond's nephew, George Washington Dumond, for one, would become Pleasant Township's "elected" assessor in 1856 and later serve as Belmond's sixth postmaster. And, Dr. Cutler's son, George Cutler, would fill the post of county auditor; George's future wife, Martha Morse, was the daughter of prominent area judge. Only a few years after this dress-rehearsal "war" between vying intra-county power blocs, at age 41 Dr. Cutler would enlist in the Union Army and serve as captain, mustering out after eleven months in July 1863 in St. Louis, Missouri.

For the Luicks' part, Henry saw to it that his wider clan fared well. To cite just a few examples:

- Catherine Luick's future husband, Adrian Elder, would serve as drainage commissioner as well as be repeatedly elected county supervisor.
- Melissa's older brother, Anthony Overacker, would fill the position of coroner.
- Although not an elected post, Fred Luick's public service would include—as a soldier at 26—"marching to the sea" in General Sherman's scorched-earth action across Georgia.

*1868 depiction of Sherman's march through Georgia, 15 November to 21 December 1864; Fred Luick, circa 1910*

- And, Henry, head of the Luick clan in Iowa, would become the chair of the Wright County Board of Supervisors as of New Year's Day, 1861, and be appointed to a four-year term as county judge on 8 August 1863—a post he'd leave cloaked in local disgrace, having...

But, that juicy tidbit was revealed in the conclusion of volume 1, *Roots of Darkness*; back to our story:

> At last the dinner was over and the convention again got busy, and all the candidates for county officials were placed in nomination, all going to Franklin Grove with one exception, namely coroner. My father was nominated for justice of the peace, a position he was alter elected to and held for years. Otis Grove had at that time a settler named Morgan, and he was named justice of the peace at that point. The shrewd Dr. Cutler had the idea that the remaining number should be conciliated and the leading one, old Mr. Ford, was nominated for Coroner. I was at Ford's when the old man came home, and I have had a thousand laughs over the affair. Mrs. Ford was rather a bright woman, but extremely illiterate, and the old man the very opposite. The Ford boys and I were conversing on the events of the day, but had paid no attention to the matter of the nominations. The Ford boys saw the old man approaching with slow, but steady steps, and on notifying the old lady of his approach, she eagerly said to the old gentleman, "Pa, what did they give you?" Ford answered, "They gave me crowner (coroner), Mama." Then came the explosion, his wife exclaiming, "To h_ _l with your crowner, who will ever hang or drown themselves to give you any business?"

The election was held somewhat later, in Franklin Grove. John Rowen again was on hand, and

> again there was fun. It was held in Henry Luick's cabin; now came the clash of the Iowa and Boone Rivers. It is sad to think that Boone River had suspicions of fraud on the part of the virtuous residents of the east side of the county, but she had, and was duly represented at the election at the Luick residence [so] the conflict was on, and it really looked like a fight a number of times between [men representing the differing sides] but cooler heads prevailed and fights were prevented.
>
> I have often since that faraway time thought about the nerve [of the representative from the Boone River faction] in boldly facing the hostile crowd. This was only the commencement of war between the Boone and Iowa Rivers. The final result was the location of the county seat at what was then known as Liberty [today "Goldfield"]. In a later struggle the Iowa won out, the county accepting a proposition of a woman named Wheeler and locating the county seat at what was known as Ontario and, my, my, was it not a whooper of a town – on paper.
>
> The Wheelers, brother and sister, the sister being the responsible party, surveyed out a town of 640 acres. The reader may guess what was shown on the blueprints in the line of improvements, all for the benefit of the eastern speculative purchaser of town lots, but as a matter of fact, only one building was erected, a two-story frame building, a courthouse built by the Wheelers, but the county business was not done there. Ontario was located near the old John Brooks farm about four miles from Rowan. Exciting times those were and Wright County has never known hotter political campaigns than were the county seat campaigns of those days.

Well, once again, we're ahead of our story... so:

---

As the Luicks crawled across the prairie in their groaning covered wagons, they had more pressing worries on their minds than squatters and future possible political squabbles. For Iowa

> was Indian country and roving bands of Sioux, Fox and other tribes were a troublesome consideration to be reckoned with. The Indians usually were friendly, but there was always uncertainty as to what to expect.

*Native Americans camped out on the Great Plains, mid-19th century*

While ever fewer in number, the Native Americans of the eastern Great Plains still standing their ground in the middle of the 19th century knew what was coming—and they didn't like it. Most alarming of all, the intruders' encroaching settlements multiplied so quickly: The indigenous people's world was disappearing ever faster, per the quickening tempo that newcomers crossed the still-bridgeless Upper Mississippi and poured out onto the prairie.

The early whites traveling, trapping or even living among the natives knew what was coming, too. George Catlin, who became a famous frontier painter-historian, spent several months in Iowa during his tours of the American West. He made trips around its eastern region about this time and described it as:

> The whole country that we passed over was like a garden, wanting only cultivation, being mostly prairie. Keokuk's village is beautifully situated on a large prairie on the bank of the Des Moines River. Dubuque is a small town of about two hundred inhabitants, all built within two years. It is located in the midst of the richest country on the continent. The soil is very productive, and beneath the surface are the great lead mines, the most valuable in the country.

*early map of Muscatine Island and burial mounds*

Geo. Catlin.

I left Rock Island about eleven o'clock, and at half-past three I ran my canoe on the pebbly beach of Mas-co-tine [today "Muscatine"] Island. This beautiful island is so called from a band of Indians of that name, who once dwelt upon it, is twenty-five or thirty miles in length, without a habitation on it, or in sight, and throughout its whole extent is one great lonely prairie. It has high banks fronting on the river, and extending back as far as I could see, covered with a high and luxuriant growth of grass. The river at this place is nearly a mile wide. I spent two days strolling over the island, shooting prairie hens and wild fowl for my meals. I found hundreds of graves of the red men on the island. Sleep on in peace, ye brave fellows, until the white man comes and with sacrilegious plow-share turns up your bones from their quiet and beautiful resting place!

*per the original* History of Iowa *captions: "Keokuk, Sac chief," "prairie chickens" and "Appanoose, Sac chief"*

I returned to Camp Des Moines, musing over the loveliness and solitude of this beautiful prairie land of the West. Who can contemplate without amazement this mighty river eternally rolling its surging, boiling waters ever onward through the great prairie land for more than four thousand miles! I have contemplated the never ending transit of steamers plowing along its mighty current in the future, carrying the commerce of a mighty civilization which shall spring up like magic along its banks and tributaries.

A harbinger of attitudes to come—notions held by Belmond historians cited in this book such as Albert Lee Luick and Elizabeth Lieuwen, subscribers to the idea that aboriginal peoples of North America were "savages" but they, themselves, belonged to the "bringers of civilization"—Catlin prophesized:

The steady march of our growing population to this vast garden spot will surely come in surging columns and spread farms, houses, orchards, towns and cities over all these remote wild prairies. Half a century hence the sun is sure to shine upon countless villages, silvered spires and domes, denoting the march of intellect, and wealth's refinements, in this beautiful and far off solitude of the West, and we may perhaps hear the tinkling of the bells from our graves.

Catlin's vision sounded grand—for anyone other than those already at home in that "vast garden spot"—but it was also, again as the Germans say, "music of the future." For the time being, there were

few settlements between Dubuque and [the Luicks'] destination. Wright County had not yet been established as an Iowa county. Henry took a prominent part of its establishment and became the first County Judge. He was prominent in many ways in the development of the community. In 1853, the nearest trading posts were Cedar Falls and Fort Des Moines, both about 100 miles away.

*early Fort Des Moines, flooded—later Iowa's capital city, Des Moines*

In such an era, in an area much in flux, the few non-natives' daily existence on the frontier was marked by both rare opportunities as well as deadly dangers. And, they remained dependent on the few outposts of "civilization" that made planting new lives in the wilderness possible in the first place—such as the fortress-cum-trading-post and provisional regional seat of government, flood-prone Fort Des Moines. (At that time, who would have guessed that one day the spartan, crudely-built stockade would be Iowa's capital city, with a population of hundreds of thousands.)

As his son Albert Lee Luick later wrote, German-born David Luick, came west with Henry Luick and

was one of the first to settle at Belmond. Soon after arriving, David picked out the land that he wanted and started for the Land Office at Fort Des Moines to file his claim for the 320 acres and to pay the necessary filing fee of $400 [for land where] a good part of Belmond now stands. He often mentioned to me what a rugged trip it was for him. There were no roads or bridges and he only knew the general direction across this wild, wet prairie on his horse. There were numerous creeks and rivers which he had to swim, and his horse often mired down in the rich Iowa soil. He said he was sure he walked more than half the distance, stopping often to build a fire to dry his clothes and cook his food. He carried the $400 gold filing fee in his money belt, and the weight of it was a problem. He became blistered and chafed around his waist and it was painful. Fortunately, there were a few settlers from whom he got shelter and direction, and in due time he arrived at the Fort Des Moines Land Office and filed for the land and paid the fee. I have a tax receipt dated at Fort Des Moines for [the] 1854 tax; also the Government Patent for this land signed by Franklin Pierce, then President of the United States.

One passing, pesky problem with claiming as one's own and settling the prairies, however, was: T'was already occupied! And, the straggling natives still left in Iowa in the middle of the 19th century didn't exactly welcome the interlopers among them—as my family was to learn, firsthand.

David Luick's unexpected, unwanted encounters with Native Americans in the earliest years of his family's settlement of the Iowa prairie speak volumes about how larger events played out face-to-face between the increasingly disenfranchised and those hoping to assume their corner of the sky.

David lived with Henry's family and started to develop his land by breaking up some of the virgin sod with a new moldboard plow which he had secured when they came through Chicago. Such a plow had then only recently been invented. This tool turned the sod in a wonderful manner, and he planted corn and seeded wheat. As there were no local markets for farm produce, [however,] he turned to trapping and he became very capable and successful at this. He did very well, since fur-bearing animals were very plentiful. He usually worked the near-by streams and lakes. And, he related the following incident to me:

Once in the spring of '54 [David Luick] had built a shelter in the bank of Little Wall Lake to get out of the weather and to take care of his catch. While he was busily engaged with his pelting, a band of about 50 Sioux Indians pounced upon him without warning. They were decorated in their war paints and feathers. Since he was miles away from any white men, he recalled that if ever there was a "scared Dutchman," it was he. The Indians proceeded to strip him of his gun and knife and most of his clothing, and pretended they were going to take his scalp. They took what tobacco he had and laughed and howled at his fright. After having all the fun they wanted, they gave him back his gun and powder horn, but kept the tobacco and went on their way. He said it seems they were on the warpath against the Tama Indians.

*Tipis by George Catlin (1796-1872) in mid-1800s painting of Sioux village*

There he was—David Luick stripped of weapons and most of his clothes, alone and terrified. Were it not that his short-term captors were presumably enroute to fight the Meskwaki living in today's Tama County, in East Central Iowa, the incident likely would have ended much differently.

On Albert's father's next direct encounter with the disappearing Native Americans, however, he was not alone. Still, he again narrowly escaped disaster, when:

> ...the following fall David joined two other men on a trapping expedition to northwestern Iowa, around the Spirit Lake district and on to the Little Sioux River. They built a shelter for themselves and their horses on the south bank of Lake Okoboji, about where Arnold's Park now stands. They were highly successful in their trapping during the winter of 1854 and 1855, and had just returned to their camp, preparing to return to Belmond some 100 miles away, when a large war party of Sioux Indians came in on them and in no uncertain terms ordered them to get out of the Indians' hunting grounds. They felt the Indians meant business, so they did not stop to pack further but started at once for Belmond and did not stop until they arrived a few days later. They were lucky they had sold their furs and had their money intact.

The year after the Indians had ordered the trappers out, five or six New England families came to the very spot where the men had had their camp and built log cabins and settled on the land in that locality. These people were just nicely settled when, early in the winter of 1856 and '57, an outlaw band of Sioux suddenly came in and massacred all except three women, who were carried away. My father and others joined the militia from Webster City and Fort Dodge to try to intercept the Indians, but they were unsuccessful since the Indians had fled to the Dakotas. The militia buried the bodies of the victims. My father said that the scene of carnage was horrible, with bodies scattered in the snowdrifts, tomahawked, cut and scalped. This incident, "The Spirit Lake Massacre," has been recorded as the worst Indian disaster in Iowa history.

My brother David's namesake predecessor, however, wasn't the only Luick to experience tense moments with the departing natives. Perhaps career-minded Henry was off becoming a prominent early citizen-judge of the up-and-coming county, hunting with a neighbor, or just being busy, carting grain to be milled in or hauling supplies back from faraway Cedar Falls or Fort Des Moines. In any event, one time, while solely in charge of the Luicks' long-sought log cabin built by the long-departed trapper, Melissa was confronted by natives in her family's home who refused to leave it empty-handed.

Young Omahaw, War Eagle, Little Missouri and Pawnees, *painted in 1821*

The Sioux had reacted hostilely towards settlers for some time, but the European-Americans at Franklin Grove worried little, as the next "Indian camps" were said to be in Northwest Iowa. One day, however, some natives suddenly showed up at the Luicks' door. As Aunts Mattie and Marion told me—then a novice, teenage historian around the time of the Bicentennial:

The redmen forced their way into the Luick cabin and demanded food. Melissa, with thoughts of the recent Spirit Lake massacre on her mind, gave the braves and their chief some biscuits. Then, distracting them with one hand, she pointed behind her back toward a window to little Louis with the other. An understanding Louis stiffly inched along the wall to the window and when the unwelcomed visitors looked the other way, pushed it open, sprang out onto the ground and ran for help. By the time Louis and a group of men returned, the Indians had left.

When the Luicks first settled in what they referred to as "Franklin Grove" Native Americans lived nearby from time to time, but not continuously. Born in 1860 to Henry's brother, Albert Lee's trapper-cum-farmer father David Luick, Amelia (Luick) Mallory recalled

being a little afraid of the Indians when the school children occasionally visited them. Admitting they were friendly Indians, she said she was astonished one day as she witnessed a sample of Indian discipline. A small Indian lad had misbehaved in some way and he was grasped sternly by the nape of the neck by an elderly squaw and propelled to the bank of the river. It was winter, but a hole had been chopped in the ice and the squaw forcibly doused the errant boy up and down in the frigid water. Mrs. Mallory said she could still envision that little fellow running to the warmth of the fire to dry his clothes and warm his shivering self.

A little more than two decades after the Luicks and the other first European-American settlers arrived in the area, the few remaining-albeit-transient Native Americans had ceased seeming to be dangerous; rather, they'd come to seem to many as curious, even ridiculous. The 20 April 1877 issue of the *Belmond Herald*, for example, reported

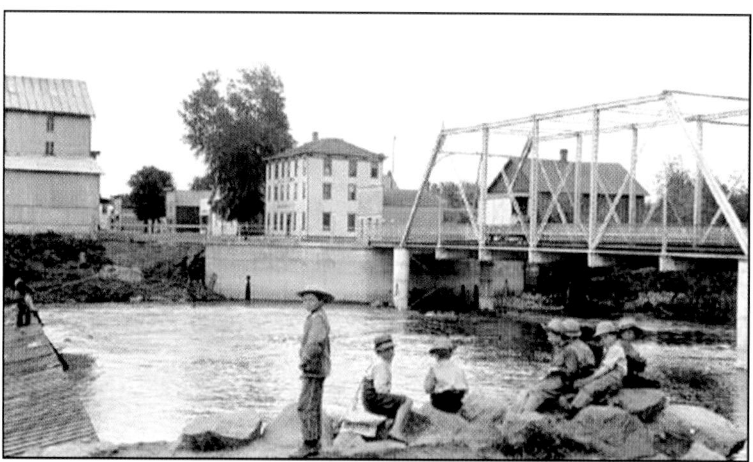

*boys playing on the banks of the Iowa River in Belmond, circa 1905*

> Below town at Pike's Grove, there has been a party of Indians camped [and among them is] a "medicine man" who is "up to snuff." He recently cured a Mrs. Brayton of Otisville, who had the scrofula [tuberculosis of neck lymph nodes] badly. 'Tis also said he offered to perform other miraculous cures at Otis, but the afflicted lacked faith in him.

———

*Quakeress in typical 19th-century "plain dress"*

The controversial Native-American medicine man, however, wasn't the only "character" to populate early Belmond, according to the town's historical society's research. Respectively born in New York and Pennsylvania, Rensselaer "Anson" and Melissa (Burman) Gray

> were the first family to bring horses and cattle and so helped the other settlers get a start in the livestock business [in 1854]. All three sons of [by-then] Widow Gray enlisted to serve and two of them died from disease during the [Civil] War. After Grandma Gray's family grew up she became the first practical nurse in this locality, and also knitted stockings for the neighbors' youngsters. She lived in the southeast part of the woods and would take her covered knitting basket on her arm and walk miles to visit some friend or neighbor, knitting briskly as she walked along. She was a Quakeress and could repeat the Bible and the dictionary at great length. She was always a welcome caller and sometimes stayed a week with her hostess, but often the children of the family were a little frightened upon seeing her in the morning sitting up in bed with a white night cap on her head, smoking a clay pipe.

The earliest settlers at Franklin Grove didn't have to worry about physical harm happening to them only at the hands of the last remaining Native Americans, but from their own family members. One story that Aunt Mattie relished retelling every time she had a chance was that of her father's brothers "and the ghost in the cemetery one night." As she told it,

Growing up on the Iowa frontier, Henry and Melissa's children shared many adventures—like the time Michael vowed he'd break little Sylvester of the habit of staying at a friend's house until late at night. At the time, the Luicks lived on the old homestead, and Sylvester's friend lived down the road, past the cemetery and around the bend. One evening Michael told his parents that he'd slip down to the cemetery—as Sylvester always took a short cut through there—crouch behind a tombstone and when his four-year-younger little brother strolled by, pop up with a sheet over his head and "scare the livin' daylights out of him." Henry and Melissa agreed that would be a good lesson.

Michael crept to the cemetery and hid according to plan. It being a full-moon-lit night, Sylvester acted sort of spooked anyway; he carried a club with him for protection. As he carefully walked past the gravesites, Sylvester quietly whistled and kept an eye open for trouble. Just as he passed a recently erected tombstone, a "ghost" suddenly stood up and moaned painfully. Sylvester took his club, walloped the ghost on the head, then high-tailed it for home.

> When he reached the safety of the house, Melissa nonchalantly asked if anything unusual had happened on the way home. "Yeah" Sylvester sputtered, "I saw a ghost an' killed him good!" Stunned, Melissa quickly drove the buggy to the cemetery and brought half-conscious, lump-headed Michael home.

*1804 engraving of London's Hammersmith ghost*

Perhaps the inclination to commit shenanigans is, like some other deviant behaviors, genetically coded and passed between generations. As Michael's son—my great-grandfather George's cousin, Adelbert "Dell" David Luick—later admitted, when asked for a *Belmond Independent* articled published 8 August 1946 what he did for fun as a boy,

> We used to steal watermelons. Of course, we had all the melons we could eat right in our own patch, but they tasted better when we stole 'em!

Regardless of what Dell or other young local melon thieves might have thought, their misdeeds were, indeed, noticed—as announced in an unnamed Belmond paper on 27 August 1879:

> MORE DEVILTRY – Thieves also riddled Wm. Luick's melon patch. Mr. L. knows the parties too, and it is through his generosity that an example is not made of them. Hardly anyone would object to going away with a few melons, especially big hearted Wm. Luick, but to have one's crop completely ruined by hoodlums, is certainly aggravating in the extreme.

*Roland, William & Ernest Luick, circa 1908; William Luick home, circa 1900; father "Mike," baby Ralph Cortland, great-grandfather Michael & former-watermelon-thief grandfather Adelbert "Dell" Luick, 1918*

---

Despite distracting moments of danger from "Injuns" or comic, soon-healed antics by their own children, the pioneers' life focused, necessarily, on basic day-to-day, hour-to-hour survival. With few tools, only the most basic technology at their disposal and little means of controlling or mitigating the effects of weather, the first settlers' lives were dictated by nature's whims. One of the most dangerous aspects of the climate the newcomers found on the prairie were its extreme swings in weather patterns. The first winter after Henry Luick's immediate family had joined him, for example, was mild:

> Wild ducks and geese never left all winter; the children gathered butternuts and walnuts from the woods and went barefoot. Game was plentiful; fish filled the river and elk came in droves to the water for a drink.

If their report now sounds fantastic, we know that the first non-natives who had ventured out onto the prairie took exact note of existing supplies of wildlife and fluctuations in weather, as their lives quite literally depended on both. As one chronicler of Iowa's early settlement wrote,

> Swarms of muskrats inhabited every pond [or slough]. They were utilized to supply the family with groceries. Muskrat pelts were always suitable for cash at the nearest town where buyers had agents to gather up all kinds of furs and hides of wild animals. During the first year of life on the prairie, before crops could be raised for market, thousands of [pioneer] families were dependent upon trapping for the cash they must have. The money was used to buy bacon and coffee. [...] Deer and prairie chickens furnished meat for a portion of the year. Some money was indispensable for fuel, and such scant groceries as were indulged in.

*muskrat (Ondatra zibethicus).*

The busy settlers, though, found (or made) time to pen letters to loved ones left behind "back East"—and those letters must have glowed with fanciful tales of adventure—for an excited reply to one of their communiques survives. In it, twenty-year-old seminary student William Luick—Henry and David's kid brother—begs his brothers to save some of the big game for him:

Ann Arbor, Mich.
Feb. 14, 1855

Dear Brother:

After so long a time since I received your letter, I will attempt to write a few lines to you. Myself and all the family are unusually well but uncle's folks have been quite sick, but are better now.

I have been to school most of the winter. We are most covered up with snow, it is all of two feet deep and the cross roads are all banked up. It is almost four weeks since it first commenced snowing and keeps snowing most every day.

I got a letter from Catherine the other day. They are all well and John says if he can sell, he shall come and buy where you are as soon as he can. And there is no mistake but I shall come some time. I want to see the country and shoot some elk and buffalos.

Woofsells folks are all well. Father traded his horses with Woofsell for a span of colts and a yoke of oxen. Woofsell traded them off to lim Coloman. Woofsell has a colt he has been offered $115 and $109 in money.

Now as soon as you get this I want you to write to me how many buffalo, elk, deer, bear, foxes and wolves you have killed and how you like the country now, and what you have been doing all winter.

All the connection send their best respects, and remember that I am your most affectionate brother.

William luick

The following winters however, knew nothing of mildness or mercy. According to Edwin Ballou, who came from Ohio to stake a claim in Wright County's Iowa Township, the winter of 1856-57 was

> the worst I have ever known. Snow fell in November, and on December 1 a heavy snowstorm began that lasted three days. Then the wind came from the northwest and drifted the snow 15 feet [about five meters] deep. The last of December, I

*19th-century sketch of man downed while hunting among elk and bison*

started for Cedar County for supplies. I came back in February, by way of Iowa City, and followed up the river. The many teams on the road had caused the snow to drift into the track until it formed a solid turnpike four feet above the ordinary level. I was two weeks in reaching Alden [a distance of about 150 miles/240 km], where I left most of my load, and went home.

*Edwin Ballou, before 1889, and a 19th-century image of an Iowa settler and team trapped in a blizzard*

Another source described conditions in early Belmond at the end of the winter of 1856-57:

A snow drift extended from the top of the hill across the river[.] This drift, level from the hill top, was 35 to 40 feet deep [10.5 to 12 meters], and when the river broke up in the spring, the water melted the snow and left an arch of snow over the river. There were times of blinding blizzards, which had a free sweep over the open prairie, when the pioneer would fasten himself to a rope, tied to the cabin, so that he could find his way back to the house when he went out to do chores.

———

If they survived nature's rages, the Iowa frontier's first non-native residents had to simply eat.

Farming was not profitable, since there were no markets. The settlers raised enough wheat and corn, however, to feed their livestock and to take to the mill at Cedar Falls to provide flour and corn meal for their families. Wild game was very plentiful at that time—elk, deer and a few stray buffalo. Wild ducks, cranes and prairie chickens were in abundance. [Michael Luick's son, Dell, later said that prairie chickens were so numerous that "they rose in clouds as hayfields were cut."] Trapping was the most profitable vocation, since there were plenty of fur-bearing animals such as beaver, mink, otter, muskrats and their pelts could be sold or traded for necessary staples such as sugar, salt, tea and coffee, shoes and clothing. The wants of these people were not great, and they seemed to know how to provide somehow for most of their needs. Nearly every pioneer had his own smokehouse for smoking the hams and bacon and for preparing the usual barrels of corn beef, and jerked meat hung in the loft for drying. The women gathered supplies of wild strawberries, cherries and plums, from which they made jams and jellies for their larder. There were also vegetables from the gardens stored in cellars. Really, they lived very well. While there were no doctors or nurses, these pioneer women knew how to take care of the ill and sick. They learned how to use many herbs and Indian remedies that they practiced with great success.

In 1951, local historian Elizabeth Lieuwen recounted in her presentation to the Wright County Historical Society, the existing foodstuffs available to the early settlers—a natural and gratis abundance which helped them survive those first harsh years, so far removed from supplies and trade. Alone the tree varieties the pioneers found upon arriving in Franklin Grove, for example,

> included cottonwood, willow, walnut, butternut, hickory, hard maple, sugar maple, elm, basswood, ash and sumac and hazelbrush. The wild fruits included plum, chokecherry, black cherry, crabapple, black haw, while the berries to be found were gooseberries, black currants, strawberries, blackberries, raspberries, elderberries and wild grapes. These were very important food items to the pioneers. Everyday fare of the pioneer was corn bread or Johnny cake, mush and milk, wild meats and gravy. Dried crane and prairie chicken breasts were an occasional dainty. Pumpkin sauce and sorghum served as dessert and eggs of wild fowl were used as food.

Another chronicler of early pioneer life on the Iowa prairie noted that before grist and flour mills could be established in newly settled areas,

> grain was ground into flour between flat stones and sometimes in hand coffee mills. Much corn was eaten after it had been parched, and rye, similarly treated, was a substitute for coffee. Green corn was dried and, when cooked with beans, made succotash. This was relished by the pioneers. To sweeten their foods, they secured honey from the bee trees, and later they made molasses from cane which was grown like corn.

Even crude sweeteners, however, couldn't change the settlers' essentially monotonous diet, whose staple meat consisted of

> pork, fresh and fresh-salted for winter use, pickled or smoked for summer use. They had plenty of wild meat, too, but quail and prairie chicken was in excess and they became tired of it. The appetite for pork seemed more continuous. It was said, "Corn bread, with pork and rye coffee, formed the prairie bill of fare, with an occasional dish of mustard greens." Sometimes added to this meal were venison, dried pumpkin, hominy, wild game, and a few additional vegetables.

At least initially, the staple sugar that sustained the first European-American settlers came to them in the form of "common hominy so much relished by them," a simple starch. Producing the substance without the aid of machinery, however, wasn't so simple, as it consisted of

> boiled corn from which the hulls had been removed with hot lye, thus called lye hominy. What was called "true hominy" was made by pounding the corn. True hominy was made in a mortar-like hole in the top of a stump. The corn was placed in it and beaten with a maul. When it was sufficiently crushed, the bran was floated off in water, and the delicious grain boiled like rice. The early pioneers in this section of Iowa agreed that wheat bread, tea, coffee and fruits were luxuries, reserved for "company" occasions.

*late-19th-century Illustrations of Iowa pioneer women weaving and spinning wool, from* History of Iowa

Besides food, the same local historian recorded conditions under which pioneers secured clothing, much of which was not only homemade, but handmade.

> Every farmer kept a flock of sheep. In earliest times, the carding, the spinning, and the weaving were all done by women. There was a spinning wheel in every home. Often there were two—a large one for wool and a smaller one for flax—and one loom might serve many families. Linsey, or linsey-woolsey, was made of linen and woolen yarns, the wool serving as the filling.

The unnamed author took note of gender-based divisions of labor. As she or he pointed out,

> Men rested between their jobs, but the women did not. They wove the cloth and knitted the stockings. When they could not make new cloth fast enough, they patched the old. Even then, they could hardly keep their families out of nakedness. One woman of those times said she had often sent her children into the woods on the approach of strangers, because they did not have clothes enough to make their bodies presentable.

Conditions changed swiftly and radically once machine-produced cloth became available.

> When the settlers first began to buy cotton goods, the clothing came in plain colors and it was dyed to suit individual tastes. Walnut bark and hulls, sumac, madder, indigo and other native materials were used as dye-stuffs, and the resulting colors were often hideous. The skins of wild beasts were also used in the making of clothing. With industrious mending, the clothing was made to do long service. But, it was all in the pioneer lifetime.

Being basically well provided for by Mother Nature, family-raconteur Albert claimed:

> Really, [the first settlers] lived very well. While there were no doctors or nurses, these pioneer women knew how to take care of the ill and sick. They learned how to use many herbs and Indian remedies that they practiced with great success.

Albert's tale conveyed such a lovely, almost ideal life that the Luicks supposedly enjoyed on the Iowa frontier. Other chroniclers, however, were less kind when describing the environment and the difficult living conditions they caused. As a Belmond Historical Society team reminds us,

> Prior to 1854 few white men had traversed the prairies and valleys of what is now Wright County. It's difficult to picture the hardships endured by the pioneers as they slowly made their way toward a new home. There were no roads, only poorly marked Indian trails; there were no plowed fields, only the ponds and sloughs of wetland prairie, with forests along the riverbanks.

According to Edwin Ballou,

*19th-century scene of breaking a path through the snow with oxen*

> In April 1855, myself and family moved [with John Rowen's family] to Wright County. We had a pleasant time until we reached Eldora [in adjacent Hardin County, to the east], then came the sloughs. We attempted to cross one with five yoke of oxen hitched to one wagon. Down went the wagon to the axles, and the harder the oxen pulled, the deeper the wagon sank. We were obliged to wade in the water about two feet deep and carry our load out. This was my first experience with the sloughs. Eldora is about 40 miles [60 km] from my place, but it was our nearest post

> office and blacksmith shop, and there was no mill within 100 miles of us. We brought provisions enough with us to last till fall, then I went to Marshalltown, 70 miles [about 113 km] distant, for flour.

Life on the frontier was not easy—for anyone, of any age. As an elderly woman of 83, at the time of Iowa's centennial in 1946, David and Sarah (Overacker) Luick's second daughter, Ida (Luick) Morse, recalled hardships as well as "stolen pleasures" from her pioneer childhood. Among other stories in the article the *Belmond Independent* featured about her in its 18 July 1946 issue, she recounted how

> Cedar Falls was the nearest adequate trading post and it was there that the men went in their wagons to stock up for the winter. On one occasion, an early blizzard lasted so long that household provisions reached a frightening low before [her father, David Luick] could get his wagon through to Cedar Falls and back [a round trip of 160 miles, about 260 kilometers]. When their provisions ran low, their meals consisted of dried prairie chicken breasts and corn meal mush made by grinding corn meal by hand in a coffee grinder.

Securing adequate food supplies constituted only one headache for the regions' first settlers:

> Pioneer families faced additional hardships in their early years in Iowa. Constructing a farmstead was hard work in itself. Families not only had to build their homes, but often they had to construct the furniture used. Newcomers were often lonely for friends and relatives. Pioneers frequently contracted communicable diseases such as scarlet fever. Fever and ague, which consisted of alternating fevers and chills, was a constant complaint. Later generations would learn that fever and ague was a form of malaria, but pioneers thought that it was caused by gas emitted from the newly turned sod. Moreover, pioneers had few ways to relieve even common colds or toothaches.

In a more pleasant vein, Albert Lee Luick's 14-years-older sister, Ida (Luick) Morse, also remembered

> the momentous visits of the itinerant merchant who carried an enticing array of tin ware, yard goods and odds and ends which helped relive the monotony of frontier life. There were also the occasional visits of west-bound caravans [of emigrating settlers] and the frequent appearances of Indians begging for pork and corn meal.

Ida and Albert Lee's father, industrious David Luick, soon constructed a sorghum mill, so

> the family enjoyed its own molasses year-round. [...] Beef was dried around the fireplace and potatoes and crab apples, cabbages and turnips were thriftily stored in [outdoor] pits or in the cellar. There was dried corn, and mince-meat was made from the crab apples and gooseberries which grew in abundance. Eventually, wintertime came to be a season without fear of hunger.

*1868* Harper's Weekly *picture of itinerant peddler stopping at a farm*

Ida's older sister by three years, as a girl Amelia (Luick) Mallory especially prized the crab apples. On 25 July 1946 a *Belmond Independent* article claimed that

> When she sees earnest young Belmond students topping off their lunches with candy bars and ice cream cones, it reminds her of the favorite lunch box confection of her day. Crab apples from the grove had their stems removed and into the cavities went sugar and cinnamon. They were baked whole in the fireplace.

---

Besides meeting the basic need of finding fulfilling food, that of securing adequate shelter also posed a challenge for pioneers—both over one's head and on one's body. As Ida (Luick) Morse explained,

> Clothing for both men and women was homemade. Calico or gingham dresses were considered "dress-up" clothes and little girls were proud of their ruffled pinafores. Every woman knew how to knit and young Ida was no exception. She knit her first pair of stockings (for a doll) when she was five.

Even as the offspring of pioneers, some of Iowa's first European-American settlers were still children, nonetheless, needing schooling as well as time to play. Years later, Ida recounted that

> The schoolhouse was located near where the cemetery now is located and much of [the pioneer children's] fun centered there. The youngsters used grapevines for jumping ropes and smooth boards for sleds. Dances were held in Pierce's Hall and on Sundays it was the church, with its pulpit filled by a [Methodist] circuit riding preacher. Young folks enjoyed rides in bobsleds or sleighs with bells ringing merrily as the horses jogged along.

*teacher and pupils at recess at schoolhouse near Hickory Grove*

No matter how the first school's first pupils reached class, all their efforts would have been in vain were it not for the region's first teachers. As well-educated adults able to focus on anything other than daily survival were rare commodities on the frontier, often inexperienced teenage girls found themselves at the front of class—but teaching, rather than being taught.

As Elizabeth Lieuwen explained:

> The teacher in Wright County in an early day was required to teach spelling, reading, writing, arithmetic, geography and English Grammar. The last two subjects were sometimes omitted if the teacher was not prepared to teach them. The teacher's examination was usually oral. Although the early settlers were interested in education and supported the schools earnestly, a few people thought the children were taking too many subjects and there was danger of the pupils becoming to [sic] highly educated and not fitted for practical life.
>
> The first school was held in a little log building, roofed with bark, that had been used as a dwelling, at the west side of Franklin Grove. Isadore Fisk Rogers taught this school in 1856, she being a young girl of fifteen. Soon after this, "A little red school house" southeast of town, near the present site of the cemetery, was started and taught at one time by Miss Susan Church Hiams, Miss Eleanor Dumond and Miss Alice Packard (later wife of Fred Luick).
>
> This building consisted of one room with no [sheltered] entry. The pupils sat facing each other on two benches built along the longer sides of the room, with their backs against the wall. Before each two children was a desk made of boards. There was no maps or charts of any kind and the only equipment consisted of a wood stove, a teacher's table and chair, and a black board was in fact a board painted black.

Later, after the focus of early settlement shifted a mile or so northwest, from the Luicks' scattered hamlet of Franklin Grove to what became a platted town with grid-like streets, the crude one-room facility no longer sufficed.

The first school in Belmond was taught in a granary on the hill by Jane Oliver, who was paid by subscription the sum of $18 a month. The County Superintendent visited school on horseback about once a year. A frame building was built on the hill in the early '60s and in it was conducted the largest school in the county. With Wm. Finch as teacher, Rev. J.D. Sands also taught in this building in '71 and '72. The children on the hill went to this school until the Independent District downtown was formed.

In the earliest days of non-native settlement of the prairies, cut lumber or even rough-hewn logs with which to erect buildings were sparse, so building separate structures dedicated to "non-essential" uses such as school or churches was a luxury. Rose (Whited) Garth, whose family first stayed with Henry Luick's when the four Whited brothers and their dependents arrived in Franklin Grove in spring 1855, later told of exceptionally cramped initial living conditions, given the lack of ready building materials.

The brothers built a log house that sheltered their families for the winter. There was a cookstove in one corner and beds in the other three corners [one for each brother—William, Isaac and Stephen—with a wife and children, respectively all in one bed. Unmarried] Levi and a young man cousin slept in the loft. The next spring two other homes were built.

"What would the pure food man think of our milking in a wooden pail?" Rose asked rhetorically in an undated *Wright County Monitor* article about her family's early life on the mid-19th-century frontier. "But" she noted,

it was scoured white with rushes. The water pail and wash tub were of wooden staves; we did not know the galvanized tubs and pails. Wooden bowls were used for butter and chopping bowls, for mixing bread and washing dishes. Gourds were used for dippers, receptacles for salt and for soft soap. Springs for beds consisted of a rope put through holes in the sides and ends of the bedstead and stretched tightly in squares. The mattress was filled with straw.

Until families with the capital necessary to purchase an inventory could arrive in the wake of the trappers, surveyors or sod-busting settlers to set up the first, primitive stores, consumer wares remained sparse, expensive and a luxury. What tools, furnishings or supplies did not come into the area in a pioneer's wagon had to be improvised on-site or, later, traded for once enough extra produce had been raised to sell. Rose recalled years later that the nearest markets were

distant and families lacked for many things before conditions were right to venture with the oxen and a load of wheat to Cedar Falls. Once when [her father] was coming home from Cedar Falls, just beyond [the next, young county seat to the east] Hampton he came through some woods and two large timber wolves followed him. The oxen needed no urging and ran for their lives. The wolves soon turned back.

When the Whiteds could not reach a mill to have grain ground into vital flour, Rose's mother

would boil wheat. It would be better than a package of wheat we buy now. Or, she would hull corn (take the hull off with lye). This is still good eating.

More plausible and terrifying than a rare and unlikely wolf attack, the first settlers

were always in fear of an attack by the Indians. It was about the time of the Spirit Lake Massacre [where about forty settlers perished in mid-March 1857] when a horseman rode into the community and gave the alarm that the Indians were coming. The families gathered at the

*Native Americans chasing a pioneer's covered wagon—into an ambush*

Dumond home, where the women and children were housed. The men took their teams and plowed furrows and laid up sod, watching all night, but no Indians came.

Rose also remembered, however, lighter moments in an otherwise taxing life on Iowa's prairies.

It was a gay time for the children when father hitched the oxen to the wagon and took us with a basket of lunch to spend the day in the grove, stopping on the way to take in a neighbor family with an equal number of children. We would come home with bags of hazelnuts, walnuts and butternuts for winter evenings. On the way home older children would run races with the oxen. Sometimes father would have a funny streak and urge the oxen on and leave the Whited and Overacker or Jenison children far in the rear for the others to laugh at.

Despite the remoteness of life on the frontier, far from large or well-equipped settlements "back East," the adults' lives were not totally without edification or entertainment. Rose noted:

The Whited family took the *New York Tribune*, edited by Horace Greeley, for several years. Mrs. Whited took *The National Era* published in Washington. [The landmark abolitionist tract] *Uncle Tom's Cabin* was published in it. When they did not have envelopes for letters, a sheet was folded, leaving the outside blank, so there would be a flap which was closed with a stick of warm sealing wax.

UNCLE TOM'S CABIN;

OR,

LIFE AMONG THE LOWLY.

BY

HARRIET BEECHER STOWE.

VOL. I.

ONE HUNDRED AND FIFTH THOUSAND.

BOSTON:
JOHN P. JEWETT & COMPANY
CLEVELAND, OHIO:
JEWETT, PROCTOR & WORTHINGTON.
1852.



*title page of 1852 edition of* Uncle Tom's Cabin *and an illustration from it showing Mrs. Smyth, a Quaker*

---

The pioneers' letters and diary entries routinely referred to frequent disease if not death overtaking them, their loved ones or neighbors. As Iowa historian Dorothy (Hubbard) Schwieder documented, "One women, Kitturah Belknap, had lost one baby to lung fever. When a second child died, she confided in her diary:

I have had to pass thru another season of sorrow. Death has again entered our home. This time it claimed our dear little John for its victim. It was hard for me to give him up but dropsy on the brain ended its work in four short days[.] We are left again with one baby and I feel that my health is giving way.

Crude medical culture and recurring waves of epidemics born of unsanitary conditions claimed thousands across the prairie every year in the early decades of non-native settlement. A notice titled only "GOING" in an uncited Belmond newspaper announced on 13 April 1877 that

Several families of Belmond have gone away to avoid the scourge of diphtheria now raging here, and in their temporary stay abroad, we are afraid they will run into something equally as fatal – the scarlet fever. The disease is getting widely circulated in many neighboring counties east and is proving nearly as disastrous.

Less than two years later, on 19 February 1879, a similarly terse notice in another unnamed local broadsheet warned of another dreaded, albeit non-contagious killer, "THE WEED:"

> A medical professor says tobacco is killing more people than whisky. Particularly the smoking of cigarettes is baneful. The arties become excited and ruptured by it.

In an era when many farmers converted grain into the more easily stored, ever-sellable and lucrative form of whiskey, Devil Drink posed a real and lethal threat to communities as wholes. Touting one local response to what was condemned as a creeping social cancer, a *Dubuque Herald* article reprinted in the *Wright County Monitor* on 28 September 1870 boasted that in Belmond

> There has been considerable interest manifested in the temperance cause here; it is probably due to this that we have no saloons in the place.

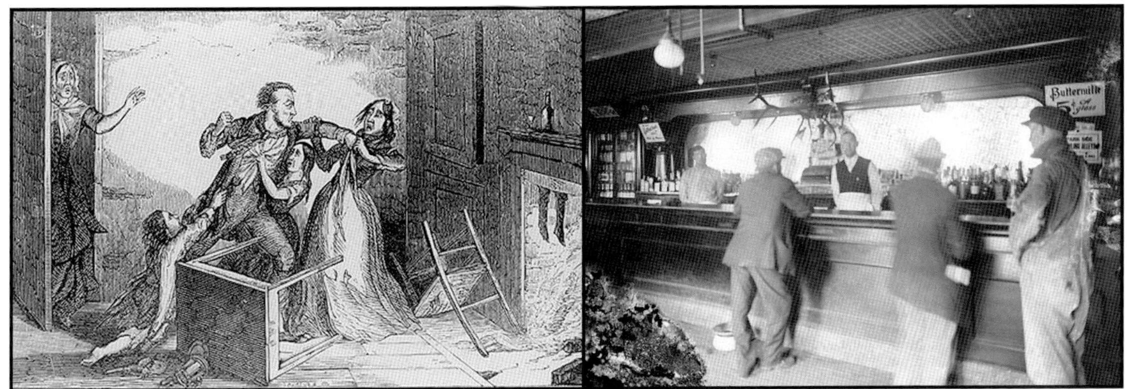

*1871 cartoon, with caption "Quarrels between Mr. and Mrs. Latimer, and Brutal Violence between Them, were the Natural Consequences of the Frequent Use of the Bottle"; a saloon in Belmond, despite claim of none "in the place"*

At the same time, on 20 April 1877 the *Belmond Herald* printed a contradictory report of alcohol's purported properties:

> A French doctor claims one-half the so-called drowned persons are buried alive and that they be brought to life by proper treatment after having been "several hours under water." His remedy is to get out the water, pour in and inject alcoholic stimulants, and uses a whip energetically, or hot irons in bad cases. He says that life remains longest in the intestines, and that they may be stimulated to such an extent by heroic treatment that the heart will resume its action.

Any fantastic claims from across the Atlantic aside, the frontier town's first doctors, nurses and, before them, midwives had their hands full, trying to improve the growing community's collective health. According to Elizabeth Nieuwen,

> Dr. [Lewis Hezekiah] Cutler was perhaps the first physician to locate in Wright County. His name is associated with several lines of business in the early '50s. He built the first frame house here. He commenced practicing medicine and for many years was the family doctor for all the families in the county. He rode his horse from the settlements in Belmond to those on the Boone River when there was not a tree or house to be seen between the two rivers.

In her series featuring early Belmond residents, Belmond journalist Phyllis Robinson honored the untiring efforts of another of the area's first doctors, G.F. "Mac" McBurney. In a *Belmond Independent* article featured on the Fourth of July 1946—Iowa's centennial year as a state—Robinson reminded her readers

> Any community owes an unpayable debt to a doctor, but to Mac is accorded a unique sentiment created by long years of sympathetic and efficient doctoring. One hears again and again, "He brought all my children into this world and I don't know what I'd done without him," or "The night was never too bad for Dr. Mac and he always came no matter what," or "He saved my son and I'll never forget it."

Robinson said the pioneering doctor's story of more than a half century of service evoked

> horse and buggy days, of low ungraded roads and untiled fields. [...] The eternal battle of mud was very real to the doctor, who sometimes found the roads impassable for his buggy and team of roans. If so, he took to horseback or hitched his bay to a cart. He recalled a time that he walked five miles up the railroad track to attend a man. In those days a doctors' battle was a double one – against disease and death, and against the elements.

*women sorting mail in a Belmond-area post office, about 1890; a 3-cent U.S. Postal Service stamp*

Articles in Belmond's first newspapers suggest that apparently the elements hindered the work of not only traveling doctors. Early mail carriers, for one, battled the worst of weather served up by Mother Nature, too. On 19 January 1877 an uncited Belmond paper announced "LOST:"

> In front of J.S. Pritchard's residence in East Belmond, yesterday morning, a team of horses, the U.S. mail sled, and the driver, E.A. Howland. Nothing has been found but Uncle Sam's mailsack, and it is feared that the property, together with the martyred driver, is a total loss. The government offers a reward for his return, dead or alive. P.S. – He was sober.

Stagecoach drivers, too, struggled to do their job despite the wide-open prairie's harsh climate. On 14 January 1880 an unnamed Belmond press announced "DELAYED:"

> Last Friday was probably as disagreeable a day as we have had this winter. The wind was very keen and carried sharp, cutting snow at a lively rate. All the stages due this point were delayed until the next day (Saturday) except on the Hampton route. Mr. Knipple successfully weathered the blizzard and came in on time; but the Webster stage did not leave that place at all, and Luther Loomis, on the Alden route, pulled the shoes off his horses and stopped at Otisville. But all hands are now making regular trips, over most awful rough roads.

Luther Loomis' determination to deliver the mail regardless of conditions won the farmboy from Oswego County, New York, much esteem in his adopted community. According to *History of Belmond*,

> In 1868 he took a contract for conveying the mails and driving stage from Belmond to Alden, Garner and Webster City, which he followed until the railroads usurped the business. During his service for the government he had to contend with numerous hardships, struggling through mud and breasting the severe snow and hail storms, at times when his very life was endangered. Yet he fearlessly sallied forth in the discharge of his duties, never missing a single trip, but always ready to go.

Hindrances to the stage getting through came not only from below in the form of mud or snow, but also from in front in the form of prairie fires, or even from above as funnel clouds.

History of Iowa *images of a stagecoach encountering a prairie fire and of a tornado whirling across the land*

In the early years of its existence, getting word to the remote frontier outpost remained paramount if challenging. As late as fall 1854 Franklin Grove's few residents

> received mail at Beriah Wright's supply store in Hardin City, until it went into decline and Cedar Falls began the popular trading point and post office. [Melissa (Overacker) Luick's older brother] Simeon Overacker carried the mail on foot, receiving $5 per trip [80 miles/130 km, one-way], the amount that was donated by individuals of the settlement.

In 1854, Belmond struggled to sink roots well beyond the realm of contiguous settlement in Iowa.

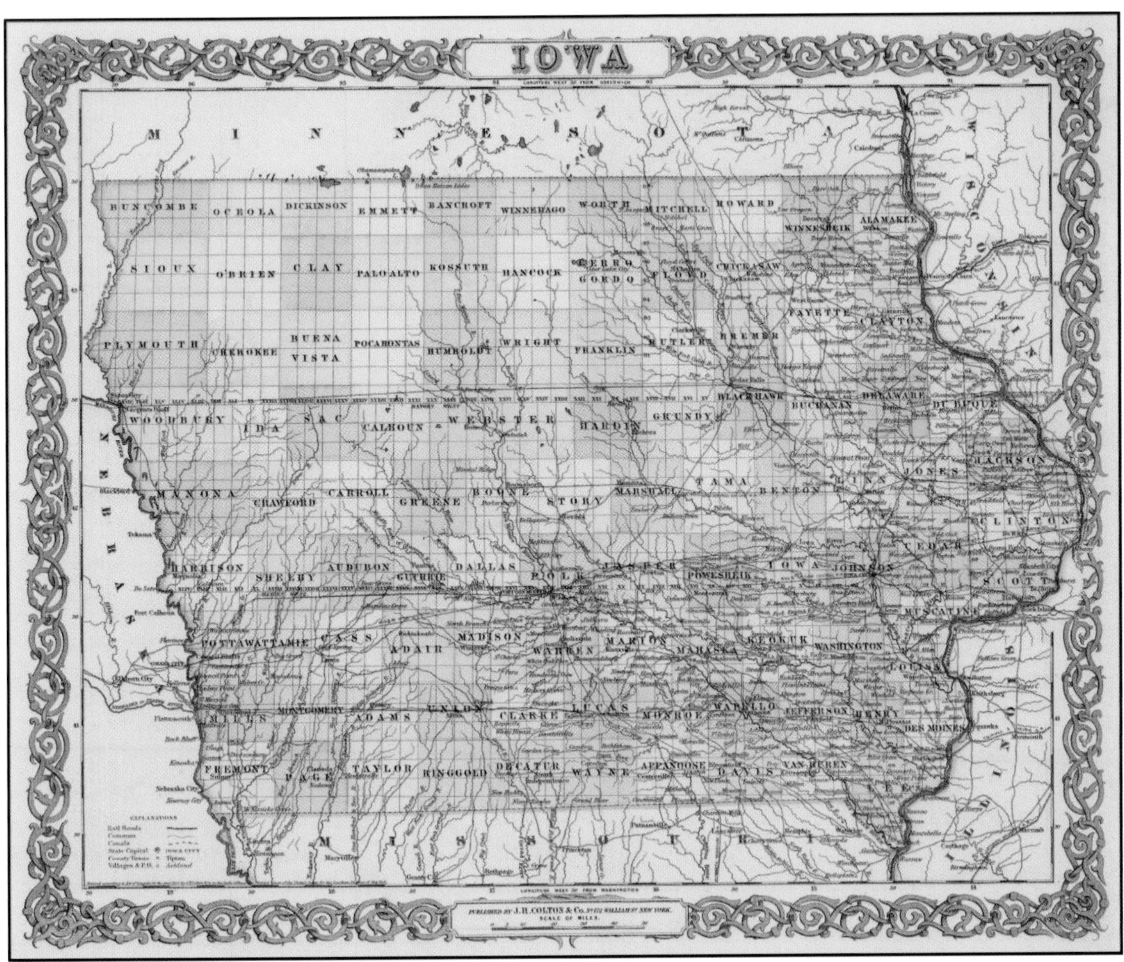


*Colton's 1855 map of Iowa: Wright County (third row from top, center) shows no roads or settlements*

In turn, Iowa lay well beyond the reach of established amenities in the United States. While the first European-American residents on the North Central Iowa prairies wished for a swift connection to points east, it would take years before even basic supplies, let alone "luxuries" like mail service would reach the fledgling, far-flung community.

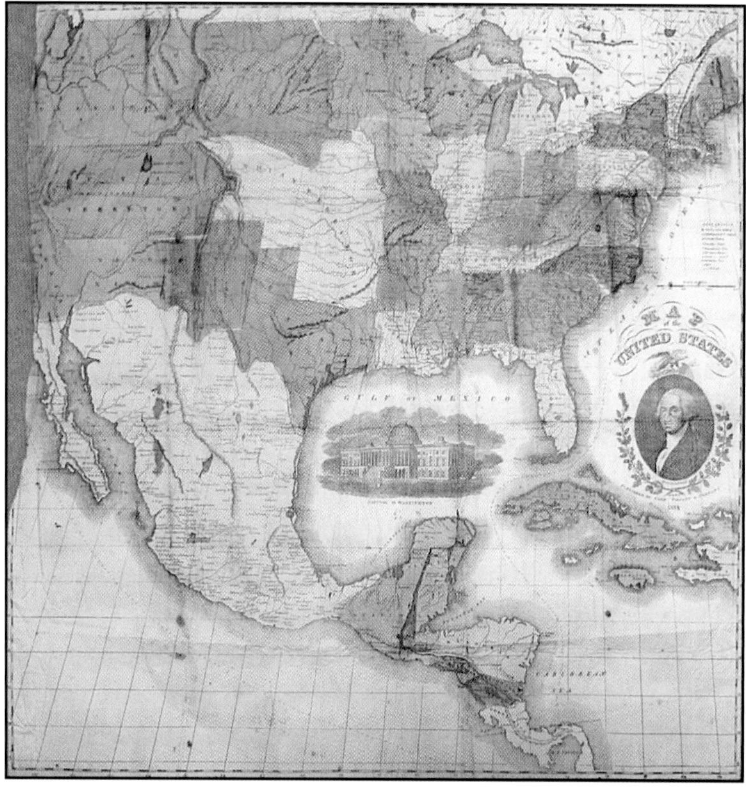

*1854 map of the U.S., Mexico and part of erstwhile British Upper Canada*

As recounted by Elizabeth Nieuwen:

> When the earliest settlers came to Belmond there were no railroads in the whole State of Iowa. All mail and goods stopped on the other side of the Mississippi opposite Davenport. When in '56 the Chicago and Rock Island crossed "The Father of Waters" the scattered pioneers of the prairies hailed the fact with joy. The same year "The Iron Horse" reached Iowa City [and later] Eldora [in adjoining easterly Webster County,] and mail was brought that far, though perhaps it would lie weeks until someone passing through Wright County would deliver it to the settlers.

As inconceivable as it might be today,

> Roads at this early day consisted of mere tracks, the route being decided by the first teamster who happened to pass that way. Bridges there were none, the streams being forded where encountered, and marshes avoided as best the unfortunate could. For several years the road from Belmond to Horse Grove was east of and around Franklin Grove, a distance of about fifteen miles, nearly double the length of the course pursued by a crow passing between the same points.

Any difficulties the first settlers of what would become "Belmond" faced receiving post, however, were little compared to, oh, possible locust inundation, prairie fire, drought, buffalo stampede, becoming lost in a freezing blizzard, slow starvation or a sudden Indian massacre. Early pioneer life on Iowa's wide-open prairies wasn't for the frail or faint of heart.

In order to face all that adversity, soon after the pioneers adequately tended to their basic worldly needs, they turned to satiating their spiritual ones. Beginning in the 1840s,

> the Methodist Church sent out circuit riders to travel throughout the settled portion of the state. Each circuit rider typically had a two-week circuit in which he visited individual families and conducted sermons for local Methodist congregations. Because the circuit riders' sermons tended to be emotional and simply stated, Iowa's frontiers-people could readily identify with them. The Methodists profited greatly from their "floating ministry," attracting hundreds of converts in Iowa's early years. As more settled communities appeared, the Methodist Church assigned ministers to these stationary charges.

Among the early members of Belmond's newly-founded Methodist church was the ever-growing contingent of Luicks living nearby. After Henry and David's trail-blazing arrival, other siblings and their extended families began arriving. With them, came other leading "first families" of the new settlement. Whole clans and circles of kin began appearing from Michigan, Indiana, Ohio... a myriad of other places.

Despite a seemingly endless series of hardships they faced during their first years in Iowa, by all indications the Luicks seemed to thrive in their new, final home in the New World. If they could survive there long-term would depend on the stability and vitality of the community, of the circle of other families or individuals who would choose to settle around them. Unlike Ann Arbor, where Heinrich, Katherine and their three young children found an existing social structure to which they had to adapt, on the almost-empty Iowa prairie the stand of trees their now-grown sons and daughter knew as "Franklin Grove" had almost none. But, the clever Luick clan well knew how to leave their lasting mark on that tabula rasa, and to do so to their advantage.

---

## chapter 12: first came farming

The Luicks came to Iowa for one thing: land. And, they meant to make the most out of the Iowa River Valley's deep, rich black soil. So, they wasted no time in transforming what they found into what they thought they wanted it to be.

*Evangelical Church and congregation in Wisner Township, Franklin County, east of Belmond; circa 1920*

Some seventy years after my family ventured from the woods of Southeast Michigan to the nearly treeless prairies of North Central Iowa, the *Belmond Independent*'s editors reviewed local agriculture's development. As excerpts from its 30 July 1925 feature article show, already then the people of northeast Wright County were keenly aware of how painstaking the process of building farms where there had been none, had been. This was possible, as a number then present were still alive in 1925.

The pioneer farmer tilled his land and harvested his crop in strange and peculiar ways when compared to the modern methods used by farmers today. In the spring of 1854 the Luick family, the Grays and the Overackers broke the virgin prairie soil with a walking plow. At planting time, holes were chopped in the sod with an ax, and the seed dropped in by hand. Hence the "sod corn" of the early days. Cultivation was with a hoe and with a one-row single shovel walking corn plow. The farmer could not ride, for there was nothing to ride on. The old single shovel cultivator was made by the blacksmith in a rude fashion, and the timber used in its construction was hewed by hand from native timber from Franklin Grove.

The first year nothing but corn was planted; the second year, some wheat was sown. Oats were not planted until several years later. No rye or barley was grown until quite a few years later. Harvesting was by hand, no matter what the crop. Corn was husked. Wheat was cut with a scythe, the old-fashioned "cradle," and then raked and bound by hand. The rake was similar to the garden rake of today but with wooden teeth. The grain was raked to a pile, then the rake held on the shoulder while the grain was gathered into a bundle and tied by hand. A good yield was 30 bushels of wheat to the acre.

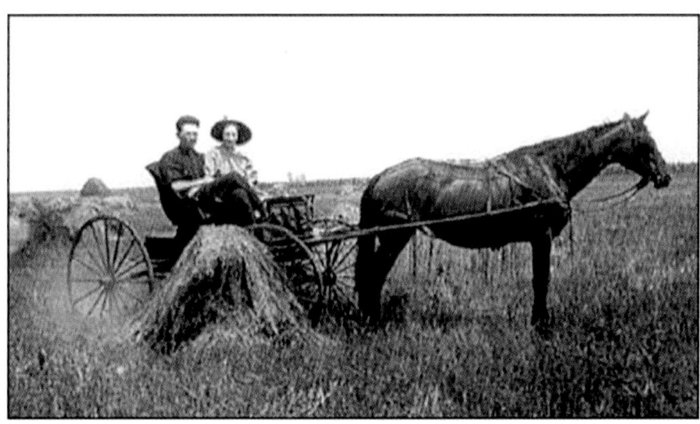

Threshing of the grain was accomplished by the "flail," a short wooden handle with a piece of whang leather fastened to the end. The grain was spread out and beaten with this flail until the grain was separated from the straw.

There was no such thing as a local market for any products then. Corn and wheat were hauled to Dubuque on the Mississippi River, the nearest market then. Later it was hauled to Iowa City, and still later to Cedar Falls. Some of it was sold to the mill at Dubuque, some ground into cornmeal for Johnnycake and into flour for bread, for the pioneer's own use. The flour was mostly of the graham character due to the fact that the mills were not equipped to bolt the wheat.

There was no such thing as a granary. Consequently, grain was piled on the ground or dumped into rail-fence cribs, until it could be disposed of.

Early stock was extremely limited. The Luicks had four horses, the Grays a number of cattle. Anthony Overacker had one milk cow, the only milk cow in the entire outfit of pioneers.

Through the Grays the early settlers were able to get a start in the cattle line. Mr. Gray brought the first stock of any character in his cattle, and the rest of the pioneers gradually built up their herds from his stock. The horses were of the Morgan type, small but tough and capable of standing hard usage. Oxen were used altogether for farming and practically all the hauling for a number of years. A good team of oxen was the prize possession of the pioneer family, and each aimed to get a team of the best animals it could.

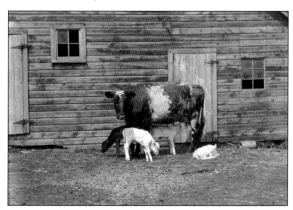

Farm buildings were makeshift and built of logs. The barns were covered with straw. There was no lumber of any character to be hand. Everything used had to be hewn by hand from the native timber. Doors were made by hewing a log to the required thickness and length. Windows were out of the question, and the first log cabins had none. Later small panes of glass were secured. The open fireplace furnished heat and a means for cooking. Floors were cut from logs, hewn down to a degree of smoothness and laid on the ground or on other logs.

*Cuppett machinery shop on East Main Street; local Belmond mill, 1910s*

The mill was the first local market for grinding; the miller took a certain toll of the grain. There was very little actual money - there was no place to get it and no place to spend it. Practically everything was bartered; a load of grain was worth so much in trade for a cow or a horse; or two calves perhaps, would be worth one cow.

*frontier-era currency, licensed by the State of Iowa*

Winters in the 1850s were severe beyond comprehension of the citizen of today. In '56 and '57 four feet [1.22 meters] of snow lay on the level. Drifts were common to the top of the cabins. At one time in 1857, [Louis Luick's older brother Michael Henry] helped [their aunt Catherine's future husband] Adrian Elder feed his stock. The barn could not be seen; drifts of snow completely covered it. A hole was chopped in the barn roof, and bundles of corn fodder were let down from above to feed the stock. There were times of blinding blizzards, which had a free sweep over the open prairie, when the pioneer would fasten himself to a rope, tied to the cabin, so that he could find his way back to the house when he went out to do the chores.

Corn sold at Cedar Falls in 1859 for 20 cents a bushel. Wheat was worth 30 cents. There were no oats to sell, and no hogs. Much of the time in later years when hogs were taken to market, they were taken dressed [according to early farmer Dave Finn "like wood in a cord on wagons."]

As the years passed, improvements arrived. Buildings were covered with "shakes," a slab of wood about three feet long and eight inches in width, hewn by hand from a slab of native timber. Much of the grain was still sown by hand, and walking plows were still used. Seeders were just coming into use in the

> seventies and early eighties, as were corn planters. The one-row walking cultivator was still used. At this period there came the first harvester, the "Marsh," which still required that bundles be bound by hand. The early threshing machines were of the merry-go-round variety, horse-powered, and not many years later, there was a steam-powered thresher in the country. Warren Rankins owned one of the first horse-powered threshing outfits and threshed much of the grain in Wright and adjoining counties.

*Belmond-area threshing scenes, both including the tractor-powered belt that made other machinery run*

> In the seventies markets for the farmer's products had advanced a little nearer. Garner, Hampton, and Alden were centers for produce. Oats were 9 cents a bushel at Garner, wheat brought a quarter. Good hogs sold at Garner for two cents a pound. Twenty-five bushels of corn per acre and 30 bushels of oats were the yields. Farm hands were getting $15 to $18 per month. Eggs were worth ten cents a dozen, butter at seven to eight cents a pound.
>
> In the 1880s the first self-binder, the McCormick, came in, a wonderful invention and a wonderful help to the farmer. The first railroad, the Iowa Central, coming into Belmond in 1881, brought the elevator and furnished the first local market for grain and corn. It was an epoch in the lives of the settlers. G.H. Richardson operated one of the first elevators in the county at the Iowa Central.

*one of Belmond's three depots; the station master in his office—note telephone in the upper-right corner*

> Agriculture is the foundation of America's peace and prosperity, and through their sons and grandsons, the early pioneers are still building the new empire.

Of course, any "empire" is won through small "victories"—in an agrarian one, by daily battles like taking out the slop and bringing in the eggs. The myriad tasks that comprised farm life on the Iowa prairies of the mid-19th century were determined, in large part, by something as basic as the weather.

> Even though farmers changed their agricultural production [with mechanization and the railroad], farm work continued to be dictated by the seasons. Wintertime meant butchering, fence mending, ice cutting,

and wood chopping. In the spring, farmers prepared and planted their fields. Summertime brought sheep shearing, haying, and threshing. In the fall, farmers picked corn, the most difficult farm task of all.

*Belmond-area womenfolk taking a rest from all that endless toil*

Farm women's work also progressed according to the seasons. During the winter, women did their sewing and mending, and helped with butchering. Spring brought the greatest activity. Then women had to hatch and care for chickens, plant gardens, and do spring housekeeping. During the summer, women canned large amounts of vegetables and fruit. Canning often extended into the fall. Foods like apples and potatoes were stored for winter use. Throughout all the seasons, there were many constants in farm women's routines. Every-day meals had to be prepared, children cared for, and housekeeping done. With gardens to tend and chickens to feed and water, farm women had both indoor and outdoor work. Through their activities however, women produced most of their families' food supply.

Even as they broke down the newly-plowed sod, the pioneers began to build up herds of livestock, as especially hooved animals constituted "moveable wealth." According to the article as preserved by the Belmond Historical Society, the early farmers of North Central Iowa commonly raised sheep. Michael Henry Luick both kept a large flock on his own farm and sheared sheep for other farmers each spring; his younger brother, Louis Lee, and nephew Henry Lorence Luick often joined him in sheering swaths through local herds, large and small.

In contrast to moveable capital such as livestock and grain, the quality and lay of the land itself meant all the difference between just surviving or truly thriving as farmers on the Iowa prairies. On 30 April 1890 a Belmond newspaper reported that frontier-trapper-cum-farmer David Luick, for one,

*Dell, son Mike, Curtis, Michael and Henry Luick shearing sheep; 1910s*

> is a happy man, and well he may be, for he has struck a fine flowing well on the Hathaway farm, in the little creek which runs through the portion east of the road. It is a strong flow, rising 12 feet in an inch pipe, and adds a good $500 [over thirteen-thousand in 2014 dollars] to the farm.

A pioneer farmer's distaff typically brought with her to the prairie more than just thoughts of water pipes or other such practicalities. David Luick's brother William's wife, for one, thought of esthetics, too.

With true womanly love of the beautiful and thoughtfulness for the future, [Rose (Pierce) Luick] had brought in her trunk from her Illinois home willow trees, which she planted, and these were the first in the county. These served to add to the attractiveness of their pioneer home, a home always open to weary travelers.

Grafting a thriving, successful—not to mention attractive—farm to the prairie's floor depended not only on what was below the ground, but what supporting structures ambitious settlers erected above it. On 15 January 1879 the *Belmond Herald*'s editor recorded the most recent developments he witnessed at one of the area's more prospering farmers:

*pioneer farm family posing with seedlings and wood-frame buildings*

It was our good fortune to pass New Year's Day at the home of [Massachusetts natives] Mr. and Mrs. Frank [and Carrie (Cheney)] Christie, near Hickory Grove. We went for the ostensible purpose of a visit to eat turkey, to see that farm and that big barn, and to have a good time on general principles. The weather was piercing cold, but we accomplished everything undertaken – especially the turkey eating. Frank raises an excellent breed of turkeys, and if we "made our mark" on that day – or on that turkey – it must not be wondered at.

*Frank; grandkids: (back) Ira, John, Ethel, (middle) Frank, Goldie, (front) Gladys, 1898; Carrie (Cheney) Christie*

The home of these agreeable people, Mr. and Mrs. Christie, is just to the southwest of Hickory Grove, and their lots may well be said to be "cast in pleasant places." The native grove is not near enough and too far east to afford shelter to the farm, but large, thrifty cottonwoods, popples [sic], maples, willows, and the like, of a dozen years' growth, stand thickly on the north and west (put out when the farm was first opened), affording the grandest protection imaginable. It seems like living in the shade of a dense wood. Their commodious house stands south of this body of timber; and still a little father south and west is that fine new barn we have before mentioned. It is the central figure of the improvements, and where the principal part of the moveable wealth of the place will be garnered from year to year.

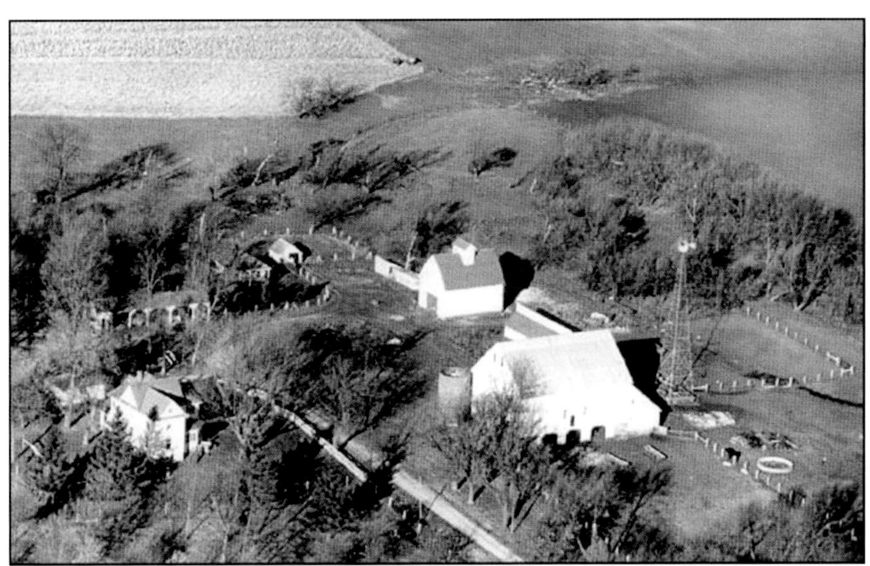

*Frederick Simerson farm, typical of the Upper-Midwest built in last half of 19th century, with large grove*

The building is 40' x 68' [12.20 x 20.73 meters]. The ends and north side rest on a solid wall of prairie [fieldstone] "hard heads," laid up with a skill and exactness that is remarkable. It is decidedly a fine piece of mason work. On the south side you enter the basement. This will be boarded up and the interior partitioned off for cattle and hogs. The second floor will accommodate 12 horses, has grain bins, corn cribs, two driveways and a bay. Above this floor is the main mow for hay, capable of holding 100 tons. The whole of this mammoth affair, 60' x 48', 40' [18.30 x 14.63, 12.20 meters] high, is to be fitted up in approved style. It is not yet complete, but will be next season.

[A Civil War veteran and one-time White House guard,] Mr. Christie is one of the well-fixed farmers of Wright County. He works about 360 acres of land. He has now 80 head of cattle, and a fine drove of hogs. The location of the place cannot be surpassed. His land is rolling and dry; a number of acres are in tame grass, and the plow land under the best cultivation. But how was this all brought about? How was this beautiful home created, with its many desirable surroundings? By industry, temperate habits, good management and indomitable will to succeed. "God helps those who help themselves." May Mr. and Mrs. Christie live long to enjoy their prosperity, is the sincere wish of the writer.

*Hayo Goeman family, posing behind the farmyard gate in winter, with a team of workhorses; circa 1900*

Almost without exception, the house, barns and other farm buildings the first settlers erected in North Central Iowa followed unwritten "rules." Those early-established norms in design, construction techniques, materials and resultant appearance resulted in a pervasive uniformity in the area's visual culture. The "template" that left its indelible stamp on rural America until today had an in-town equivalent, too. It also determined durable, outward forms of settlement that cannot be separated from the inward form of the American heartland's social fabric. That deep, lasting imprint, in turn, directed the flow, the eventual course of the entire nation.

Such templates were copied, then replicated in uncountable communities, in thousands of counties across the country. The story of one, then, can be seen—at least in broach strokes—as representative, as "the central story" of thousands.

---

**chapter 13: templates for "civilization"**

The settlement of what one day would become "Belmond" spoke volumes about what sort of people my Luick ancestors were, as well as the daily-life world we, their descendants, would know growing up, decades later, on the Iowa prairie. As Albert Lee Luick, born 1877, retold:

> Soon after Henry, Jr. and David Lick arrived to make their home in this Iowa wilderness, many other pioneers began to arrive. One of these was Archie Dumond, who came in 1855 to put in a dam across the Iowa River to furnish power for the grist mill and saw mill he was to build and operate successfully.

Initially the settlers had little choice but to build their first longer-term shelter out of logs, given the unavailability of sawn lumber and the widespread use of sod houses, which only came into widespread practice further west, some time later. While hunting wild game or scavenging for wild edible plants supplemented their meager diets, the area's earliest pioneers had no choice but to purchase staples such as ground flour or cornmeal faraway, and ride or carry it in. Hunger for substantial foodstuffs, then, dictated that mills were among the first businesses to be built. As windmills would only later be light yet durable enough to be practical or cost-effective, and wood remained scarce, water power proved essential in securing enough food for all to eat.

In a 1978 essay, shot-gun-toting Cloe Jenison described how *The Old River Dam* was erected, in part with help from her grandfather, Joseph Bud Jenison, and great-grandfather, Elias III:

> Men with oxen, mules and horses agreed to build stone boats to go along the river to the north of the settlement and pull rocks to the site they had chosen. Men without animals and equipment offered to get into the river and push and roll the rocks to make a damn high enough to hold the water back and to make the power needed to run the mill. The water in the river was low at the time so they were sure they could build a dam. It took many men to roll the rocks into the water and rolled into place, piled one on top of another until they had the dam the height they wanted. They used an inclined plane built of split logs from Franklin Grove to move the rocks up one on top of another. After many, many days the dam was completed.

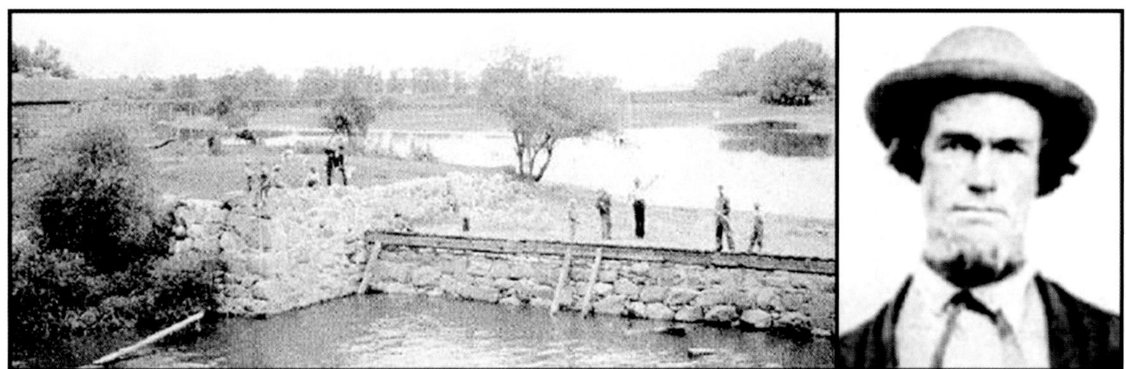

*men and boys on the Iowa River dam in Belmond; Melissa (Overacker) Luick's eight-year-older brother, Simeon, whose grandson, Albert Lee Luick, played on the damn as a boy, growing up in the town his father, David, settled*

Despite the settlers' best efforts, however, after only a few months' use the initial mill industrious Archer Dumond constructed washed downriver by floodwaters in spring 1856. Still,

> Archie Dumond was a resourceful and progressive man, and in order to build the home he planned for his family, he found clay along the Iowa River bank which he thought would be suitable for brick and so he built a brick kiln and produced the necessary brick for building the home that [stood] as a landmark to his resourcefulness [until destroyed in the 1966 tornado that flattened much of Belmond's historic core in mere minutes]. This house was the rallying place for the early settlers to come during the many Indian scares of that time.

*house Archer Dumond built—first brick one in Belmond area, which boasted an etched-glass front door*

Ironically, only a few years before the same hill where the settlers established a refuge from feared attacks by the region's original inhabitants was the site of the last inter-tribal "Indian Massacre of 1852." Half a decade later, the Dumond family's home served as the focus of the settlers' stand against a feared reprisal by Native Americans—ancient peoples desperate to stop encroaching "pale skins" such as my Luick, Overacker, Jenison or other ancestors already there.

The Belmond Historical Society's exhaustive study of the town's biography, *History of Belmond, Iowa 1856-2006*, recounts both incidents in telling details:

# Indian Scares

### Indian Massacre of 1852

Belmond Cemetery Hill was once a bloody battle ground for one of the last Indian battles known in Iowa. Peace now reigns where once the air was filled with war whoops and screams of the dying.

The U.S. Dragoons pre-dated the U.S. Calvary and were some of the first white people to lay eyes on the plains and prairies of Wright County. They were known as "mounted foot soldiers." The "Neutral Strip" was a 40-mile-wide strip of land that had been established by the U.S. Government in 1830. This land was meant to be used as a buffer zone and the tribes had agreed not to cross it and thus keep the peace. A portion of the Strip was in Wright County and this was traveled and patrolled by the United States Dragoons who were constantly on the lookout for Indian trespassers and white whiskey peddlers.

In 1852 the friendly but weak Winnebago Indians, assisted by the U.S. Dragoons, constructed a sod fort on a small hill north of Franklin Grove as a means of protection for themselves against the strong, savage Sioux Indians. The location of this mud fort is where the present day Belmond Cemetery is located. In 1852 this was quite a large hill; it was in later years when the first plot for the cemetery was planned that it was razed down to its present height.

It is reported that in 1852 the "wily Sioux, in numbers of about 1,000 came down on the little fort and captured it, killing most of the members and taking the remainder as prisoners."

Runners were dispatched after the attack on the Winnebago by the Sioux and they soon reached the Dragoons who then saddled and mounted their horses in haste and overtook the Sioux. The Dragoons defeated them, killing many and returning the prisoners to their families.

The few Indians left living in Franklin Grove were eventually moved north by the government, but they told their story to Mr. Beebe and his sons who first settled in Franklin Grove in 1853.

Later, when Mr. Beebe and his sons sold their "claim" to Henry Luick and new settlers began arriving in this area, the ruins of this fort were still to be seen. The families repaired the sod fort and used it for many years. Years later when the land was broken up for farming purposes by Mr. Luick, arrowheads, bells, tomahawks, a scalping knife and other relics were found.

### Indian Scare of 1857

The news of the horrible butchery of the Spirit Lake Massacre in early March 1857 spread all over the northwest and filled the settlers with the greatest alarm. Every preparation was made by the few settlers of the infant village of Crown Point which was renamed Belmond.

As many people fled their homes for Webster City, a number of men met at Dr. L.H. Cutler's store in Belmond and organized themselves into a military company for defense of the settlement with Dr. Cutler as captain.

Once this organization was effected, the men immediately set to work and erected a mud fort. Even though some families had left to seek safe abodes, the greater portion had remained and even the wives of the brave men who formed the military company volunteered to remain and share the fate of their husbands, cooking and doing everything in their power to assist them in their labors.

The mud fort that was constructed sat near Mr. Dumond's house and as many as 32 women and children stayed at the Dumond home while the men piled sod and laid up logs for more solid protection. This hastily constructed mud fort overlooked the Iowa River from the west and it stood in evidence for many years of one of the many fears faced by the early pioneers.

For better security, the women were all gathered into the one log cabin while the men remained in the fort and established a regular routine of military discipline. Pickets were established and sentinels posted. They knew well what kind of enemy threatened them; the Indians were cunning, crafty, shrewd and treacherous. Knowing this they were ever on the alert and always attentive to duty.

After several days had passed and they had heard nothing from their brother settlers on the Boone, O.W. McIntosh and Thomas Sheets were dispatched on a scout mission to learn how matters stood. Their instructions were to return in 24 hours.

On reaching the Boone they found all still and silent, as if death had entered every household and swept up with one fell swoop all their families. They turned their horses toward Webster City and continued to find every settlement completely deserted. They feared the worst had happened because even though there was no sign of bloodshed, there was also no human face to be seen.

On and still on they went, yet they found nothing but deserted country until they reached Webster City. It was at this place where the settlers had repaired to upon receiving the news of the Spirit Lake Massacre. All here was excitement and agitation as the people were busily engaged in fitting out an expedition for Spirit Lake.

All this time the people at Belmond were in the greatest anxiety, from the reports that were brought to them by people from the north, they expected the Indians would shortly be upon them. The non-return of the scouts within the time stipulated also added to the reigning anxiety that was felt by the whole community. Thirtysix hours had passed and there was no sign of the scouts. The township was convinced something had happened to the scouts or they would have returned.

*19th-century depictions of "Massacre" and Abbie Gardner's kidnapping; Dakota Chief Wanata ("Charger")*

It was determined necessary to send out two more men, so on the same afternoon George Dumond and Aaron Dukes were dispatched on a similar reconnaissance as the former two.

Upon reaching the Boone, Dumond and Dukes found the same death-like stillness that the preceding scouts had experienced. They headed their horses down stream with precaution marking their every movement. With revolvers in hand and ready for any emergency that might arise, they continued downstream, but no human form was to be found and the scouts made the decision to continue on toward Webster City.

While moving along cautiously and ever on the alert, they suddenly heard something moving through the brush! The night was dark and what or who it was, they were unable to ascertain. Being true western men and possessed with more than common courage, they were bound to determine whether the sound that had startled them was caused by Indian, man, beast or goblin. For this purpose, they charged towards the noise, firing their revolvers all the while, only to find upon arriving on the spot, that whatever it was had fled.While resting for a moment, they suddenly heard the sound of something going across the prairie at great speed! They lost no time in idle meditation and striking their rowels into their horse's sides, dashed on at full speed.

In the darkness of the night there was nothing to guide the horsemen but the sound of the hoof beats of whatever, or whoever, they were pursuing. On they raced until they overcame it and discovered, to their mortification and chagrin, that it was nothing but a poor old cow that had been browsing among the brush.

This little incident, however ludicrous it may seem, had the effect of changing the monotony of the journey of the scouts. It had caused them to pass over a considerable distance of the way in a much shorter time and a short time later they spotted a party of men coming up the river on an expedition similar to their own. They instantly spurred their horses on to meet these men, but ended up startling the other party so severely that they instantly wheeled about and galloped off at a speed that rendered all efforts to overtake them useless.

No other incidents transpired the rest of the way to Webster City where they found the two scouts that had preceded them and a great portion of settlers from along the Boone. The next day, after inspiring new confidence in the hearts of those who had left their homes, the four scouts started on their return trip to the mud fort.

While this reconnaissance to the Boone was being made, the party at the mud fort had been reinforced by a company from Alden, some 30 miles down the river. No information had reached the garrison in the mud fort since the first scouting party was dispatched and the greatest anxiety was felt by all. They were determined, however, to remain steadfast and if the Indians did attack them, they would defend themselves and their homes to the very end.

Fortunately, such an emergency did not take place, for on the return of the scouts they were informed that the cause of all the danger from an Indian attack was over.

Upon receipt of this information, the garrison was disbanded and each man returned to his own domicile to follow the peaceful routine of everyday life.

Thus ended the great Indian scare of 1857.

Once the feared but mostly exaggerated "Indian threat" had been unquestionably eliminated, settlers streamed into Franklin Grove and rapidly began establishing a Euro-American world.

Mr. Howland built a store building on the west side of the river and conducted a General Store. Mr. Pierce came from Illinois and built several store buildings and put in a General Store on the side of the river near the mill. Dr. Cutler put in a drug store; a blacksmith shop and wagon shop were also started with many other services that made this a real trading center.

An experience repeated so many thousands of times, in so many thousands of frontier towns across North America, from the first English colonies to the last homesteaders' supply towns in Alaska in the mid-20th century, it left indelible marks on the American character. In shortest order, the growing town experienced an accelerating occurrence of numerous firsts:

*Griesey's store (bottom left), bank and harness shop: In 1867 Spruce Street (now "Main") was a dirt path.*

Illinois-born Abner Cox established the first blacksmith-gunsmith shop on the Hill, already in 1855. Pleasant Township's first justice of the peace and Catherine Luick's future brother-in-law, James Elder from Pennsylvania, performed the first marriage ceremony in the future "Belmond" by uniting 15-year-old Ohio-native Catherine McNutt and John Rowen, 18, from Connecticut, on 16 March 1856. Reportedly, Louis Luick was among the first "white" baby boys to be born in Belmond—fittingly, on the Fourth of July 1856. Reverend Andrew McNutt preached the first sermon and established the first church, a Brethren one.

Some settlers, however, did not wait for outside agents to organize religious services on the prairie. Elizabeth Lieuwen, for one, recounts how the first families living near hers

> organized a Sunday School, which was held in the Pierce schoolhouse [for twelve years]. Sometimes we had preaching services. John E. Rowan of Clarion, Conrad Fatland, and Wm. Shillington were the ones that I remember who came to preach. Later [...] Rev. Viola Smith, an ordained minister in the Friend's church, preached regularly. Probably because our numbers were small we were closely united and the members of this group who are living, have for twenty-five years met in annual reunion.

Nieuwen's detail-rich narrative chronicles how, as an example of congregation-building across frontier America, in Wright County

> The congregational church was organized in 1867 with twelve charter members. [...] It was the pioneer of this denomination in Wright County. Father J.D. Sands was installed as its first pastor, coming in 1869 to do missionary work [and according to Lieuwen] John Dozier Sands was the most outstanding man in the early history of Wright County; Belmond was proud to claim him as a permanent resident. He was born in England and was in the British Army which came to Canada to put down the Papineau Rebellion. He served four years [and after being] discharged entered Grand Signe Academy in Montreal, mastering the French language. In 1844 he entered Yale Theological seminary and graduated in 1847. He came to Iowa at the outbreak of the Civil War, when he went as chaplain of the 19th regiment, Iowa Infantry Volunteers and served until the close of the war.
>
> In 1871 he was elected County Superintendent of Schools on the Republican ticket. That gave him a wider field of work, preaching and lecturing in all the schools that he visited. In January 1872 as he went on horseback to Clarion to his official duties one terrible stormy day, his dwelling burned with all its contents, without insurance. His large library insurance of $1800 had just run out. The forty on which he lived [...] was purchased with a legacy. When he was not preaching he was ditching his land or working in the harvest fields with his neighbors.
>
> As time went on his work enlarged until he preached twice on Sunday and five nights during the week, one circuit being in Hancock County and one in Wright. Mrs. Sands always accompanied him and they organized the Congregational Churches of Clarion in 1872, Eagle Grove, 1881 and Rowan in 1890.
>
> Thus through storm and flood, heat and cold, with his face turned steadfastly toward the New Jerusalem, he toiled on and never asked, "What will you give me?" This man, a Greek and Hebrew scholar seldom equaled, with a perfect knowledge of the French language, a man who could have commanded a munificent salary in many an eastern city, toiled on here for 34 years and probably never received over $400 a year for his services, an example of self-sacrifice seldom equaled.
>
> The present Sands Memorial Church stands as a monument to his memory as does a splendid granite shaft in Franklin Grove cemetery, paid for with gifts from admiring friends and parishioners and on which is inscribed the words, "Preacher, Patriot, Pioneer."

A man later to play a central (albeit involuntary) role in the ultimately unhappy marital resume shared by Henry and Melissa (Overacker) Luick, Connecticut-born Charles Johnson (cited on the 1860 census as a "master carpenter") built Belmond's first brick house—for ambitious Archer Dumond, who had just constructed the area's first kiln. And, according to compiled research confirmed by Don's team, Canadian-born Isadore Fisk Notestine

> taught the first school in the area in a log house, which was erected by Anthony Overacker on the west side of Franklin Grove; a brick schoolhouse was built in 1857 across the ravine northwest of the Dumond house [but] burned in 1863.

Even primitive schoolhouses, though, have to be furnished and supplied—at least with basics.

> The first merchandise probably ever sold over a counter in Wright County was from the stock put in by Jules Cowles in July 1855. The first frame house was built in 1856 by Dr. Cutler, in which he opened his store. O.O. Kent built the "Red Ranch" hotel on the Hill around 1857; it was a large square frame building and for years was one of the two hotels of the town.

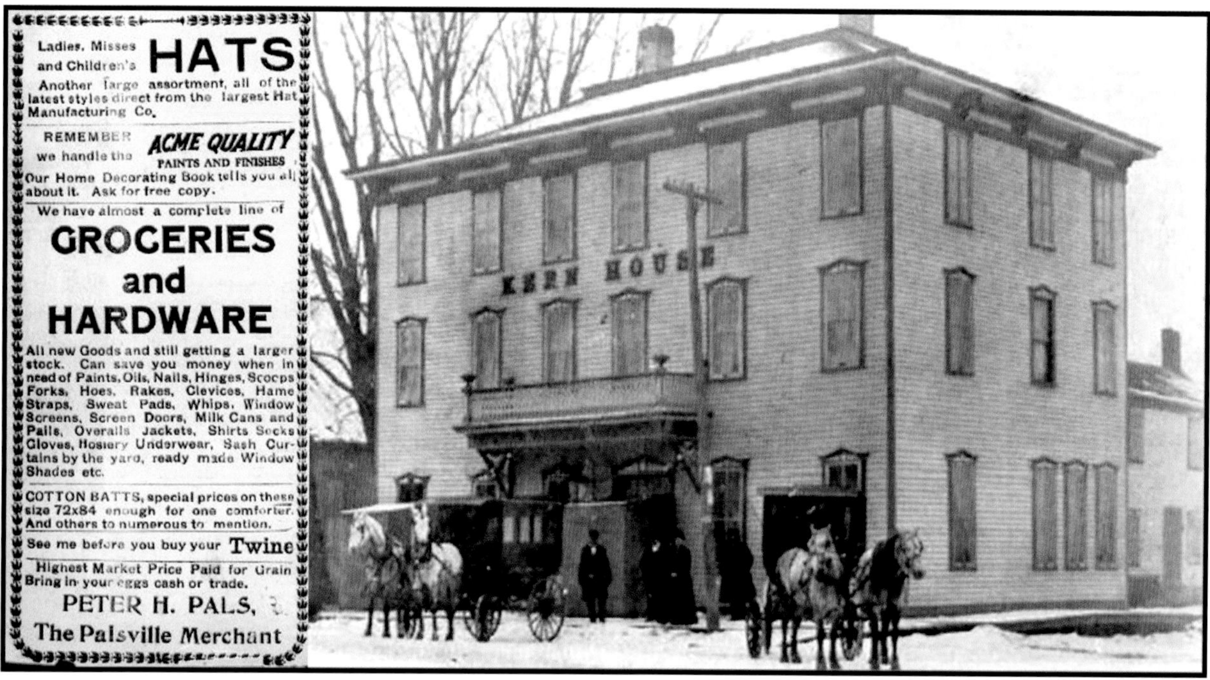


*Kern House Hotel on Main Street, Belmond, early 1900s*

Building all those "firsts" would have been for naught, however, had there been no way for people living outside the fledgling community to access and thus be able to patronize them, too. The need to connect the young settlement—officially named "Belmond" only three weeks earlier—to a wider world led, then, to another "first:"

> The first entry in the Wright County Road Book, dated July 7, 1856, recorded a petition from Anthony Overacker for a road; Henry Luick, a Pleasant Township trustee, was appointed to view and locate the road, which was established in 1856. The so-called Belmond Road led to the county line and was the chief highway in early times in Wright County, as over it went all the travel from the Belmond area down the Iowa Valley to Alden, Iowa Falls and Webster City.

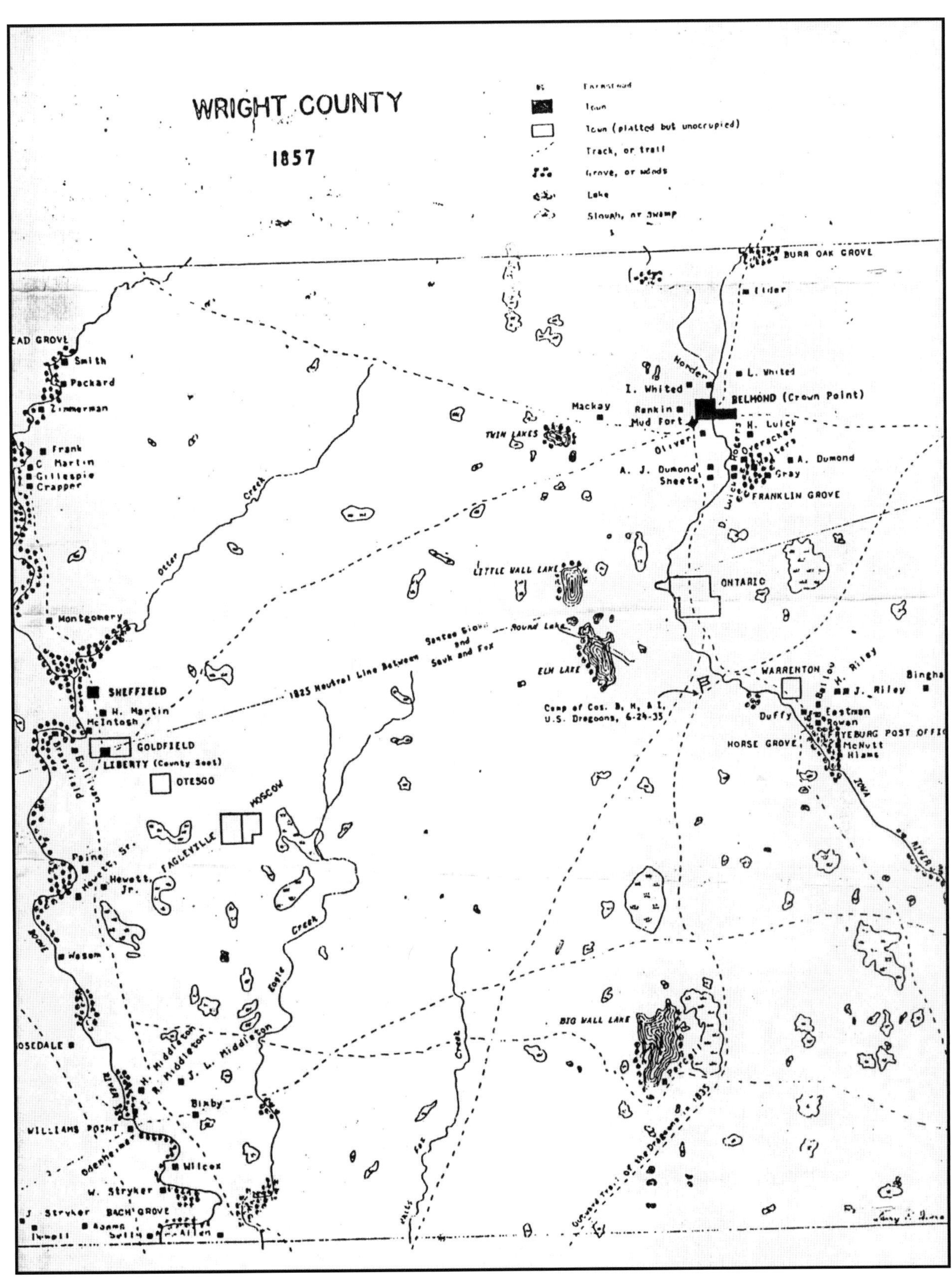
WRIGHT COUNTY
1857
Town
Town (platted but unoccupied)
Track, or trail
Grove, or woods
Lake
Slough, or swamp
BURR OAK GROVE
BELMOND (Crown Point)
Mud Fort
TWIN LAKES
FRANKLIN GROVE
LITTLE WALL LAKE
ONTARIO
Round Lake
ELM LAKE
1825 Neutral Line Between Santee Sioux and Sauk and Fox
WARRENTON
Camp of Cos. B, H, & I, U.S. Dragoons, 6-24-35
HORSE GROVE
SHEFFIELD
GOLDFIELD
LIBERTY (County Seat)
OTESGO
MOSCOW
EAGLEVILLE
BIG WALL LAKE
WILLIAMS POINT
BACH GROVE
Otter Creek
Eagle Creek
Iowa River
Boone River
Smith
Packard
Zimmerman
Montgomery
McIntosh
Paine
Wesom
Bixby
Wilcox
W. Stryker
J. Stryker
I. Whited
L. Whited
Mackay
Rankin
Oliver
A. J. Dumond
A. Dumond
Sheets
Gray
H. Luick
J. Riley
H. Riley
Duffy
Eastman
Rowan
McNutt
Hiams

As hoped, that early connectivity helped fan the new settlement's rapid growth. According to the *Belmond Sesquicentennial*, in 1864 William Luick's future father-in-law

> came to the community with a fortune already made [and] built a magnificent store, his business consisting of dry goods, boots and shoes, hats and caps, Queensware, hardware, and millinery goods. [...] Soon after the war it was rumored that a $10,000 man was coming to Belmond. Smith D. Pierce from Illinois established the industry of cheese making that gave farmers a market for milk. He had a nursery of fruit trees set out that started fruit growing around Belmond. Mr. Pierce died in 1884 and "Capitalist" was listed as his occupation on his death record.

It would be myriad "capitalists," millions of entrepreneurs who came to the American frontier looking to make their fortune, who would transform a wilderness into what the newcomers called "civilization." That New World they were establishing grew, though, one project at a time:

> By 1870 Belmond had three stores, one grist and sawmill, a cheese factory, two blacksmith shops, one harness maker, one boot and shoe maker, two practicing physicians, one carpenter's shop and one agricultural warehouse. Gurley Pritchard published the first newspaper in 1873 called *Belmond Mirror*.

Not only the young town's residents heralded its growth and prospects for same. On 28 September 1870 admirers from Dubuque chimed in the *Wright County Monitor* that the town

> lies in a county in which abounds the most beautiful and picturesque scenery to be found anywhere in the State of Iowa; a country which abounds with high rolling prairie, beautiful groves, transparent lakes, and above all a healthful climate [that] makes it perhaps one of the most desirable localities in which a man could desire to locate.

*early view of west end of Belmond's Main Street, circa turn of the last century*

> Belmond, the metropolis of this county, is a fine village and is [...] improving as rapidly as the pressure of the times will permit. It is finely situated, being on both sides of the Iowa River[.] It contains six stores, all of which are doing a good business. Dr. L.H. Cutler has just completed his splendid building; and is rapidly filling it with a good assortment of dry goods and groceries. As the doctor is a thorough businessman, and one of the "go-aheads" in everything he undertakes, we can predict to a degree of certainly that his business will prove a success.

Outsiders' esteem for emergent Belmond continued to swell for years. Less than a decade later F.J. Evans, editor of the *Iowa Falls Sentinel*, penned a guest article that appeared in the *Belmond Herald* on 25 June 1879. In it Evans described what he, his wife and two other couples saw on a recent outing that provided the article's headline, "To Belmond and Back – What Was Seen by the Way."

> Belmond is a pleasant little town of about 400 inhabitants, nestled down on the banks of the Iowa River at a point where two railroads are ere long destined to cross. And I may here state that they are both graded to and beyond this place. Belmond has a grand future before it, surrounded as it is with rich farmlands, and the prospect of two railroads within a year or two, business will surely be living there before long. The country around Belmond is rather sparsely settled as yet, and the open prairies afford lots of feed for stock, and it is estimated that there are 20,000 head of cattle being herded in Wright County this season. The people of Belmond are blessed with the spirit of public improvement, and we noticed they were grading their streets with gravel. J.J. McAlpine, who has heretofore been in the drug trade, has sold his stock of drugs and is arranging his store building for a hotel.

Just seven years later observers from the *Des Moines Leader* shared their impressions of "Belmond, What It is Doing Now, and What It Expects to Do" in a special *Belmond Herald* article 15 September 1886. Excerpts from it testified that

> This beautiful little city of 1,000 inhabitants is situated in [a] portion of two townships – Belmond and Pleasant – the greater part of the business portion in the city lying in Pleasant. [...] When we visited the place first, 18 years ago, it was a small hamlet, giving very little promise of the thriving business place it has since become. On the south of the city, but in close proximity, is Franklin Grove, a very nice body of timber, which relieves the prairie of its otherwise monotonous appearance. The surrounding country is an undulating prairie of great fertility, most admirably adapted to all purposes of farming. A prosperous and enterprising class of farmers cultivates it. Among the pioneers of this region we find David and William Luick [...] and others, who have been here nearly, if not quite 30 years. They had faith in this portion of the county and their reward has come. [...]
>
> The situation of Belmond is delightful. A dry townsite, excellent water power, wide clean streets, good sidewalks and crossings, neat, attractive private dwellings, nice shade trees, and substantial business houses make a combination worthy of special mention. The social and business elements seem to vie with each other for the welfare of the place, and the stranger who enters its gates is impressed with the idea that "peace reigns within its walls, and plenteousness within its palaces." [...] There is a large school building with four departments, and an attendance of 300 pupils. The Catholic, M[ethodist] E[poscopal], Congregational and German Evangelical [Lutheran] are the church societies, each owning its edifice. [...] Of professional men, besides the clergy, there are four physicians and five lawyers. The souls, the bodies and the rights of the people should be well protected in Belmond.

*Belmond's first large schoolhouse, with pupils below and teachers seated in windows, shown in the mid-1870s*

We met and did business with [...] representative men of the place, via: G.A. Thompson, miller, who is improving his mill as fast as possible to keep up with the demands of the country. His flour is in great demand and is sold within a 130 miles of Chicago. Mr. Thompson is a veteran of the Mexican War and lately met with his old comrades in Des Moines. Though his hair and beard are white, his bodily strength seems undiminished. [...] H.F. Kahl, the blacksmith, manufactures a spade that is extensively sold, and which for durability and workmanship takes the whole bakery; Bert Wilson, the barber, has razors hard enough to shave the cheek of a democrat [...] Frederick Luick is one of the most successful farmers and stock raisers of this section, and [...] Charles Jenison, David Luick and [others] all belong to the hard-handed yeomanry of Wright County...

The *Belmond Herald* is a weekly paper edited by S.A. Keeler, and keeps its tenders supplied with choice Republican Doctrine. If Bro. Keeler was a little more liberal minded, his democratic subscribers of whom he has a great many, would like his paper better...

Last but not least, the Kern House, the only hotel in Belmond – but no other is needed, for the proprietor, Mr. Case, cares for the traveling public in a manner entirely satisfactory. A good table, good rooms, kind attention, a free bus to and from all trains, and a livery stable in connection with the house, incline pilgrims to consider it a very desirable stopping place.

A wagon factory is very much needed, and Belmond offers special inducements to anyone who will go there and start one. A linseed oil mill and a low factory would also do well there and the water power is one of the best in the state. Should anyone who reads this article feel induced to go to Belmond to live or engage in business, he will find an excellent class of people and a welcome general and sincere.

We omitted the fact that we also met his honor, Judge Ben Morse, of the Supreme Court of Michigan, a clean-cut democrat with an enviable war record. The Judge carries an empty sleeve. He is visiting relatives in Iowa [including his nephew, Ida (Luick) Morse's husband, Willard.]

Political passions or affinities notwithstanding, after so much exponential growth in such a short time—in the course of about half of a then-average life expectancy for babies born in 1880—less than half a century after it was founded as a political entity, Wright County's map looked completely different from that patchwork drawing of just two decades earlier.

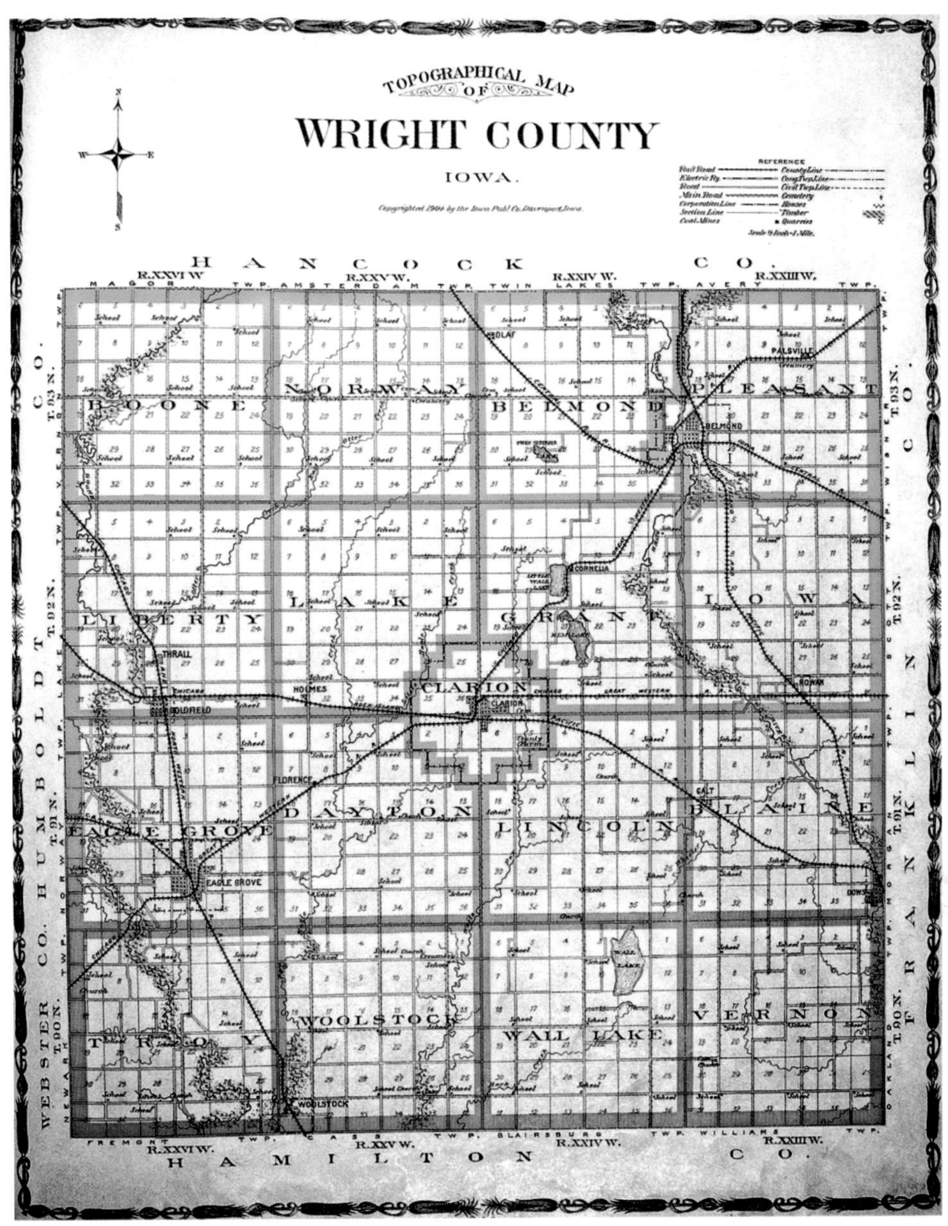


*1904 map of Wright County, Iowa, fifty years after first non-native settlement*

———

Among those who preceded them to Ann Arbor, the Luicks were one of numerous families. In what became "Belmond," however, they were among the first few—as seen in the handful of names that repeatedly resurface in the town's earliest recorded history. A fervent, years-long chronicler of the town's development, in their extensive history of Belmond, Bancroft & Co. offer a review of the pre-prairie life of one leading figure as a telling case study:

As a young man Archer Dumond moved from Seneca County, Ohio, to Indiana, where in 1834 he married Elizabeth Martin. Two weeks following their marriage the bride's uncle married her half-sister,

Deborah. In 1854 the Dumond and Martin families left their homes near Crown Point in Lake County, Indiana and—joined by Dr. Lewis Cutler and his two sons from Stephenson County, Illinois—arrived to stake claims near "the Hill" on the Iowa River's west bank, opposite the Luicks' settlement near Franklin Grove. There,

> The three families immediately commenced building a log cabin beside the Iowa River near where the first mill was later erected and all 21 persons lived through the summer in that cabin. Before long, Mr. Dumond erected a new log house for his family, this one on the Hill west of the Iowa River [and named it] Crown Point. Later in 1855, many Dumond relatives from Seneca County, Ohio, began their westward trek to the new settlement in Wright County.

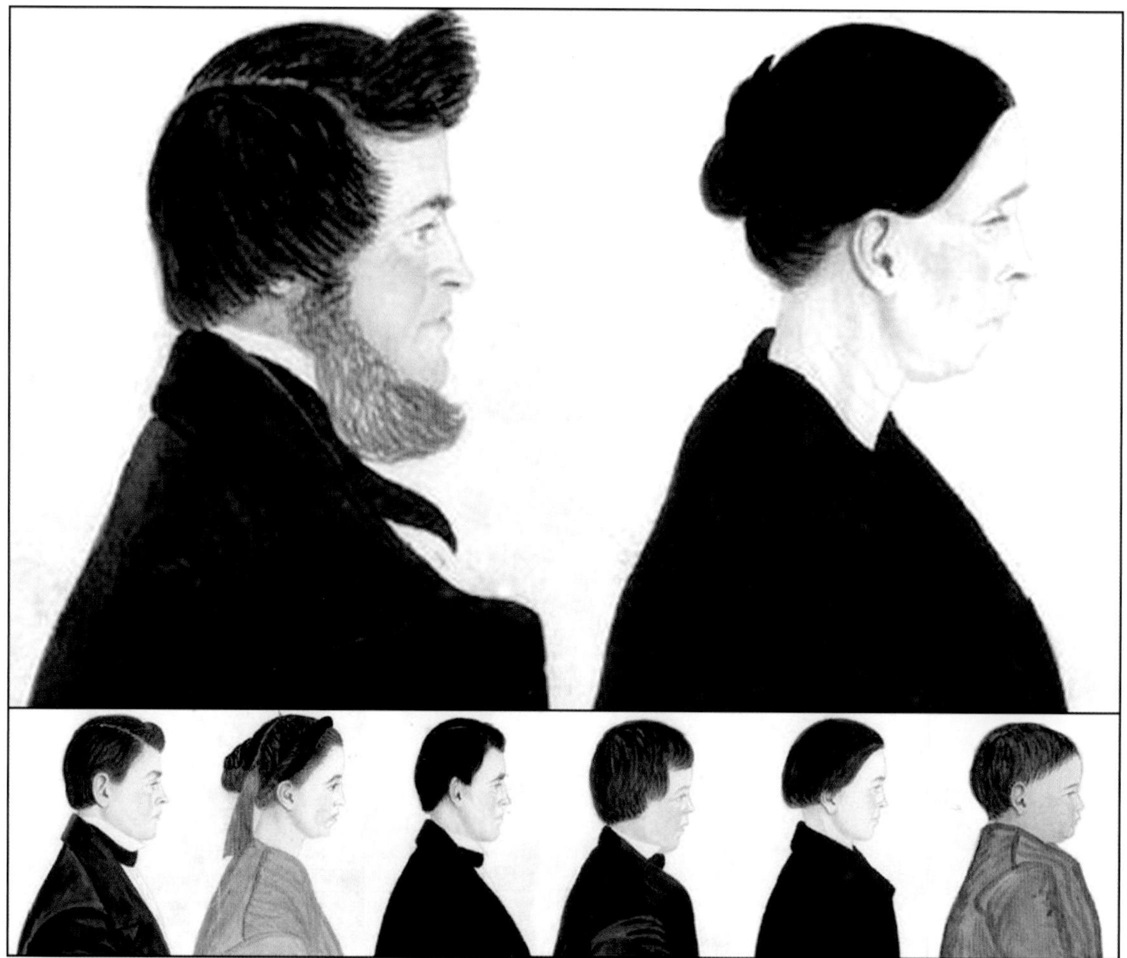

*Archer & Elizabeth (Martin) Dumond; children: Elias, Eleanor, George, Theodore, Benjamin and Harriet*

Mirroring the same dynamic taking place all across the 19th-century American frontier, settlers tended to move en masse from existing communities—in this case, first from Washtenaw County, Michigan, then, later, especially from Lake County, Indiana. Glowing letters sent to kin "back East" lured many to join relatives or former neighbors in some far-flung settlement "out West." On 28 August 1855 Judge S.B. Hewett, Jr. of Eagle Grove Township, penned this account:

> Some things will be unpleasant for a few years. There is not much society here such as you have in the East, but soon will be. Soil is deep, dark and very rich, is easy to cultivate and rapidly raising in value. Land is being taken up by speculators fast. One man has a tract of 120 acres, with 40 of wooded land, that he will sell for $800; 10 to 15 acres broken on it, on which you could raise all you can eat for the next year certain. He has a poor cabin in which you can live for a while. I think he will take $600 if you show him the money. In coming out you will have to sleep on beds on the floor after you cross the Mississippi, but that

> will not hurt either of you; it did not hurt me. You should have a pair of stout horses and a yoke of oxen, a wagon which is strong, so you can use either horses or oxen. Buy this east of the Mississippi River; also cows of good stock as you can find. [...] If your father comes, have him bring his carpenter's tools with him. He will want them to build your house with. About money—bring all you can; 'twill pay better here than in the East. Bring $1,000 certain. Ship beds, etc., in large chests and trunks. They will not get here for two months after you arrive if you send by freight. So check them and pay the excess baggage; then they come when you do. Come soon, as the land office land is going very fast.

*1840s Iowa;* The Sailor's Wedding *(1852) by Baltimore painter Richard Caton Woodville, who studied in Germany*

Not only did such homogeneous, acquaintance-driven settlement patterns create lingual uniformity from, say, Pittsburgh to Denver, but also relative cultural similarity across the entire Midwest. And, they took many place names with them, propagated generation by generation the length of the Heartland, so that today one can find clusters of, to cite one example, "Mount Vernon," "[New] Lisbon" and "Jordan Grove [City]" in Ohio, Indiana, Illinois and Iowa—no doubt transplanted by westward-pushing members of the same families, hailing from the same stations in their multi-locale frontier careers.

Less abstract than pronunciation or sociological patterns, practical prairie pioneers "took care of their own"—especially of those newly arrived from "back home." As Don's local-history team points out,

> Food and shelter were the primary concerns for the pioneers. The wagons into which [they] had packed their meager belongings were sometimes converted into dwelling places while the family's first crude dwelling was quickly constructed. Most often, however, those who had come before opened their doors to the new arrivals. They always found room for one more in a house where every inch of the floor was covered with beds. All newcomers needed a place to stay 'til they could build a cabin; no one was turned away. As long as there was a mouthful of food in the house, it was freely shared with others.

That early spirit of taking care for the common good, to the benefit of all, survived in rural America for many decades. Although its members pursued individual dreams throughout, at least for the first generations following our pioneering ancestors, a widespread shared belief in an intertwined fate helped their communities weather many a trial—dust bowls and Great Depressions, world wars, economic booms or busts, even radical cultural revolution. But, now?

---

**chapter 14: a name endures**

Some frontier communities enjoyed boom. Some weathered busts. Some experienced both. All were forever colored by how they dealt with either, for only out of pooling their resources, sharing their burdens and celebrating their achievements did a collective identity eventually emerge. And, as the suggested "Crown Point" was already taken, that local distinctiveness begged to be named.

*Emily Dumond, who inspired "Belmond"*

> Mr. Howland built a store building on the west side of the river and conducted a General Store. Mr. Pierce came from Illinois and built several store buildings and put in a General Store on the side of the river near the mill. Dr. Cutler put in a drug store; a blacksmith shop and wagon shop were also started with many other services that made this a real trading center.

Well, almost. Later, the young burg's first postmaster, Archer Dumond had several daughters. The oldest, Emily, apparently was quite a looker—the "Belle" of the town. The settlers' first choice of a name for their envisioned community was "Dumond" but there was already a post office in Iowa registered with a similar name, "Dumont." As they had to craft one of their own making, they fused "Belle" with... To this day, "Belmond" in Iowa is the only place in the world known to have that name.

*a festive occasion on Belmond's Main Street, circa 1910*

---

"Belmond" is not the only one-of-a-kind name in the world. Another is "Luick."

Growing up, I always wondered what my surname meant. Gramma Luick had punted with "It was the name of that village back in..." but even as a mere lad I could smell something fishy in the stale tale she spun. So, me being me, I kept asking—everyone I thought might know... until I found someone who did.

Eugen's clever (and only) daughter of two children, Margrit Luick had left our ancestral home on the banks of the Neckar River—which flows through the heart of *Schwaben* like a main vein—and went up-river in 1966 to the ancient university town of Tübingen. Sitting as it does on a rocky spine along the lazy Upper-Neckar, these days equipped with pole-pushed flatboats filled with the love-struck or leisure-seeking, it seems a bit like a Medieval, Germanic Cambridge.

*Eugen, Elisabeth, Margrit & Michael Luick in Esslingen, April 1982; student protest at the Technische Universität, Berlin, protesting the West German government's adoption of "Emergency Acts," May 1968*

Studying there until 1971, right through the turbulent second half of what we think of as The Sixties when we think about that time of strident protest at all, Margrit joined all the shrill political demos, all the smoke-filled jazz-club bashes and fist-in-the-air street clashes, all the late-night, wooly-eyed philosophical debates—the very "radical-student stunts" that sofa-soldier Dad and my three maternal uncles decried from the safety of their Sunny Circle retreat. When Bud cheered "the cops" as they "cracked open a few heads" I wonder if he had red-headed Margrit Luick's in mind.

Along with French, German and ethics, Margrit studied linguistics, so can say with certainty that "Luick" comes from the Flemish name of the now-Belgian city of Liege. Substantiated by other Luick-line researchers in Swabia, we know that reform-minded folk from "Luik" left the Catholic-contested city in one of the recurring waves of Reformation-era fluctuations. Our ancestors fled religious intolerance, following first the Rhein, then the Neckar, in search of the safety afforded them by Protestant Württemberg, which declared itself "*evangelisch*" as of 1543—only twenty-seven years after Martin Luther nailed his 95 Theses to the solid, massive doors of Wittenberg's stolid, passive church that had no idea of the storm his few hammer strikes were unleashing.

Linguistically, "The 'c' has no meaning" Margrit tells us authoritatively. "It's simply an *Auslaut-Verhärtung*, a Germanification of the Flemish name for the town that refused to tolerate personal freedom."

---

## chapter 15: a lasting legacy

Regardless of how Belmond's founders eventually named their emerging prairie town some three centuries later, far removed from the religious rebellion of their people's turbulent past in sectarian-sensitive Europe, it grew—fast:

> In about 1856 the first addition to Belmond was laid out and registered, located on the west side of the river. With the steady flow of new settlers coming in and with the maturing and marrying of the children of the early pioneers, the community continued to grow. The fertile soil lying all around it was developed into wonderful farms, and homes were built for miles around. The village became more important with many new homes, schools and church buildings.

As Don's team reminds us, "Many pioneer settlers did not live to see the prairie blossom." Infant mortality rates in the rural Midwest remained high for much of the rest of the 19th century, as did the percentage of woman dying during childbirth. Adults died young compared to today; what are now simple maladies, easily cured, then quickly claimed thousands. Recurring epidemics of typhus, cholera, influenza or—less often but often deadly—tuberculosis raged across the prairies in turns. Of course, violent crime or suicide, though seldom, were not unknown.

As noted by Don & Co.,

> The first burial ground selected was the high ground, overlooking the river, north of the Dumond brick house. Mary Sheets Dukes, the wife of Aaron, died [before 1856 and] was the first to be buried there. Her baby was soon laid by her side. [...] During the winter Mr. Arnett, who lived at Twin Lakes, was frozen to death while attempting to walk from his home to Belmond during a blizzard and was also buried in this ground. There are no stones marking these grave sites and the exact location of this cemetery is no longer known. In 1857 the Belmond Cemetery near Franklin Grove was set apart and soon after, Rensselaer Gray, who was about 58 years old, died of consumption (tuberculosis) and was the first burial in the new cemetery. [ML-T's great-x4-grandfather] Elias Jenison died October 2, 1857, and on May 18, 1858, heart-attack victim Archer G. Dumond was laid to rest in this cemetery. He had celebrated his 50th birthday six weeks earlier. The inscription on his stone [below, left] reads, "Asleep in Jesus, blessed sleep, from which man ever wakes to weep."

*Archer Dumond's gravestone (left), in one of the oldest sections of Belmond's hilltop cemetery*

Enduring the dangerous hardships presented by taming a rich-yet-wild prairie both required extraordinary stamina of body and soul, but also was the stuff that seemed to confirm a common belief that our pioneer ancestors were cut from special cloth, that those who survived such ordeals and toil were divinely endowed and specially blessed. In turn, such a sense of outstanding character and unique accomplishment fed a mostly unspoken yet somehow clearly conveyed belief *au courant* in my youth in America's "exceptionalism."

Surely, many of those present at the public observance of Belmond's first century of existence found their community—their picture of America in miniature—"exceptional." Under the headline "Colorful Pageant, Giant Parade, Hits of Centennial Celebration," the *Belmond Independent* reported on 16 August 1956 that the resultant parade,

> approximately 100 units long, won the praise of an estimated 7,000 onlookers. An estimated 1,500 people attended the opening night's performance of the pageant, "Journey into Yesterday," about 1,200 attended the following night. All of the 19 scenes in the six episodes contributed to the pageant's look into the past. The alumni meeting at the high school gymnasium drew an estimated 750 to 800 persons. Seventeen acts competed in the Centennial Amateur Show with the first $50 first-place prize going to a Hampton tap dance team. First place in the waltzing contest went to Mr. and Mrs. Ed Gabrielson. Lester Gabrielson won the "Best Beard" award. The award for the oldest costume went to Mrs. R.B. Piper, whose dress was 120 years old.

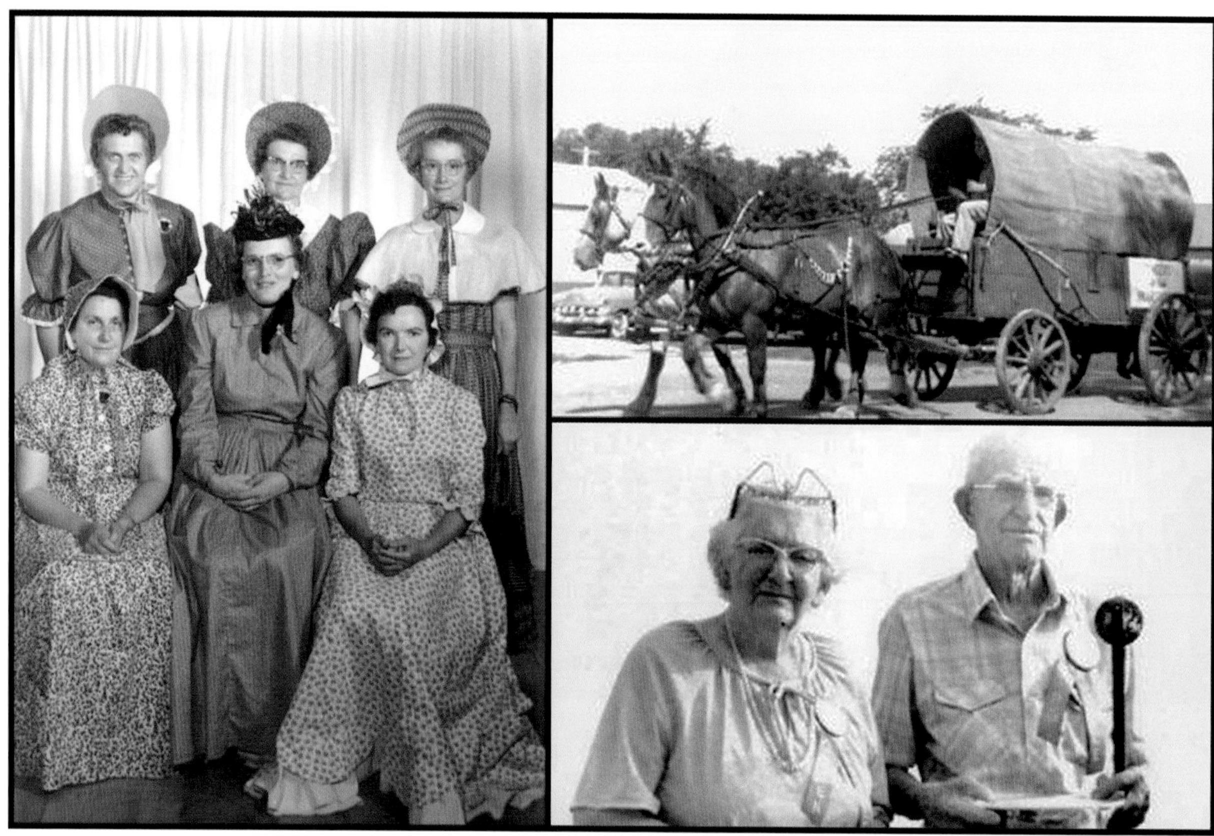

*Mattie (Luick) Ross and Marion (Luick) Smith, back row of Belmond Centennial-celebration scene, 1956; covered wagon displayed in Centennial parade; 125th–party hosts Edith (Luick) Hill and Albert Luick, 1981*

Twenty-five years later, in 1981, Mattie (Luick) Farmer and Marion (Luick) Smith's older brother, Albert, served as "king" and Edith (Luick) Hill "queen" of Belmond's Quasquicentennial, its 125th birthday. The *History of Belmond* Sesquicentennial recorded that

> Crowds watching the parade and grandstand fireworks production were estimated from 5,000 to 10,000. At the program held in the park [the] queen and king for the four-day event [...] were descended from the Luick families who were Belmond's first settlers[.] The pageant held on Thursday and Friday evenings at the Luick auditorium had about 700 people in attendance at each performance. The pageant reviewed Belmond history in verse, song and short dramatic pieces. Free dances were held on Main Street on Friday evening.

Both Belmond birthday celebrations—as well as that marking its 75th, in 1931, which featured Louis Luick's violin playing, "the bones" played by Dell Luick and a quartet with an "H.J." Luick—highlighted the achievements of "civilization" that the pioneers had established on the wide open prairies of North Central Iowa since 1850. Each balanced on the mostly unarticulated yet unmistakable assumption, that the New Canaan our ancestors had built constituted a feat of biblical proportions. Feeling ordained in our destiny, we felt we belonged to a much larger historical drama—to the story of building America.

That confident pride rang loudly, for example, at the end of Elizabeth Lieuwen's 1951 speech:

> Today Belmond is as progressive a town as you will find anywhere in the State of Iowa. It is a city [of 2,173 inhabitants] beautifully located on the Iowa River, at the juncture of three railroads. It is easy of access as Highway 69 runs directly through the town.

*aerial view of Belmond (1940s), looking west to east: The 1966 tornado destroyed some 2/3rds of Main Street*

It has modern and up-to-date stores, good banking facilities, a live, up-to-date newspaper, seven churches, a fine school system and a hospital with doctors and nurses, the very best. The biggest project now on the agenda is the building of the New Community Hospital which will begin in the spring. Two leading industries, the General Mills, Inc. Soy Bean Plant and the Thompson Hybrid Corn Company give much employment and impetus to industry.

It is a place of beautiful homes, fine people and a good place in which to live. "Anything in the way of progress," Belmond has it.

Ladies and gentlemen, we give you, Belmond.

*scenes of "everyone's hometown," Belmond, Iowa—the porch scene, 1910s; a Main Street scene, 1916*

The cultural legacy of Manifest Destiny colored not only uncritical narratives offered by the children of pioneers in the hyper-patriotic 1950s, but an entire nation's, until the present day. For Albert Lee Luick's part, that son of some of the prairie's first settlers believed that:

> The fortitude, integrity and character of these early pioneers established Belmond as an ideal, progressive and friendly place to live—typical of the hundreds of such communities scattered over the Iowa prairies to make Iowa the wonder state of the Union. Belmond celebrated its Centennial in 1956 with an appropriate pageant and celebration. What wonders the first century has wrought from the wild prairie of what we see today. This is America.

———

**postscript: primordial warrior genes**

Tuesday evening, the 8th of July 2014: I scurry down the deserted streets of Esslingen, wondering if a neutron bomb has killed all the *Schwaben*—or perhaps extra-terrestrial beings have kidnapped them an' whisked 'em all away to some distant planet to be slaves. There's no one to be seen, no noise except the occasional *"Hurra!"* being screamed from darkened dens, illuminated solely by the glow of crowded television screens broadcasting live FIFA's World Cup soccer match between Germany and jinxed Brazil.

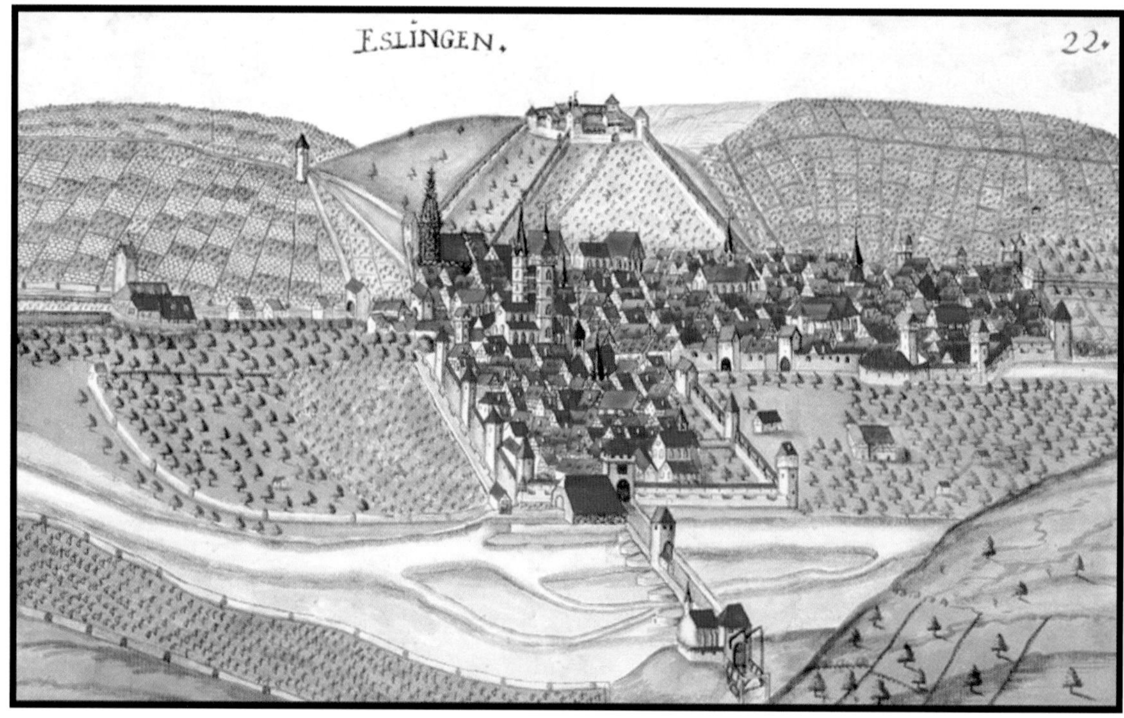


*"Eslingen" as engraved by Andreas Kieser in 1685*

I'm already late for dinner with Jochen and Iris Luick, their now-grown son Konstantin and his girlfriend, Michaela Müller. Yes, I can honestly deflect the blame for my being late (as usual)—this time on our absent cousin Margrit, with whom I spent too many swiftly-evaporating hours plotting the book we wish to publish about her father Eugen's bicycle journey to the Holy Land and Egypt, winter 1932-33.

As I race up to the Luicks' door and frantically press the bell, I hear another roaring wave of *"Hurra!"*

Sweet as ever, Jochen's wife, Iris, opens the door, smiles broadly and brushes me in past her. As she casts an eye up and down the street to see if anyone detected my violating the unspoken rule of being off the streets whenever Germany plays a World Cup finals game, she urges *"Komm doch rein—schnell!"*

I join my German cousins for an umpteenth meal, pleased to see them again—sporadically but loyally, ever since that initial visit in 1982, during my Easter break from Ermysted's School, some three decades earlier. In the meantime, now-deceased Karl and Ruth's son, Jochen, has himself grown bald and gray; still sporting an unstinting smile, big-souled Iris, too, shows Time's relentless grind. And, their "baby" who once played on the cool-linoleum floor of my Berlin apartment a quarter century ago, is now a grown man with a steady girlfriend and a solid job as a Swabian stone carver. Yes, Time *does* fly.

*Michaela Müller, Iris (Glaser), Konstantin & Jochen Luick, at home in the* Esslinger Altstadt*; 8 July 2014*

Over dinner of *Linsensuppe* and *Salat*, Jochen relates, unsolicited, a story I'd never heard but lived.

*"Ja"* he begins, *"mein Vater Karls Großvater,"* his great-grandfather, was a *Gendarm*, a paramilitary police officer in Meißenheim, a village on the banks of the corseted Rhein, not far from Strasbourg. *"Ja*, he vas a stronk, a berry stronk *Mann*. He hat many sons *und am Freitag* evenings, if dey drunk too much—" Jochen struggles to continue in English, *"—er hatte kein Problem, seine eigenen Söhne..."*

Jochen's tale makes me smile as I picture a resolute, little Luick man strut into a rowdy pub, decked in a sober-but-imposing police officer's uniform, barking orders to the well-lubricated crowd, then marching his several inebriated adult sons off to the village jail at sword point (in those pre-gun days).

*"Ja"* Jochen explains, Luick men were always known to be forces to be reckoned with—resolute, yet fair. "Dey alvays got vhat dey vanted" Jochen notes, and while not tyrants, their single-mindedness earned them *"Respekt"* among their neighbors. "De Luicks" my distant cousins hits close to home, "dey alvays knew vhat dey vanted—*und* how to get it. De udders alvays felt a little fear in front of de Luicks."

Noticing that the relentless clock already has reached Ten to Late, I excuse myself as having to catch an early train to Dresden in the morning. We hug and bid each other *"Tschüss!"* as I set out the door.

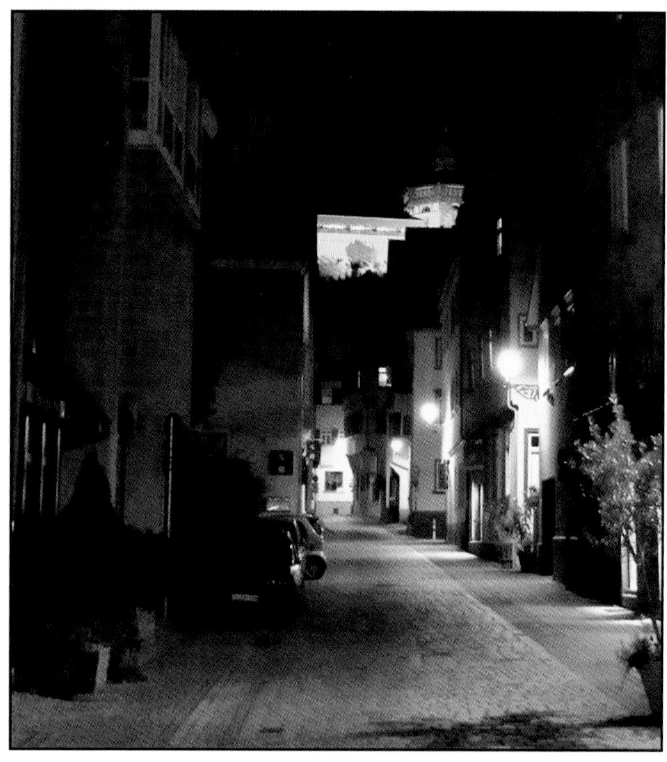

*Esslingen's* Burg *overlooks the old* Reichsstadt*, day and night.*

Passing again through the abandoned streets of my father's family's ancestral hometown, my mind reels with images of other forceful, uncompromising Luick men seizing the world by the tail and refusing to let go. Noble-thrashing Heinrich jumps first into my mental inventory of restless, aggressive Luick men. Next, I think of his son, "Mad Bobcat" Henry and the county-seat war he instigated, then steered to fit his covert career goals. Or, latter, his simply seizing his neighbor's wife and high-tailing it Down South, before trekking back to Württemberg long enough to pocket tens of thousands of dollars in gold. And, in my cramped, busy brain, I see carefree Louis, instrumentalizing his entire brood so he could play his fiddle and make the people of Belmond dance. Then, there was George, the ambitious social-rebel duped by the Klan—followed by Donald, who rejected a pretty, devout wife to chase a transient teen lover for a few years. And, Bud? There was another force to reckon with—just like his second son still is.

I meditate on thoughts of Andreas, the German gene researcher I met in Morocco, and of American James Fallon's "warrior gene" theory—to me so plausible a road map of my paternal heritage that I fear I'm an unwitting poster boy for it. This legacy, a curse-cum-blessing, both drives and leads me every day.

Tripping over Esslingen's cobblestones, I think of the ancient Neckar behind me even as I envision the Iowa River lumbering by in front of me: Just then, an endless column of hungry buffalo—those massive Monarchs of the Prairie—begins to approach, then ford the untamed frontier river stretching in front of my pioneer family's rough-hewn cabin door. My body's near the Neckar but my soul lingers on the Iowa.

In one moment, I twinge when I think of my father's people, of the generations immediately preceding us, and of all the baggage they so expertly left us, buried deep yet trip-wired. In the next, when I think of less gutsy, even more insane lineages, I feel a sense of gratitude, an appreciation for the kind of neurological and genetic correlates of psychopathy that lead me to be restless and aggressive, to fight for what I want or think is right. The complacent Europeans—they don't have that acculturated response nearly as much as we who turned our backs on the Old World and set off to build a new one.

By now fairly springing through the narrow lanes of Esslingen's medieval heart, I finally feel fully free.

*the countryside around Grötzingen, part of today's Aichtal, the region near Esslingen that "my" Luicks last left*

---

# PART VI
# The Mother Lode

Although the myth of the "self-made [wo]man" remains a pillar of too many Americans' romanticized narratives about our people's experiences in the New World, in truth no one could have transformed the North American wilderness nor now can correct the country's current course alone. It took—and will take—above all communities, or at the least "families" in whatever constellations that might be. Key to understanding what America has been, what it has become and what it yet could be, is dissecting what makes us who are "American" different from those who are not. What distinguishes us children of immigrants and pioneers from those with whom we once were related but no longer are? How did we change, evolve into something else, something new and unique in the world? How did a myriad "we" become a meaningful "us"—and how might our future be better than the fractured present portends? How might we become more of what we were always meant to be—free, exceptional and trailblazing? Surely, the heights we might yet reach can only be built on the firm foundation that we've already laid.

The children of immigrants Heinrich and Katherine (Gerstenmaier) Luick who left Michigan for richer, cheaper lands in Iowa reflect the experiences of millions of Americans, from the colonial period on the East Coast to, in some forms, present-day Alaska. Given the representativeness of both their trials and achievements, their specific biographies—as recalled by swooning Albert Lee Luick looking back a long century later, or as found in third-person accounts or subsequent obituaries—offer edifying case studies of the pioneer experience on the American frontier of the 19$^{th}$ century: a nation's fate, in one family's.

Generalities are not as insight-shedding as specific examples, as macro patterns or trends are often most easiest found and more fully understood on micro levels. As such, David Luick's unexpected, unwanted encounters with Native Americans in the earliest years of his family's settlement of the Iowa prairie—to cite one example—speak volumes about how larger events played out face-to-face between the increasingly disenfranchised and those newcomers hoping to assume their corner of the sky.

The "Indian wars" that took place in the New World were no doubt horrible experiences for those involved, on both sides. What David or Melissa [see related stories, earlier in this book] experienced was tensely unpleasant at the least, and potentially deadly, yet did not resemble the wars that other Luicks experienced in the Old World. While one branch of my Luick family left Germany, the other stayed: Both were forever changed, even marred, by what Life presented our people—and how we responded to it.

---

Some twenty years after my initial visit to Luick relatives in Esslingen over Easter-break back in '82, while interviewing fifty former WWII-era German prisoners of war for the TRACES project, I learned that some young German men opposed to Hitler in specific, to war in general or to both sometimes shot themselves in the foot, purposely mangled a hand or in some other way rendered themselves unfit for combat at the front. Whether or not drafted Eugen welcomed contracting typhus while fighting on the Eastern Front, my distant cousin's being sent to Urach, in our family's native Swabia, to recuperate from his illness gave the frustrated artist an extended spell of sketching the local scenery, rather than shooting the distant enemy. Eugen even had the time to assemble an exhibit of his work. By July 1944, though, his recovery had progressed to the point where he could be sent to Dresden. With its Baroque silhouettes and, nearby, "Saxon Switzerland," he reveled in whiling away time in "Florence on the Elbe." His artistic gain, though, almost cost him his life, had a single bomb fallen where he was at the time.

Eager to paint life rather than extinguish it, Eugen used every opportunity to leave the *Kaserne*, the military barracks where he spent ten months being readied to be returned to the collapsing Eastern Front. Most days, seeking motifs, he'd scour Dresden, which even in wartime shone with the pomp and treasures the former, 953-year-reigning royal family of *Sachsen* had showered upon their *Residenzstadt*, their capital of what before the Wettiner foolishly backed losing Napoleon had been their kingdom reaching as far east as today's Ukraine and northwest towards Hanover.

*the Sophienkirche rising beyond end of the Zwingergarten; the Augustusbrücke leading to the "Old City"*

One day, however, in mid-February 1945, Eugen received an order to go into Dresden's city center on *Wehrmacht*, on official German-army business. What he found surprised him—as he later recounted, around the time of our meeting in Esslingen:

> Out of the bombed cites of the west came refugees [who] sought a feeling of security. From the east streamed endless columns of those seeking help, weakened by hunger, shaken by the cold and driven by fear. Millions were on the run. Cinemas and schools served as emergency shelters, other public spaces were full, the city spilled over with people. On the afternoon of 13 February an order led me to the main train station. The halls and platforms were overfilled, so passage was a good as impossible. It was mainly woman, children and old people. They were fleeing from the Russians and felt halfway safe here, because they had at least found a roof over their head—yet only hours later they died a cruel death; in the main station alone the number of deaths was said to be eight thousand.

Prior to the fully unexpected bombing, later that night, however, life in wartime Dresden lurched on, as "normal" as possible during the accelerating collapse of the Third Reich. As Eugen made his way that day through what for centuries had been "the Florence of the North,"

> The [main shopping street,] Prager-Strasse offered an unusual scene: people, who dragged with them their worldly possessions, many from Silesia, with horse-drawn wagons, hand-pulled carts—a parade of misery. A carefree, playing gang of children with painted faces reminded me that it was carnival. [Dresden's central park, the] Grosse Garten and the meadows along the Elbe were one large military

> camp. One saw in the people the stress of their flight, the sadness and desperation, but also the hope of survival. Many endured their fate with admirable composure. Since the Russians had crossed the Oder River on 8 February, the growing stream of new arrivals increased day and night. The till-then cheery city took on an alien face.

Only two days before, on Sunday, 11 February, as church bells called the faithful to worship, Eugen had been enroute to visit the Zwinger, the Saxon kings' statue-laced pleasure gardens, when he suddenly stood still. Struck by the momentary splendor of the view of the *Frauenkirche*, Our Lady's Church, from one of the city's main bridges, he spontaneously set about capturing the instance with watercolor. Happy with his impromptu artwork, he then continued—never imaging that this would be not only his last, but likely the last-ever painted image of the intact Baroque city on the Elbe.

As Eugen later wrote, "Two days later, hell broke loose." The events that followed on Carnival Tuesday, on 13 February 1945, unfolded with an unexpected swiftness and furry, best captured with Eugen's own recollections:

> Shortly after 10pm a full alarm followed without pre-warning. Marking planes set off flares. At 10:13 demolition bombs shook the city, knocking in the windows and blowing off the rooves. At that point a hail of firebombs began to transform Dresden into a sea of fire. After midnight a second massive attack followed with heavy demolition bombs. The main targets were the *Grosse Garten* and the meadows along the Elbe, where tens of thousands of those who had been able to escape the earlier firestorm hell had fled. On the next day a third attack in the time from 12:12 to 12:30 completed this work of destruction.

*Indiana-born German-American Kurt Vonnegut was a prisoner of war who survived the bombing of Dresden. He said "Florence on the Elbe" became a hellish inferno, then a gutted, charred ruin, in a matter of minutes.*

> The Allies reported of successful air strikes on German cities, in particular Dresden. Spread over a span of fourteen hours, counted together in just sixty minutes one of the most beautiful cities on our planet was laid to soot and ashes. It was an inferno like nothing before ever seen by human eyes. The number of dead could not be confirmed. The first estimates moved between forty and three-hundred-fifty thousand. According to an announcement on 20 March 1945, 202,040 dead were registered. No one dares say how many nameless are waiting for judgment day, buried in caved-in deep basements or in enormous bomb craters, in turn filled in from subsequent demolition bombs. Until the 13$^{th}$ of February the city was for its 600,000 inhabitants and estimated half-million refugees one of hope for a sense of security and survival. Still, Dresden became in one night the greatest mass grave in all of history. [...] It grew ever quieter. Over an area of twenty-eight square kilometers [10.8 square miles] all life was extinguished. The last large German city was, without any military necessity, leveled to the ground. [British] Bomber general Harris could be satisfied with his photo collection of destroyed German cities and bring it to a close.

If there had not been enough death and destruction enough, more would follow—the subsequent devastation of which Eugen was to personally witness and, forty years later, record in gruesome detail.

> The last act of the tragedy played out in the following days in the streets leading out of the city, where strafing fliers—true to the orders they'd received—hunted refugees and those fleeing with machine guns, and thus achieve further "successes."

The burial troops were deployed in the ruined area. Corpses were recovered out of the filled-in basements, as far as they were accessible and the emitting heat allowed. One laid them out in rows next to each other on the *Altmarkt* [the Old Town Square] and other available spaces: the shriveled mummies and the fire-charred. Those still most resembling human beings were those who'd suffocated for lack of oxygen.

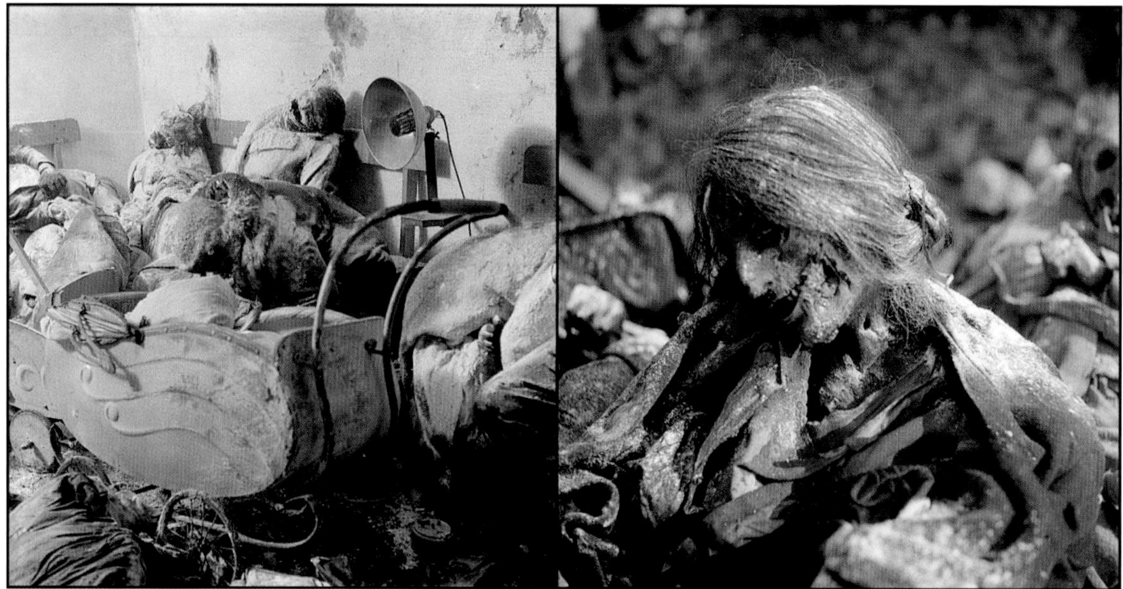

*The dying Nazi regime exploited the bombing of Dresden for its own, desperate purposes. The caption its propaganda agents gave the above photos included "A mother turned stiff by death over her twins' baby carriage" and "A female corpse in an air raid shelter." Objectively, such deaths truly were torturous ones.*

Now and again civilians and soldiers were to be seen, searching among the dead for relatives, acquaintances or friends. On the remains of walls hung scraps of paper meant to relay signs of life. Often consisting of only a few words, they were sobering signs of love, worry, fear and hope.

Four decades later Eugen deemed that "Less helpful were the large posters from [Propaganda Minister Josef] Goebbels" hung around Dresden soon after the bombing by still-faithful fanatic Nazi followers. They exhorted:

People of Dresden! The Führer [Hitler] knows about your suffering and need. Do not succumb to desperation. Don't capitulate! The Führer will avenge you! In a few days will come the great reckoning. Prevail until the most glorious victory in German history!

---

"History" is usually determined by unexpected, often uncontrollable forces. And, as cliché has it, it's often "written by the victors." The history of European settlement of New-World lands around the globe, then, would be written not by native peoples, by those vanquished and largely extinguished, but by those who assumed the land the natives previously had inhabited and then made it their own.

In the absence of protracted, wholesale wars—with Iowa's aboriginal inhabitants, with Southern slaveholders, etc.—the Luicks who had ventured to the heart of the North American continent in the middle of the 19$^{th}$ century mostly, at least outwardly, thrived... but not without much effort.

Now, some examples, stories of my people as individuals—first as told by Albert Lee Luick:

[His father] David, upon returning from his last trapping venture, settled down to farm in earnest and to develop and improve his land. He lived at first with his brother's family, and there were now many new settlers locating in the area, which became a very active settlement. A dam was built across the Iowa River, then a flour mill and a saw mill. Now that settlers could have the logs sawed into lumber, David began to cut walnut logs from the abundant supply in Franklin Grove and use them to build a house. When the logs had been sawed into lumber, and were well seasoned and ready for construction in the spring of 1857, Simeon Overacker—a brother of Melissa, Henry's wife—came with his large family from Ann Arbor. They brought with them Katherine and Frederick Luick, so all the brothers—except for John—and their sister were now early pioneers of Iowa. John remained in Michigan.

Simeon Overacker was an experienced carpenter and was engaged by David to build the house he planned with lumber cut from Franklin Grove. The doors were heavy walnut slabs cut from Franklin Grove. The doors had hand-wrought hinges and latches make by the local blacksmith. The construction was very good, since Simeon was a skilled workman. In 1859, David Luick and Sarah Overacker were married. Sarah, the eldest daughter of [Melissa (Overacker) Luick's brother] Simeon and Caroline Overacker, was then only 16 years old but had grown up in this pioneering environment and was very capable. They started housekeeping in the walnut house with little furniture, but they obtained the necessary furnishings on their first trading trip to Cedar Falls.

*Sarah Lucinda (Overacker) Luick, circa 1890; a typical "American Four Square" house in Belmond, about 1910*

Sarah kept a neat and orderly house, and was such an exceptionally good cook that her recipes were much sought after by relatives and friends. Her wild strawberry, cherry and chokecherry jams and jellies were most delicious. She became an expert seamstress and dressed her daughters and herself in the latest fashions, to the admiration and envy of the ladies of the community. David was a good, practical farmer. His livestock was always sleek and well-fed. He tilled his land with great care to produce the best crops. They were known for their hospitality, and no traveler was denied food or shelter. The settlers, many from faraway places, who came with their grist to be milled or to trade at local stores, were always welcome to make this home their headquarters. These early pioneers were very helpful to each other in times of sickness or sorrow, always willing to share with each other. David and Sarah took their place in local activities and community affairs and in raising their family, which consisted of Amelia, Ida, Emma, Mabel and Albert Lee. David was active in forming the first Town Council of Belmond. He also was instrumental in forming the Independent School District of Belmond and was the first president of the board of directors and remained a director for many years. I am highly honored to pay homage to these very wonderful people, my parents.

While one of the most colorful of Heinrich and Katherine Luick's descendants to push westward, David wasn't the only one to thrive in Iowa. His brother William—even if he had to walk a couple hundred miles to get there—was another. Again, as retold by Albert Lee Luick:

William Luick was the first child born to Katherine and Henry after coming to America and settling the farm near Ann Arbor. He, their fourth son, was a sturdy, active boy. His parents, ardent Lutherans, chose this son to promulgate their faith. He was sent to a seminary at an early age for that purpose, but William got the lust for the west and his desire to join his brothers in Iowa overcame him. When his brother David returned in the fall of 1856 to Michigan for a visit with his family, William joined him for the return trip. They traveled by train and ferry to Dubuque and then started to walk the 200 miles to Belmond, since there were no trains and few stages west of Dubuque at that time. It was a considerable undertaking. Often while they were on their way, winter storms set in with heavy snow and cold on those open, bleak prairies. They nearly perished, but finally succeeded in reaching their brother Henry's home after this perilous journey—their feet, hands, ears and faces badly frozen.

*Rose Belle (Pierce) Luick, circa 1900; William Luick's farm, east of Belmond—among the first in Wright County*

William was an industrious man and worked with his brothers for a couple of years before acquiring land of his own just east of the town of Belmond. There he broke the virgin soil and established himself as a successful farmer. He married Rose Pierce, a wonderful person, the daughter of one of Belmond's early merchants. They were active in the early life of the community and their home was always open for gatherings. They did their share of making this a friendly place to live. They had [five] children—[Sarah, who died, age 10,] Smith, Ernest, Alma and Cora. Uncle William was truly a wonderful character.

Rose Belle Pierce, the woman William chose as his wife, was descended from Roger Williams, the New England religious free-thinker and colony leader. According to family historians "a woman of forceful character and loveable disposition," Rose

> was born in Oswego, New York and reared in Du Page County, Illinois [just west of Chicago. She] brought in her trunk from her Illinois home willow trees, which she planted and these were the first in the county. These served to add to the attractiveness of their pioneer home, a home always open to weary travelers.

Rose was the daughter of Smith Pierce, who built one of the first stores in Wright County, about whom colorful details remain. According to the *Belmond Sesquicentennial*,

> In 1864 Smith D. Pierce, who came to the community with a fortune already made, built a magnificent store, his business consisting of dry goods, boots and shoes, hats and caps, Queensware, hardware, and millinery goods. Rose Whited Garth wrote, "Soon after the war it was rumored that a $10,000 man was coming to Belmond. S.D. Pierce from Illinois came and established the industry of cheese making that gave farmers a market for milk. He had a nursery of fruit trees set out that started fruit growing around Belmond." Mr. Pierce died in 1884 and "Capitalist" was listed as his occupation on his death record.

Shopkeeper's-daughter Rose was said to be "of forceful character"—but she wasn't the only Luick clan member to fit that description. Being of "forceful," though, is not the same as being of "decent" character—as proven by her brother-in-law Henry Luick who, some eighty years before his grandson George Michael Luick did the same, ran away with a neighbor's wife, then laid low south o' the border.

As cited in volume one's conclusion, at around the end of America's Civil War, Henry did, indeed, flee Iowa (as a contemporary parody later lampooned) "one early morn" on a romantic retreat of two years in Missouri—as the judge well knew to do, leaving a legally-safe state line between now-criminal them and their still-lawful mates back in Iowa. And, as in the parody, after returning—supposedly repentant—to their respective spouses for less than a month, left them once again, this time irreversibly.

In case the stage upon which such an involved drama unfolded was not cluttered enough, this farce's plot thickened. It was innocent enough that Lydia Marie (Lathrop) Johnson's eleven-year-younger sister—the widowed Sarah Jane (Lathrop) Baker—married Henry and Melissa's oldest son, Michael Henry, in 1865. Finding his new daughter-in-law's older sister—Belmond master-carpenter Charles Johnson's wife, Lydia—simply too alluring to resist, of course Henry had ditched his frontier-worn wife of over two decades, Melissa, for the more delicious neighbor lady.

*Time's endless march: Michael Henry Luick's direct male descendants—his son Adelbert (holding great-great-grandson baby "Michael M."), his grandson "Michael G." and great-grandson, Cortland Luick, circa 1946, a full century after Henry Luick first came to Iowa as a young surveyor.*

To complicate the webs between those of consenting age in the Luicks' later shared domicile in Oskaloosa even further, Henry and Melissa's 20-year-old Sylvester married Lydia's daughter, Irene Marie Johnson, on 25 September 1868—a week and a day after Irene turned eighteen, a month before Irene's mother and Henry legalized their till-then illegitimate relationship... So ran my German-American roots.

———

When they set out for the United States, the Luicks had not left "Germany" at all.

In spring 1833, as the family received official permission to turn their backs on the Kingdom of Württemberg forever, there *was* no "Germany:" The crowded Central-European powerhouse that we mortals alive today know as a (re-)unified county—one of the world's wealthiest, and its fourth largest economy—is a modern construct. Forged through Prussian wars of conquest of the mid-19$^{th}$ century, by the time Henry Luick returned there in late 1872—almost forty decades after leaving as a nine-year-old boy with his parents and two younger brothers—Württemberg had ceased to exist as a sovereign state. In its place, when Henry stepped off the ship from *"Amerika"* he found a recently-declared *Reich*. The new "empire" defiantly proclaimed in 1871 in Versailles' Hall of Mirrors stretched from reclaimed Alsace-Lorraine in the west to the East Prussian plains buttressing the also-expanding Russian empire, and from the snow-peaked Alps in the south to the tranquil shores of the Baltic Sea in the north.

Henry had left a Germanic realm with as good as no factories, a pastoral patchwork of duchies and kingdoms, of sleepy medieval towns—many with city gates, towers or even parts of crumbling walls in place. The bustling, swiftly urbanizing and mechanizing "new Germany" that he returned to now as a middle-aged man scarcely resembled the comparatively languid, shabby and, at times, starving place he had known as a lad. But, my great-great-great-grandfather wasn't there for tourism—rather, for gold.

*Borsig machine-construction plant in Berlin, 1847; inset (1873-1876) Paul Meyerheim's* Vor der Vollendung (Before the Completion) *at Borsig, once Europe's largest and the world's second largest locomotive builder*

As Maquoketa, Iowa's *Jackson Sentinel* announced on 14 November 1872,

> Mr Luick, an active and intelligent German of Eddyville, [Iowa] has fallen heir to $55,000 and has gone to Germany to reap his reward.

The citation that cousin Tony Luick was able to locate gave no further details, but Henry must have found his grand trip to Europe greatly rewarding as on 19 December 1873 Cedar Falls' *Gazette* reported:

> H J Luick, who was one of the heirs to a large estate in Germany, has just received his portion which amounts to $92,000 in gold. His name ought to be spelled without the "i".

Perhaps it was Vienna's stock-market crash on *Schwarzer Freitag*, the "Black Friday" of 9 May 1873, or a sudden surge in the value of the American dollar given European exchange-rate fluctuations, that somehow transformed his earlier estimated windfall of $55,000 into a reported $92,000, but in any event Henry bagged a lot. Already a man of means—having been one of the first landowners of Wright County, a commissioner and judge—the "Mad Bobcat" invested his now-considerable worldly wealth in at least one business venture, for the 1875 edition of the *Wapello County, Iowa Business Directory* lists:

> Luick, H.J., Proprietor – Luick House, born Germany, came to Iowa in 1852 [sic]

After he returned to Iowa—his pockets full of gold guilders—what had being back in Germanic lands meant to the man who brought my family to live in the heart of North America, to the world in which I grew up? I cannot know what it meant to him, to slip between worlds, but I know what it means to me.

On a personal level, after more than a dozen years of living in Germany, I know without a smidge of doubt that I am *not* a German. Yes, I feel fully bi-cultural: I function abundantly and, mostly, happily in modern Germany. At the same time, I suffer no delusions of being a "German in miniature:" I insist, for example, that everyone I meet pronounce my name as in English, not per its German pronunciation. Moreover, however, I know that my soul is ever drawn to an Anglo True North, not a Teutonic one.

On a familial level, the longer I stay in Germany and the more I get to know, to understand how the country's heart beats, I increasingly feel grateful that my German ancestors (not only the Luicks, but also the Thramses, Ehrhardts, Falks) left the country before it was one—and thus we "missed" the haughty Kaiser, hateful Hitler and headstrong Honecker (head of the East-German communist regime for almost two decades). Those decisive experiments (industrially driven imperialism, Nazism and Communism) each left deep marks on the soul of the country—stains indelible and toxic. I feel blessed, that my Luicks were free to develop beyond the constrictions of the calcified, conformist German psyche, and were spared the worst immoralities, as well as the endless stupidities of *two* deceitful, deadly dictatorships. The thought of what we might have turned into, had my family stayed, sends a shudder through me.

Instead of earth-bound farmers, would we have become blood-thirsty killers, rampaging through occupied Eastern Europe as Wehrmacht tanks rolled towards the shell-shocked Soviet capital? Would our womenfolk, instead of storing up wild chokeberry jams in dark prairie cellars, been choking to death in Prussian bomb cellars? Later, in the so-called workers' and peasants' paradise, would we have been torturing "ideologically incorrect" malcontents, "class enemies" whose only crime was to want to live free, rather than torturing willful cows whose only wish was to escape my father's curses and slaps? Would we have been any braver than the rest of the inmates who silently tolerated living in that huge detention camp called the "German Democratic Republic," rather than pulling garishly-decorated NFO floats down Clear Lake's Main Street on the Fourth of July? Would I be slaving away today in some sleek Mercedes-Benz factor in Untertürkheim, rather than over a soiled keyboard, tapping out tales from the New World? Would I be a social historian or a socialist hack? Would I be a Neo-Nazi, or a neo-con hawk?

Such ponderings, however, are only abstractions, for fact is, I spent my entire youth on the Iowa prairies. Despite having first visited Germany at 17 as part of a young-Methodist tour group from Iowa in summer 1980, then regularly crisscrossed the country numerous times as a solo tourist, I only moved to Berlin at age 30—and that without a word of German. For my great-x3-grandfather Henry Luick, however, *Deutsch* was his mother tongue, English only an assumed one. How could it have felt for him, in those pre-jet days, sojourning in *Germania*, but having been forever, deeply changed by *Amerika*?

*May's* "Schwarzer Freitag" *in Vienna and after-shock stock-market crash in New York, October 1873: Already then, globally connected markets effected the fates of millions—including Henry Luick, at the time in Europe on business.*

Even as I write this, I consider my own future fate—but Henry Luick chose his: Although at the time in question a very wealthy man, easily able to summon well-dressed Lydia to join him in savoring gilded Old-World glamor, he voted with his feet and trundled home to his lady love, back to the open Iowa prairies. As he did, Henry turned his back on the land of his birth for a second time—this time, forever.

---

All the material wealth in the world, however, couldn't shield rich Henry Luick from emotional loss or spiritual impoverishment. Two decades after his jaunt to *Europa* to cash in on his maternal treasures, an obituary published in the *Belmond Herald* in December 1893 betrayed his private grief.

> Barbara [née Luick], wife of William Hatt, died 11 December 1893. She was born in Grattan, Kent Co., Mi. on 10 April 1851. In 1853 her father Henry Luick emigrated with his family to Iowa, settling in Belmond, Wright Co., Iowa. Thus Mrs. Hatt was one of the early pioneers who suffered the privations that necessarily fall to the lot of those brave ones who prepared the way for those who followed. She moved with her mother [upon Henry's leaving Melissa for Lydia] to Michigan in 1865 and married William Hatt that following year. In 1880 she returned to Belmond with her husband and children and has resided here since then. The deceased leaves a husband and four children. [...] Death was caused from a complication of diseases, especially heart trouble brought on by a severe attack of La Grippe. Her friends have lost a most valuable helper, one ever ready to lend a helping hand, or give a word of sympathy to those in need or in trouble; while her own immediate family have lost a loving wife and mother, whose first thought was for the comfort of those she loved. Especially will her loss be sadly felt by her aged father, who still survives her and whose declining days were being brightened by her tender administrations.

*Barbara (Luick) Hatt, circa 1873*

**For some reason, Henry Luick and his children, as well as their attendants, tended to court complicated love relations—his beautiful daughter, Barbara, being no exception. Shown here in her early twenties, about the time her father harvested his family's hefty inheritance, she'd actually been married already for a half-dozen years, having been wedded soon after her 16th birthday to William Henry Hatt, eight years her senior.**

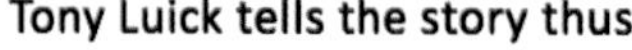

**Tony Luick tells the story thus:**

*William Henry Hatt, likely 1870s*

> In the spring of 1843, Henry Luick and Melissa Overacker married and had two girls, Barbara (1851) and Mary Catherine (1847), and five boys: Michael Henry (1844), Sylvester David (1848), Louis Lee (1857), Frank Eugene (1861) and Charles Grant (1864). [Two daughters, Rosella and Frances, died, respectively, in infancy (1855) and at age five (in 1861).] It is likely that while in Michigan, since both families (the Luicks and Hatts) lived in the same county near the small town of Franciscoville, the families were acquainted and, more specifically, Barbara Luick and William Hatt knew each other. Thus it is also likely that it was not an accident that William Hatt went to Belmond in 1867 for the purpose of seeking Barbara's hand in marriage. They returned to Franciscoville, where they were married and lived until 1880.
>
> William and Barbara had four children: James Henry (1870), Marietta "Etta" (1872), Lewis William (1878), and finally Maude Mae (1891)—when Barbara was 40. They moved to Iowa in 1880, so all of the children were born in Michigan except Maude, who was born on a small farm near Belmond. Barbara became sick with the flu only a couple of years after Maude's birth; she died in December of 1893. William sought help from family members, particular his daughter Etta (now Bakewell) and Mary Catherine (Luick) Packard (Barbara's sister) in raising Maude, as the other children were much older and mostly on their own.
>
> About 1898, 4 or 5 years after Barbara died, William remarried to Christina (Petersen). The 1900 U.S. census has William (59), Christina M. (wife; 45, born in Denmark), Malinda C. Peterson (stepdaughter; 12), and Maude M. Hatt (9) living on their rented farm in Pleasant Township, Wright Co. In about 1905, Maude left her father's house to work for, and live with, Frank and Daisy Beed at their farm near Hansel, Iowa. Willie C. Maxson, also an employee of the Beeds, and Maude were married Oct. 7th, 1908.

According to William Hatt, in 1916 he finally gave up on his relationship and allowed his second wife to "take off with his money" after liquidating his possessions. She purportedly "threw him out" and sold his house, and so he went to live with his daughter Maude and her family. For a couple of years, 1917 -1919, there were generally two and sometimes three elderly relatives boarding with Will and Maude. They were Sylvester Edward Maxson (64), William Hatt (77), and occasionally Estella (Wright) Maxson (58), who had a frequent passion for Sylvester. Gladys related years later that she was a witness to a rather heated relationship between Estella and Sylvester, the retired school teacher and the sheep herder. At that time, Estella and her husband, Frank Maxson, were separated. Anyway, the relationship with Sylvester ended with his untimely death due to the Spanish flu epidemic in 1919.

William Hatt stayed with Maude and her family until he died in 1925. He was buried in Belmond Cemetery, beside his first wife Barbara. In 1996, his great grandson had a small head stone carved and placed for William as no stone had ever been placed.

Less than five years after Death nabbed his doting daughter, Barbara, it returned to also claim the long life of Henry Jacob Luick, who, according to an obituary in the *Belmond Herald* on 16 March 1898,

was born in Stuttgart, Germany, Sept. 11, 1822 and came to Washtenaw County, Michigan in 1832 with his parents who were of Lutheran faith. At the age of 20, he was married to Melissa Overacker. Nine children were born to them, six of whom still live [...] Barbara (Mrs. Hatt) dying a few years ago. In 1853, Henry removed to Iowa, stopping near Franklin Grove. At this time, Belmond was not thought of. He was among the first settlers in Wright County, but few of whom remain to tell the story of privation and toil necessary as pioneers. In [corrected: 1868], he married Mrs. Lydia Johnson and moved to Mahaska County. Ten years they lived in Oskaloosa, returning to Belmond in [1879], where they have since resided.

*Henry Jacob Luick, circa 1890*

In his younger and more useful days, Mr. Luick was a prosperous and influential man, holding at one time the position of County Judge for several years. His death has been so closely linked with the history of Wright County, that by his death, another of the old landmarks disappears. For the past several years, he had suffered intensely, much of the time, from that dread destroyer known as Bright's disease of the kidneys. Had his constitution not been uncommonly strong, accompanied by great will power, he must have succumbed to his malady long ago. As it was, however, after a few weeks of intensified suffering, his spirit was set free on the morning of the second of March, 1898.

Besides a faithful, patient, loving wife who nursed him through his trying illness, he leaves a host of relatives and friends to mourn his loss, this being the first death in his immediate family for over 40 years. Four brothers and a sister of this family were permitted to follow him to his last resting place.

The burial took place from the home at 2:30 Thursday, and all that was mortal of this loved one was laid to rest to await the Resurrection morn. Funeral services were held at the Congregational Church by Rev. J. D. Sands at 3:30 the same day.

Having come to the New World 65 years earlier and planted the Luick lineage in a new country, thus paving the way for tens, some day hundreds of thousands of descendants to live lives fully different from what they would have known in the Old World, the "Ol' Bobcat" quietly passed on to other haunts.

---

When I was a little boy, as young as five or so, I'd go out to the gravel road that passed in front of Ashlawn Farm's fence-lined gate. I'd look to the north and study the ruler-straight road as far as I could see, to the point where it disappeared into an all-absorbing sky. Then, I'd turn slowly and do the same, to the south, 'til my eyes ran up against the towering white grain silos of the Farmers Coop in Burchinal.

I hadn't had much schooling to that point but knew enough about the world to know it was said to be round, without edges or end. It only made sense, then, that if I set off one day in one direction, along that unbending road, at some point I'd return from the other direction—and in the meantime surely have seen unimaginable sights, not to mention have had fantastic adventures along the way. "Someday" I thought to myself as I stood motionless for what seemed to be hours and stared, longingly—first in one direction, then in the other: "Someday" I promised my little self.

*Seen from the end of Ashlawn Farm's long driveway, a double rainbow beckoned me to that endless road.*

The German word for "homesickness" is "*Heimweh*"—literally "The pain of [missing] home." Its correlate, "*Fernweh*," lacks a direct translation in English, but a literal one would be "The pain of [missing] distant places," whereas figurative ones include "itchy feet," a "yen to see distant places" or, ironically, the Anglo-usurped German word "*Wanderlust*," the "desire to roam." Was my *Wanderlust*, already as a tike, specific to my unique personality formation, or did I come by it through restless genes? All I know is, I've had it all my life—and that "pain of missing distant places" has made all the difference.

---

Apparently, Henry and Melissa's third child, Sylvester, and his young bride, Irene Johnson, eventually overcame the social stigma of having been part of the complicated and questionable intra-familial marital drama cited above, for by the time of his death, Sylvester clearly had become a central member of Belmond's close-knit community—as suggested by an obituary in the *Belmond Herald* in April 1938:

> Sylvester David Luick, 89 died Monday morning at the home of his daughter, Mrs. Harry Vierkant, five miles south and two miles east of Mason City. Mr. Luick suffered a broken hip in a fall January 8th and failed to recover from the injury.
>
> Mr. Luick was born June 14, 1848 in Jackson County. Michigan and came to Iowa with his parents on November 8, 1853[.] Mr. Luick in his later years in reminiscing said that their first home was a log cabin in Franklin Grove and for two years the family had to go to Dubuque for groceries. There wasn't a railroad west of the Mississippi River at the time. The first winter was a mild one; the ducks and geese were in this section throughout the season. In 1854 a larger log house was built and the old cabin was used for a school house. More settlers moved in 1855 and the family had a neighbor - 25 miles distant. The winter of 1856 was a terrible one for the pioneers as

*Sylvester Luick, circa 1910*

snow was three feet high and the settlers' supplies were exhausted. The Indians, frightened by the threatened approach of soldiers, had just left Franklin Grove.

Mr. Luick on September 25 1868 was married to Irene Johnson, who preceded him in death December 2 1912. Surviving were four sons and a daughter.

---

Sylvester wasn't the only Luick to ever experience a life-changing event in the month of December:

Over the Christmas-New Year's holidays of 2010, a personal calamity occurred while my then-partner, Rock, his two young children and I were on a tour of ecological projects in Costa Rica. When we returned to the Loess Hills region of Western Iowa—where at the time TRACES was grafting a project for organic gardening and farming, alternative energy and (especially but not only rural) community revitalization—we found the Burr Oak Center pillaged and stripped of all that we had built up over more than a year and a half of meticulous work. Worst of all, the plundering had been done by the (erroneously- and self-named) "master gardener" who we had left in charge of safeguarding the place.

*hanging and drawing Scot John Ogilvie, 1615; the Loess Hills as seen from my Burr Oak Center bedroom*

It was devastating enough to lose so many tangible traces of so much intangible effort, but adding insult to injury were a series of injustices that left me feeling emotionally hung, drawn and quartered. For one, through an unexpected peculiarity of Iowa law, we were not allowed to sue the rouge former staff who'd robbed us, once Gary Klein had filed charges against TRACES to extract some last of his own property of his left among the booty that he was still in the process of removing when—while still in Costa Rica—I had premonitions of catastrophe at home and called the county sheriff to check the by-then-nearly-empty house. Further, Heidi Bowman, the shiftless drifter of a woman who the physically-disabled renegade gardener had recruited to help him strip the place in our absence, was a longtime and, according to her, "intimate" friend of the judge appointed to hear the subsequent one-sided trial. Rather than recuse himself due to personal bias, the about-to-retire judge refused to hear any evidence not pertaining to Gary's property in question: Despite well-documented evidence of Gary's having used the TRACES credit card to charge several thousands of dollars' worth of "intimate apparel," on-line porn sites and moving expenses, as well as proof of ownership of items he'd schlepped away with Heidi, then maintained belonged to him, the judge pushed away every page I tried, in vain, to hand the stern-faced arbiter. And, I was left to defend now-cashless TRACES on my own, since Gary—unbeknownst to us—had consulted Iowa Legal Aid before I had attempted to solicit counsel from that organization myself.

As a crowning slap to the face, Monona County's "Hang-Man Magistrate" recessed the trial in order to reconvene (are you sitting?) *in my home* at Burr Oak. Of course, Judge Nailor refused to remove his muddy shoes when he, with a deputy shadowing as body guard, came to conclude the trial with an absurd "walk-through" of the house that had nothing to offer in terms of clarifying what belonged to whom, when or for how long. When I then appealed to the Iowa Court Commissions to review such unorthodox procedures as well as my long, exhaustively documented list of instances of how the entire trial had violated numerous juristic norms, the State of Iowa's highest legal-review authorities merely sent a form letter, brushing off any responsibility to carry out its assigned duty to assure justice.

All in all, the whole affair was an assisted rape. Perversely, the perpetrator of the crime walked away a greatly enriched man, possessing considerable property and new, involuntarily-surrendered capital. And, his victims? The aftermath of Gary's heartless wrongdoing left me devastated: I felt traumatized, rendered by day sad and irritable, by night unable to sleep restfully. When I awoke each morning, I literally saw Gary's grinning, toothless face in front of my blood-shot eyes; I dreamt of the man, both in my ever-interrupted sleep as well as in the awake state. And, I felt expressly disappointed with my country, with a system that had failed to project me, TRACES' board members and all those involved—other than Gary Klein. Already disillusioned after a decade of America's fighting an illegal, unfounded war with Iraq, with a people who had done us no wrong, I now felt generally dejected by the land of my birth. Everywhere I turned I saw corruption, chaos or systematic failure. And, that broke my heart.

---

The best educated of Heinrich and Katherine's children, an uncited obituary recounted that William Christian Luick was

> the first child born to [the Luick family] after coming to America and settling on the farm near Ann Arbor. He was their fourth son and a sturdy, active boy. His parents, ardent Lutherans, chose this son to promulgate their faith. William was sent to a seminary at an early age for that purpose, but William got the lust for the west and his desire to join his brothers in Iowa. In the fall of 1856, his brother David returned to Michigan for a visit with his family; William joined him on his return trip. [...]
>
> The early migration of this family to Wright County was fraught with such dangers and hardships as only pioneers know, for it was in the winter of 1856 and 1857 that William first made this vicinity his home. One of the experiences which pioneers will never forget was what is known as the "Spirit Lake Massacre" and of this cruel scene some of the old settlers still talk. [...] William lived with his brother, David until 1859, when he went to live on his first farm, remained there until 1894. In that year he moved into another house on the farm, remained there until Oct. 4 1909, the time of his death.

*William Christian Luick, 1890s*

*Belmond-area farmstead, representative of the region and era; circa 1910s*

William was a farmer here when wheat sold for forty cents a bushel and hogs at two and one-half cents a pound. William was a member of the Odd Fellows and the Ancient Free and Accepted Masons. He was not a politician, but always voted the Republican ticket.

---

Among the debris left by an inside-job crime, I had tried to fight. When that failed, I opted for flight.

How could I stay in a country where I felt unsafe, where even the State's highest legal authority could not protect me or people I cared about from the evil machinations of twisted minds or lost souls? It seemed that politicians of all stripes had abandoned the people to focus on their own enrichment at the expense of the rest of us—a nation led by an elite clique, an occupational army of scheming Gary Kleins.

*Burr Oak's garden seen from the center's balcony; 1840 depiction of Gary's double, Guy Fawkes, plotting treason*

Ironically, the whole hateful, game-changing act Gary committed seems to have arisen out of love—or, at least, his stilted understanding of and botched attempts at securing that most fragile of human treasures. Based on what others or I later heard or saw, Gary apparently thought that by volunteering to oversee Burr Oak's gardening he could ingratiate himself to me and then, well... An intimate relationship between the two of us, however, *never* occurred to me—not ever, even once. Then, on top of Gary's unrequited infatuations for me, another love interest of his, Rock, came from Central Missouri to visit for a weekend. He left a day earlier than planned, with no wish of pursuing Gary but, rather, me—per a fleeting meeting that I neither initiated nor later could resist repeating. Problem was, Gary assumed I had secretly chased Rock after his sudden departure—which I had not. Rather than take responsibility for his own, self-sabotaging role in Rock's swift decision upon his arrival at Burr Oak to bag a potential relationship moments after he walked in the door, Gary—who has no teeth but a hunchback, a handful of chronic diseases but no material resources of his own, and many acquaintances but few faithful friends, yet had informed Rock of none of his various maladies nor solitary isolation over the several months they had phone dated—blamed his dashed hopes, undeservedly, on me.

Whatever it was that had motivated Gary to incapacitate our shared project, both its loss and his moral trespasses were too great for my conscience to cope with: I decided to flee the train wreck which I, at that time, in that place, perceived at least my life, if not the entire, surrounding New World to have become, and to seek what seemed a saner, safer refuge in—as Dick Cheney called it—"Old Europe."

The sham of a trial took less than six months, from filing to finding. In that time, our last intern and I closed up the house at Burr Oak so I could turn the keys over to a realtor, and I put all business affairs—the non-profit's as well as private ones—in moth balls. Cashless following Gary's successful treachery, I liquidated my Roth IRAs and pawned a few remaining personal possessions in order to buy tickets. I visited my beloved mother for what I realized could, plausibly, be a last time. Then, I waited in St. Paul.

It would all be so easy, run so smoothly... so efficiently, so... so *Germanic*.

To help make the whole process run optimally, I went to the busy Merriam Park Branch Library to consult the experience or wise advice of others. When I approached the reference desk and asked the bespectacled librarian "Hello. What do you have about emigrating from America?" he at first only peered up at me over the rims of his thick specs, dumbly.

"Don't you mean '*im*migrating *to* America?'" he tried to correct me.

"No—I really do mean '*e*migrating *from*' this great country of ours."

For a moment, he only looked at me. Then, as if I'd asked him what resources he might offer me to combat gonorrhea or build a concealable, body-worn bomb, he slowly stood, dropped his voice and commanded "Follow me." Our hurried hunt, though, came up empty: While Mr. Librarian and I found thousands of references to "immigrating to America" in the Library of Congress on-line catalog, among real-time reference books on the library's shelves, in magazines, etc., we were unable to uncover a single source on how to organize leaving the United States of America forever. "It's just not done" he finally concluded, then swiftly pivoted and returned to the line that had gathered at his counter.

Still, I was determined that it would all be so easy, run so smoothly... so efficiently, so... so *Germanic*:

AmTrak's *Empire Builder* from Seattle would arrive in Minnesota's capital at 7:47 AM. My friend CeCeile—a painter, local activist and TRACES board member—would drive me to the station. I'd board; we'd smile at one another, shedding bittersweet tears; then, at 8:03, the train would lurch into motion.

Fate, though, had other plans—not at all resembling my Best Laid ones:

*first in a series of Works Progress Administration art*

I'd arisen at five—soon after which I found an email from AmTrak, informing me of a delay of "a few hours." *Damnation!* I swore loudly, panicking. When I called America's national railway to inquire what was causing the delay, the woman speaking to me through a tin can on a string—for some reason with a clothes pin clamped to her nose—could only hum the mantra "Difficulties in Montana, sir. Difficulties in Montana, sir. Difficul—"

Problem was, I was fully ready to roll: My condo in St. Paul was impeccably clean, ready for the renter to move in on the coming weekend—that of Memorial Day. My too-many bags were packed, tight and impenetrable, untouchable for fear that opening this or that zipper even a smidgeon might release a nuclear reaction, setting off an unstoppable chain reaction that would turn the entire cosmos into a vast inferno of exploding, over-stuffed suitcases. And, every mental atom in my weary body was fixated on the pending departure, "The sooner the better." Still, I had no choice but to wait.

When a second email arrived, announcing another delay of "a few more hours," I despaired—for if I missed the connection in Chicago for New York, I'd lose the unrefundable passage I'd booked to Europe.

Just then, the phone rang. Thinking it was CeCeile, begging off driving me and my thousands of bags to Midway's AmTrak station, I picked up the receiver and teased "So, it's all takin' too long for ya, huh?"

"I beg *your* pardon?" a high-pitched, proper-British-accented man's voice asked indignantly.

"Oh, I'm *so* sorry" I begged, "I was expecting someone else."

"Yes, that's apparent" the old man snapped with a click of his teeth at the last "t," then continued—despite the initial awkwardness over my stupid quip—to make an offer I never could have expected.

As improbable as it seemed in that moment (and still does), almost half a year after I'd sent blind applications to every private school in Germany at which I could imagine teaching, some Waldorf school in *Schwaben* had rediscovered my inquiry "inadvertently misfiled" and now, in a pickle to fill a position before summer break, a search-committee chair wondered if I might still be interested in a job. Explaining my situation, I took his number and agreed to call a fortnight later to schedule an interview. As we hung up, I whispered "If the *Empire Builder* had come on time, I never wouldda gotten this call."

---

If "Mad Bobcat" Henry Luick was a trail blazer, his decade-younger brother David was a consolidator, a man who brought various ideas, people and strands of possibility together in order to make something greater out of them as a whole. (A third category of Organizational Human might be that of integrator, the woman or man who follows the trail blazer, picks up the strands unified by the consolidator, then digests them, breaks them down into useable parts.) While Henry charged forward, recruiting others to follow in his wide wake, the records suggest that David Luick's efforts had more staying power and left far fewer victims. If Henry's mode was to polarize, divide, then lead through cloaked manipulation—a trait I suffered greatly under and learned too well from my father's family—David brought people together, built consensus, then moved forward as a group, to the benefit of all.

His obituary, as it appeared in the *Belmond Herald* on 8 January 1912, reflects David Luick's gifts.

*Johann David Luick, 1890s*

Monday morning, January 8th 1912, death of David Luick was announced, one of the earliest of Iowa pioneers, and one of our most respected citizens. While his death was not unexpected, it was believed and hoped by those who were nearest and dearest, and by his friends who were legion, that his life might still be spared, not for the good he had done, but for the good he still could do, and which in his lifetime it was his every desire to do, in and toward all mankind.

David Luick was born at Stuttgart, Wurtemburg [sic], Germany, June 27 1832. When six months of age he accompanied his parents to America, when they settled near Ann Arbor, Washtenaw Co. Michigan, where he resided until twenty-one year of age, when he came to Belmond, Iowa with his brother Henry and family, September 6, 1853. In the year of 1859 he was united in marriage to Miss Sarah Overacker, who preceded him to the land beyond February 16, 1900. To this union [corrected: five] children were born.

In commenting upon the long life of David Luick, is to review the trials and hardships that were his as one of the pioneers, who first saw Iowa, when it was but one broad expansive prairie, in its original primeval condition, with here and there a few white settlers, and the American Indian still roaming at will. Just preceding the Spirit Lake massacre of 1857 he located upon a homestead adjacent to the scene of the above massacre. Following this he returned to Belmond, where he resided until the time of his death.

Upon returning from Spirit Lake to Belmond, Mr. Luick lived upon the farm and land that he had priorly acquired from the government. At this time intensive or diversified farming was unknown. If it had not been for the fact that he was a most successful trapper, he like other members of their order, [section missing] when David Luick was laid to rest beside the remains of his beloved wife in Evergreen cemetery. Truly, it can and must be said that his is the rest of the just.

---

I've long wanted to think of myself as belonging to "the just," but by the time I'd swept together the shards from my crashed-and-burned Big Green Dream, I felt spent. I had not had a moment of genuine rest from the instant I learned that Gary had cleaned out the Burr Oak Center until I had seen my dear mother and, as I forced myself to get into the waiting pickup, bid her *adieu* on Mother's Day morning, 2011. It was all I could do, then, to get to the point of being ready to walk away from the new biography I'd built in the United States since returning stateside from a full, functioning life in Germany the Thursday before the Tuesday attacks on the World Trade Center in September 2001.

By the time I could finally confirm that the *Empire Builder* was at last approaching St. Paul, I had been up already a whole work day, with an eight-hour train trip ahead of me, before being able to try to catch the next departure for the Big Apple with, now, hardly any transfer time left in the schedule. In any event, I had no choice but to try: Staying and living among smoldering ruins was not an option.

*an Amtrak train crossing Colorado, eastbound at Grand Junction*

My loyal friend CeCeile pulled to a squealing stop in front of my condo, I—who'd been anxiously waiting on the curb for of the day—threw in my bags and away we flew. She drove me to the station. I boarded. Once I counted my endless entourage of bags for the umpteenth time, I turned: We smiled at each other, shedding bittersweet tears. Then, the train lurched into motion.

As the train pulled out of St. Paul's AmTrak station, it was not clear to me what I "should" be feeling, let alone what I *was* feeling. Any recognizable emotion was clouded by a fog of general numbness, a muted panic brought on by the sickening realization that this was "it." As the doors of the shiny, stainless-steel car had closed and the train now leaned into a slow forward movement, there was no going back. I now was on an unintended journey, and no matter where it led me, I could never return to my beloved Midwest the same person I was in that very moment.

Once the initial shock of an irreversible break with everything I'd ever known, and anything I'd ever been, began to fade, a growing pain, a creeping nausea spread through my torso. As I acknowledged my complete aloneness as of that second—an utter solitude that scarcely would be interrupted for the next three weeks—I didn't know if I'd puke or start sobbing. The two-day train ride across the eastern half of the United States, followed by a long Memorial Day weekend in New York and the two-week Atlantic crossing on a freighter that laid ahead of me, would all be a solo trek into the Unknown. The pregnant potential of all the possibilities excited me, even while the utter uncertainty of it all cast a terror into my soul unlike few things ever had.

At that moment, the train tilted as it gained a hit of speed and threw me against the wall of the stairwell where I insisted on standing. My tightening chest pressed up against the smoky-glass window, I looked out over the Twin Cities' Midway and spied downtown Minneapolis' dozen or so skyscrapers, towering over the emerald erstwhile prairie like slender giants.

*WPA poster promoting childhood reading, late 1930s*

The high-rises looked as lonely as I felt, as I stood in that train and grasped that the past three weeks' constant parade of visiting friends and family had now promptly ceased. There would be no more lingering with cherished souls over savory meals. There would be mostly an unremarkable, quickly forgotten blur of cold snacks caught on the run as I served my sentence of months, maybe years of wandering the world in search of a new life to replace the one I had fully and irrevocably jettisoned the moment I had boarded that train.

There would be no more protracted, heartfelt phone calls meant to pay down the deficit of contact I knew was coming once I set off into the world, once I boarded this very train—a date I had made months ago yet still wasn't prepared for as CeCeile drove me through the springtime streets of St. Paul in late May. There would be no more quiet, early-morning or early-dusk walks through Merriam Park's tight rows of Victorian houses tucked behind picket fences and lilac hedges. There would be no more soaking in the last, fleeting moments of Home, before The Boundless Unknown became—once again—the only thing that surrounded me and cast my inner landscape.

At that moment, taking a soft curve, the train tipped again slightly as it headed towards downtown St. Paul. Having shifted direction, I could see Cleveland Avenue—and felt an immediate pang, knowing that CeCeile had just, minutes before, sped down that same street, to go walk Wotan, her and Terry's naughty, cock-eared mutt who—she lamented in the car as we had approached the station—had not been walked since early morning, given her having to "be on-call to haul *monsieur*."

A bit further, the train cut across "my" 'hood—past the playground at the end of the side street next to my condo, past the burned-brick, Edward-Hopperesque corner shops with their smattering of cafes and boutiques, past the old sandstone school cum community center.

Knowing that my Arts and Crafts condo apartment lay only a few streets back, past stuffy Starbucks, the busy Merriam Park branch library and the smelly, poorly-lit laundromat, a slight yet discomforting lump formed in my throat, for this was not one of my myriad road trips or jaunts away for a week or two: I was emigrating, so this was good-bye, *auf Wiedersehen*, aloha, ahoy and *adieu*! Yes, I found it all exciting—but terrifying, too.

The train then crept alongside Ayd Mill Parkway, affording a lingering glance at the route I almost always took to drive back to Iowa, to visit Mom or return to the Loess Hills for another stint of Green Living. Seeing the Ayd Mill now, I couldn't help but think of my last visit to Mason

this is the MARKET where the storekeeper buys the food and brings it to his store near your house


*WPA poster promoting buying fresh food, late 1930s*

City—ironically, and unplanned so, on Mother's Day weekend—to bid my mama a teary-eyed farewell, not knowing if or when we'd ever see each again. Even now, rocking back and forth, standing in the stairwell of this long-delayed train, I could feel, literally, a pain in my belly: the sharp slit of separation.

Despite being a trained Ph.D. in history, and although I've traversed the world countless times, only now would I truly know, on a gut level, inside my own skin, what it felt like for my ancestors—from *Schwaben*, *Franken*, *Pommern* and *Elsass*, from Lincolnshire in the English Midlands, Ulster's County Down, the hills of Wales and the Danish isles—to sever their familial and cultural tap roots, and set sail for "*Amerika*." Sure, I had lived in Europe for a total of eleven years by then, and I had crossed the Big Pond so many times I finally had stopped noting which of the uncountable flights I was on during a particular trip—but this was different. I would travel by land, one mile after the other, and then by sea, one breezy wave upon another, barreling into Nowhere.

At the moment, though, I was still at the beginning of my seemingly involuntary journey, still deep in the heart of my native Upper Midwest—with Minnesota's capital slowly passing past the window I stood leaning against, my palms pressed flat on the glass, as if to silently protest in vain this whole scene.

Was I "ready" to leave? Yes.

Did I "want" to leave? No.

---

When Heinrich Luick and his wife Katherine uprooted their fledgling family in *Schwaben* and sunk new roots in Southeast Michigan, the Luick family tree also began to sprout new branches—in the form of additional, now "American" children. Their only daughter—Albert Lee's aunt, Katherine (Luick) Elder,

was born in the log cabin near Ann Arbor [and] grew to young womanhood there before coming to Iowa to make her home[.]After living for a time with her brother Henry's family, she met and married Adrian Elder, a sturdy young man who had recently come to this section[.]They established a home on land just south of Belmond. Both were industrious, hardworking and thrifty, and built a fine home and farm where they prospered through the years.

*"Kate" (Luick) Elder, 1890s*

*Adrian Elder, circa 1890*

They used to tell how Adrian kept the early settlers supplied with wild honey. He was an expert in tracing bees to the hollow tree and extracting the tubs of honey because sugar was in short supply. He also was skilled in basket weaving, an art he had learned from his Dutch ancestors in Pennsylvania and he kept the families supplied with this important article. He also was the first County Commissioner for the district [thanks to the county-seat war led by his future brother-in-law Henry Luick] and discharged this duty for many years with wisdom and good judgment.

They were active in helping build a better community life and were always willing to do their share to improve the community. They lived a very happy life together with their three children; Charles, Katherine, and George. [They also raised Kate's 18-year-younger half-brother, Emanuel Luick].

---

The *Empire Builder* gained speed as it followed the Mississippi as that majestic river flowed past downtown St. Paul's fat banks and sleek corporate headquarters, its grand civic buildings and carefully groomed riverfront promenade. Knowing that in a couple hours it and I would part ways, perhaps for several years if not forever, I savored its familiar sights as much and as deeply as I could.

Seeing some of the several 1930s Art-Deco buildings in what's referred to as "the last Eastern city" as one crosses North America from East to West, I thought of Meridel Le Sueur and her desperate search for a job in the face of approaching wintertime hunger. Then, randomly chasing wild mental segues, I could not help but think of my diminutive granny, and of Charlotte's Depression-era decision to marry Donald, the dashing small-town Elmer Gantry who implanted in her the seeds of my family's decades-long emotional quagmire. *Was marrying him once they got pregnant* I wondered to myself, *really the only option Gramma saw?* At that instant, rather than judgment, I felt an aching longing for my dead father's dead mother—and missed them both. Despite all their wound-induced shortcomings, I would have been happy to have had either one of them sitting next to me in that devastatingly lonely moment, on that anonymous train headed to an indefinite future on my own, on a continent not my own.

Besides evoking burdened ghosts I'd rather have dodged, surveying downtown St. Paul's squatty skyline offered me other, albeit also double-edged distractions from the pain of leave-taking. Over the roof of the flawlessly renovated, Italianate-style Central Public Library, I could see the towers that ring the Landmark Center, that old Federal courthouse converted into a cultural center—the erstwhile home to the Midwest/World War II-history museum I had built and operated in the Twin Cities for three years.

*WPA poster promoting pedestrian safety, late 1930s*

Just then, the train clanked and swayed its way around the river's bend to the south, below the ancient Native American burial mounds atop the sandstone ridges just east of downtown St. Paul. Now headed towards Pig's Eye Lake, standing on that train I wondered again, for the thousandth time, if closing the TRACES Center for History and Culture just as the economy unraveled in fall 2008 had constituted a "failure" or actually a well-discerned pre-emptive measure to avoid certain financial ruin.

The track-slapping rhythm of the train, however, didn't entertain such pensive reflection for long. As St. Paul's spires and domes, high rises and low-lying river flats disappeared into the distance, we couple hundred passengers and crew were fairly barreling—if 79 miles per hour can be dubbed that, when other countries' trains reach twice that speed—along the river's edge, hugging that margin where thick stands of trees slowly gave way to stretches of open water, with only an occasional water-logged tree trunk bobbing in the gentle waves as a barge here or a solitary speedboat there cut across the river.

Soon thereafter, the Mighty Miss morphed into Lake Pepin, the wide spot in the river just beyond which Laura Ingalls Wilder was born in the "Big Woods." *Ah, my ol' friend!* I mused. *We've come a long way.* Old Man River had many years earlier come to symbolize freedom and autonomy for me. As a junior in high school, from the moment I got a license I made this or that hollow excuse to borrow the family Pontiac on weekends, then make a beeline for the Mississippi River Valley. Rarely traveling, my family spent most of its time when I was a kid on Ashlawn Farm diggin' dirt an' chasin' critters.

The first time I saw the broad, blackish waters of the Mississippi, I stood at its shores, mesmerized, soaking in the power and majesty of the Upper Midwest's answer to the romantic Rheintal. Unlike the open prairie of North Central Iowa, the winding, Palisade-abutted gorges of Northeast Iowa's "Little Switzerland" region might as well have been on another, free-er planet than the father-dominated flatland I escaped once or twice a month for most of the rest of my high school career.

As random nostalgia gave way to focused reflection on stray encounters I and my people had with Ol' Miss, I stared out the window, mesmerized by things unseen transposed over things that were. As I watched herons strut their way along the river's shallows, waiting to stab a late lunch, I remembered that *Grandma Thrams' grandparents were on the first train to ever cross the Upper Mississippi*. As I observed proud eagles scope underlying waters for prey, and bottom-heavy Canada geese try to defy gravity, it occurred to me that *Rock and I made love here one moonlit summer night, in a swaying white van with steamed-up windows*. As silly-looking pelicans scooped up fish in their elastic bills, I recalled that *I once drove the children and grandchildren of former German POWs held in the Upper Midwest during The War along that Great River Road over there—and they were astounded by the region's rugged, picturesque scenery.*

As the *Empire Builder* snaked along the long valley, I noted that the humanoid "wildlife" population on the river also was out in force. After a second endless winter in a row that seemed unwilling to give up its grip on the long-suffering populace finally did let go and spring had just irreversibly arrived, scores of boaters and of fishing men and boys—as well as a few girls—had taken to the water to commune with their deeper natures. As I rolled along on my way away from my native Midwest, four- and two-legged mammals joined animals with feathers and fins to see me off: The Mississippi teamed with Life, and that abundance gave me solace as I tried to outrun haunting, deflating thoughts of what had been lost during the disaster I'd weathered the past six months, what little was left and what might remain possible.

*WPA poster promoting protecting wildlife, late 1930s*

---

The story of Katherine's and Adrian's married life cannot be told without mentioning her prominent, nepotistic brother, Henry, for as judge he performed their wedding on Sunday, 19 June 1859. For unknown reasons, following the death of their father Heinrich in 1860, "Kate" (as she was called) took her and Henry's then-five-year-old half-brother, Emanuel, to live with her and Adrian, even though his 41-year-old mother, Heinrich's second wife Dorothea, would live another eighteen years, but apparently shunned the clan. Perhaps it was her and Adrian's kind act of kindness that predisposed Emanuel, later in life, to care for still other children in need—as celebrated in his undated, anonymous obituary.

> Emanuel Luick was born in Washtenaw, County, Michigan, January 15, 1855 and died at his home in Belmond, February 5th 1918, the cause of death being pneumonia. He was 64 years.

In infancy he was baptized in the German Lutheran church. When but 4 or 5 years old, he and his brother Gottlob came to Iowa with Henry Luick because they were left without parents and in this new country; he made his home with Adrian [and the boy's half-sister, Katherine (Luick)] Elder until he was 19 years old. At the age of 21 [sic] he married Alta Haner. Mrs. Luick passed to her reward December 19th 1916. They were not blessed with children of their own but Mr. and Mrs. Luick were so fond of children that three young people were raised to manhood and womanhood in their home. Walter who died in 1908, Jennie now Mrs. John Helland of this city and Andrew, who is at present one of Uncle Sam's soldier boys.

*thought to be "Jennie," Alta, Emanuel and "Andrew," circa 1910*

Shortly after their marriage, Mr. Luick purchased part of the farm which was his home until he retired about ten years ago. He added to his acreage until the farm comprised about 400 acres.

*close-up view of archetypal Belmond-area farmyard; notice windmill and period car parked behind the gate*

He leaves to morn his loss two sisters, Mrs. Amelia Cook and Mrs. Mary Armbruster and a brother Gottlob, all residing in Michigan, and a half brother, Fred, besides a host of nephews and nieces and many friends. Mr. Luick enjoyed a wide circle of acquaintances who can vouch for his lively interest in things rural. He was a great admirer of children. Many a child has been made happy by the treat of a kind word Mr. Luick gave it. His aggressive spirit has been a factor in the community to further interests that were prone to lag. Altogether it can be said Mr. Luick will be greatly missed by his friends, his words of counsel will be longed for by those who sought them.

———

Dispossessed of most my one-time material wealth, the title "museum director" and almost all hope of ever again being happy, sitting alone in that crowed train I longed for a few "words of counsel" myself.

The Twin Cities far behind me, the Mississippi Valley had become the consuming context in which all of my thoughts and feelings now seemed to unfold—at least for a couple hours: I could not resist its magnetic, seductive allure. With the omnipresent river just beyond the window my only constant now, the train passed fertile fields, leafy woods, pastures full of contented cows felling the tender first grass of spring, Victorian river-front villages, and quaint, brick-paved county seats like Red Wing and Winona.

With the thought *Oh, Winona: It isn't far from here that Laura Ingalls Wilder's relations—and later Ann Kew Moorehead's sisters—once lived,* I recognized how intensely aware I was, bombing through time and space, of myriad connections, past and present, familial or unfamiliar. I also realized that my mind could not imagine anything even resembling a future, anywhere, in any way.

*WPA poster promoting tourism in America, late 1930s*

Rather than what was to come, I could see only what had been—my ancestors, their trials, their accomplishments and failures; our homes and farms, perennial hopes and personal tragedies. As a social historian, I knew that one family really consists of many, of uncountable families who, together, form communities, who populate regions and fill parishes or provinces or states, who comprise nations and, in turn, occupy a diverse yet increasingly interdependent world. Sitting there on that lonesome train, I felt the presence of a vast crowd of people, both living and deceased, who had touched my life in endless ways, who had determined—whether or not I knew it or understood how—the flow of my days.

When I had survived a near-miss nuclear holocaust in October '62 and entered the world alive, after all, I inherited a complex, intricate and infinitely rich cosmos. I had not organized, invented or built a single thing; all that I came to think of as "mine" (or at least my family's) someone else had thought up, worked out or endured long enough to overcome. Millions of people, through infinite individual accomplishments, trifling and tremendous, had—together, in aggregate—crafted a world I came to take for granted, to assume was constant and assured. Now, having lost nearly all my worldly possessions and with almost no resources left to call my own, I was abandoning my spot in the New Canaan that my people had so painstakingly established; I was forfeiting their and my entire earthly legacies, in the thin hope that life might be better, elsewhere.

———

Frederick John Luick was born in Michigan, where his father Heinrich was a farmer and carpenter. Fred's mother, Katherine, died in 1843, age 43, when Fred was four. After he joined his siblings in Iowa, Fred lived with his brothers. He enlisted in the Union Army (Company C, 3rd Iowa Infantry) in 1864: By then, Fred had grown his sizable livestock herd, which a brother kept intact for him while he was gone. He served with General William Tecumseh Sherman and was discharged in Washington D.C. in 1865.

Soon after he returned to the Midwest, the young veteran took as his wife Alice Agnes Packard, a teacher at the Luick-family school. After Fred and Alice married on 7 September 1865, they commenced to amassing a farming operation which grew to over 3000 acres in size by the time Fred's life was so vaingloriously chronicled in the *History of Wright County, Iowa*, published in 1915. The author held that:

*Frederick John Luick, 1890s*

> Character of the highest class has been developed in the life and career of Frederick J. Luick, a noted farmer and cattleman, now retired, and banker of Belmond, Wright County, Iowa, who, from the small beginning of forty acres of land, has acquired three thousand acres, all located in Wright County, Iowa, besides a charming town home in Belmond.
>
> Frederick J. Luick [was born] on August 20, 1839, on his father's farm, in Washtenaw County, Michigan. [...] Wonderful tales of the fertility of the soil and of future opportunities must have been sent back to Michigan by the first members of the Luick family who came to Iowa, for one by one the remaining members migrated to this state until they were all united once more and became neighbors in the state of their adoption. Frederick J. Luick [...] arrived in 1857, the year of the Spirit Lake massacre, and amid the scenes of consequential excitement began his residence among new people and customs. He was at the impressionable age of seventeen at the time of this experience and was accompanied on the journey by Simeon Overacker and his family. For several years Frederick J. Luick made his home with his brother, Henry Luick, but after David Luick was married, resided at his home.
>
> In 1858, at the age of nineteen years, Frederick J. Luick purchased his first land, consisting of forty acres, in section 30, which he later traded for eighty acres farther north and located on the Pleasant township main road, and this, in turn, he traded into the old homestead of his brother, Henry Luick, on which stood the original log cabin, one of the first homes erected in the county of Wright. Through all of his agricultural operations, Frederick J. Luick has been interested in general farming and stock raising, and in this line has met with success.

*siblings Edith, Harold and Chester Luick, circa mid-1890s*

> In 1865 Frederick J. Luick was united in marriage to Alice Packard, daughter of Edwin C. and Caroline (Bailey) Packard, and to this union four children were born: Albert, who died when four years of age; Edith, Chester P. and Harold Frederick. [...] Chester P. is single and lives at home with his parents on their place, which is located at West Bend, Iowa. [...]
>
> The "father and son movement," though not a formal organization as it is today, had its inception among the fathers and sons of yesterday, and the ties were just as strong and true as in the present day. Frederick J. Luick formed the business partnership between himself and his son, Chester P., and their relations have remained firm through all these years. The active work and management of the farm and stock interests have been assumed by Chester P. and Harold, the father now resting from his long life of well-concerted effort and arduous toil. Chester P. specializes in Polled Angus, Hereford and Durham cattle, while Harold

specializes in Holstein cattle. Together they feed out annually about twelve carloads of cattle and five carloads of hogs.

Frederick J. Luick is president of the Belmond Savings Bank and was for twenty years a member of the Board of directors of the State Bank of Belmond. In his political faith, he is an earnest supporter of the Democratic party, but his zeal has never carried him beyond his convictions and he has always claimed the inalienable right to vote for the best candidate, regardless of party machinery. Frederick J. Luick, through diligent seeking, has found and gathered many of life's beautiful flowers, and in the seventy-fifth year of his career he can look back over a well-spent life.

*State Bank of Belmond, which Fred Luick helped oversee; circa 1915*

---

*WPA poster promoting Cleveland art exhibit, late 1930s*

The scheduled five-hour layover I was to have in Chicago between trains had evaporated into five minutes. Still, I managed to shuttle my eight big suitcases from the *Empire Builder* to the *Lake Shore Limited*. Like so oft in my frequently charmed life, a miracle occurred: As I threw the last bag into the door of the train to New York, the conductor standing on the platform hoisted a hand-held reflector into the clammy air of Chicago's underground Union Station, yelled something unintelligible to everyone and no one, blew a shrill whistle, let his hand fall and, with that, I jumped through the door past him as he, himself, scaled the steep steps, then turned and closed the door behind us. I had made it—but only just.

Taking one of the few free seats among the sleeping passengers, a backwards-facing one, the adrenalin I'd tapped to move a mountain of luggage in short order left me taxed yet wired. Although exhausted, when I tried to close my tired eyes, my tortured mind raced so that any sleep was fitful—more disorienting than regenerative. Having had no money for a couchette, I had no choice but to sleep sitting propped up against the florescent-lit train car's hard, reverberating wall. With my brain literally shaking inside my skull, my semi-conscious thoughts took on the consistency of cold scrambled eggs.

Drifting in and out of stolen moments of light dozing, each time I came partly to, I peered out to see how far the train had gone on its slow slog to the Big Apple. When I realized that we were in Northwest Indiana, for example, all I could think of was the Jennisons and the canal they helped build that helped deport the Miamis to the Missouri. Then, when the first hint of dawn revealed downtown Cleveland's skyline, I saw native-daughter Melissa (Overacker) Luick Arnold afore my eyes, dressed in calico and a pioneer woman's worn apron, her hair parted plainly down the middle and tied in the back into a tight bun, standing in front of a long line of first uniformed, then wooden-shoe-clad forefathers stretching back to Niew Amsterdam. Once the train crossed the border into Northwest Pennsylvania, it was the Shupes' and Diefenbachs' turn to turn up in drab, unadorned Mennonite garb, sans "paint on clay."

Unable to afford a cup of coffee once I forfeited any fantasies of achieving real sleep, by the time the sun had refused to back down beyond the horizon and I surrendered to my fate, I felt like a listless zombie. So, I let my heavy eyelids drop and tried to at least meditate on restful images. Perhaps it was the constant spinning of wheels beneath me or the continual flickering by of tall trees and spikey corn stalks, slender silos and towering fast-food signs, but instead I soon fell into a semi-hypnotic state. Sinking further and further into my seat, I increasingly had the sensation of falling ever backward, of almost being sucked rearward towards the East—and, of listening to myself as if a piped-in voice-over.

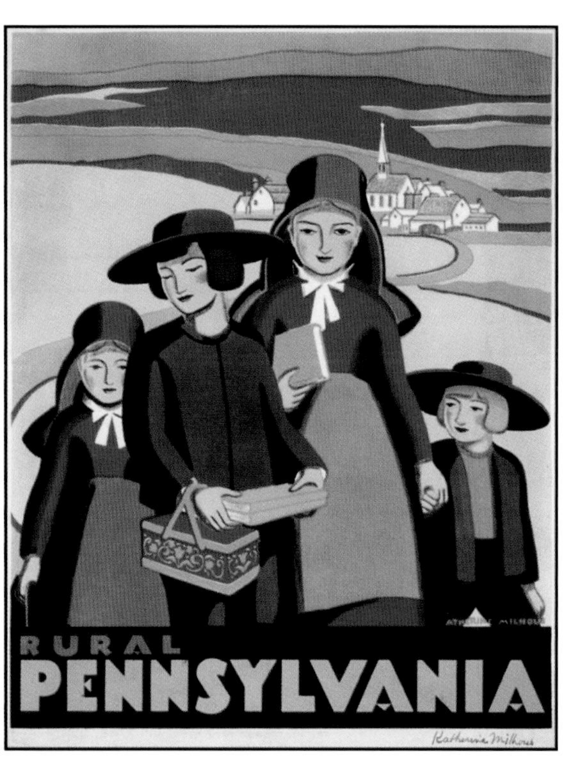

*WPA poster promoting rural Pennsylvania, late 1930s*

As the border between conscious and subconscious, of "real" and imagined grew ever fainter and more porous, I suddenly saw my great-great-grandfather, Louis Luick, as a sixteen-year-old boy, around that time that he had set off with his ma, Melissa, to trek west to California in search of the Mother Lode—ironically, about the same time as his pa, Henry, had set off east, cross-country per rail to New York, then on to Europe via ship, also in search of gold, but already panned and hammered into smooth bars. And, young Louis was in motion—but *backwards*! Instead of heading slowly westward, I observed (as if high in the sky) as he moved in reverse, east towards Iowa, in fast motion. Once, in my mind's eye, he had returned to Iowa, it seemed time fast-motioned back twenty or so years, till I saw a younger Henry and his brother, David, as they, too, scurried in reverse, over the Iowa prairies, across the Mississippi River at Dubuque aboard a ferry, via Chicago back to Washtenaw County. After yet another spring backwards about two decades in time, I could see Henry as lad of eleven, toddler David and the whole family, zipping ever in reverse to Olde Buffalo, then shooting the wrong way on the Erie Canal as far as Albany, then riding behind the newly launched *DeWitt Clinton*, followed by retracing the boat ride back down the Hudson...

And so it went, branch by branch of my entire family tree, in quick succession, like rivulets of a dissipating stream concurrently fanned out across all of America—but in reverse, retreating backwards across space and time to the point at which each lineage first set foot on the shores of the New World.

*Gosh*, I marveled silently to my stunned self, *what's all this about!*

Mesmerized by this miracle, every historian's wildest dream, I watched as the map of North America changed design and color, as if I were observing a topographical heat-lightning storm of hues and lines shape and reshape the land of my birth. *Oh, that's right* I noted, *when the Luicks arrived, there was no state or even 'Republic' of Texas, only an outlaying Mexican province dubbed 'Tejas' we'd not yet wrestled from our southern neighbors.* In 1833 California, too, was merely a shimmer in Manifest-Destiny-drunken Yankees' covetous eyes. *Only my Danes, the land-hungry Juhls, came to an 'Amerika' that had factories* I reflected: *But, all the rest? They came well before the Civil War*—and so it went, until I'd dissected the state of my nation at the point when each branch of my ancestral family tree had stretched across the Atlantic and sunk new roots. *What a different land it was then* I tsk-tsked, *no standing army, no bloated bureaucracy, no corporate whores posing as public servants, feigning deadlock in order to headlock a coalescing folk into doing its will.*

At that moment my eyes opened slightly and I vaguely registered where I was: in a train, looking out a milky-glassed window over an ugly, gaudy suburban strip lined by big-box stores hawking junk; not in the heavens, looking down over an insular young republic waiting to become a globally-interconnected powerhouse. And, I remembered that I was headed for New York City, the United States' capital in fact, if not in name. I was enroute to America's gate, about to go out where most of my people had come in.

---

Already by the time of his death, Frederick Luick had become a quiet local celebrity, esteemed by many. Years later, his admiring nephew, Albert Lee Luick, continued to pay tribute to the man as:

**Without animals, life would have been impossible in 19th-century America.**

a very kind and humble person. He had a great love for all animals and, after coming to Iowa, he worked with his brothers in looking after their livestock and was able to accumulate a considerable number for himself. It is said of him that he never retired at night until he knew all his livestock had been fed and bedded down for the night.

After returning from the Civil War and his march with General Sherman through Georgia to the sea, he returned to take charge of his herd that his brother had kept intact for him. He soon married Alice Packard, the daughter of an early pioneer family[.] Working together, they established a farm just southeast of Belmond. Through their thrift, hard work and prudence, they developed one of the most successful livestock farms in this section of Iowa. They were very helpful to many worthy early settlers in helping them establish themselves in this community, and took a prominent part in civic betterment.

---

New York was a zoo—a colorful, fascinating, exhilarating human zoo, but a zoo, none the less. As soon as I stepped off the train, I saw in the first five minutes more diversity in human appearance and behavior than I'd seen in Iowa in the past five weeks. And, I loved it.

A Quaker friend of many years, Sally met me at Madison Square Garden—that cavernous "hell" that had so frightened me as an eight-year-old Iowa farmboy visiting Gotham, summer 1971. After a long, melting hug, we set off for the Upper West Side, where she and her hubbie Chuck (who I ironically call "Chuckles" when he isn't around) put me up that Memorial Day weekend of 2011. They also put up with me, as I—still tired and still wired—had solely one thing on my taxed mind: my pending emigration.

*WPA poster promoting theater in Harlem, late 1930s*

I had been gravitating towards this moment for a long time. Soon after Rock returned to Missouri in early January to resume teaching high-school chemistry, leaving me to face the misery of cleaning up the gutted Burr Oak Center on my own, I began having nightly dreams. Each seemed merely the latest installment in an unending series, sequels in an unfolding mystery: *What's to Become of Michael?*

The motif was always the same: I found my consistently bewildered Self scaling darkened stairways, up and up and up, leading me to rickety, pre-war attics above postwar Berlin. Like a hamster scrambling through a labyrinth, looking for a way out, via menacing stairs I hurried from attic to abandoned attic, at times over tiled rooves barely supporting my sweating weight, at other times with me straddling the peak of a bomb-pocked roof, looking like a wobbling trapeze artist eager to regain equilibrium, then scurry on. Each time, I had the vague feeling of being followed, but I could never make out by whom. I always spoke in German to anyone I encountered, even though I thought in English the whole time. And, when I awoke from these recurring scenarios, I always had the sense that *Something I* need *is back there—and I need that thing more than anything else. I* need *to go back to Germany: I can't get any longer what I need most, here.*

Strange thing was, a decade earlier, I'd had similar dreams while concluding my eight-year sojourn in Berlin—but instead of attics over the reinstated German capital, I rushed through haymow after haymow in scores of dusty, rustic Iowa barns, passing across fields of brittle, golden grain along the way. And, when I awoke from those recurring scenarios, I always had the sense that *Something I* need *is back there—and I need that thing more than anything else. I* need *to go back to Iowa: I can't get any longer what I need most, here.*

---

One of Fred and Alice's two sons, their dutiful heir Chester, followed his parents lead. Later in life, Chester became a benefactor of the community of Belmond by donating funds for the Luick Memorial Swimming Pool, as well as both the Luick Memorial Auditorium and Gymnasium, which are attached to the local high school. He also financially backed other civic improvements in Belmond, most notably what by this writing has become a state-of-the-art medical center in the middle of Main Street.

The closest thing to nobility on the equalitarian prairie, already as a young man Chester's projects, movements and developments keenly interested some local readers—such as those of this account of his and his first (of three) wife's wedding, as recounted in the *Belmond Herald* on 7 August 1918:

*Sarah Martha Griesy, likely early 1910s: She had an eventful life of her own. Her obituary in the Globe-Gazette, 17 June 1935, read: Mrs. C.P. Luick, 54, daughter of pioneer residents, died Sunday afternoon at her home after a lingering illness. She was born March 6, 1881, at Carroll, daughter of Mr. and Mrs. Val Griesy. In 1885 she came to Belmond, where her father was pioneer minister, banker, hardware merchant and served as mayor. She taught for several years. She first married George Lieuwen, who soon died.*

The wedding of Mrs. Sarah M. Griesy and Mr. C.P. Luick was solemnized last week Wednesday at the home of the bride's mother in Belmond. The ceremony was performed at five o'clock in the afternoon by Rev. S.U. Leinbach, a brother-in-law of the groom, in the presence of relatives of the contracting parties.

Following the ceremony the newlyweds were driven to Clarion by [Cato] G. Griesy, brother of the bride, and left on the Great Western train for Chicago and points of interest in the east. Following their return they will take up housekeeping in the beautiful new home being erected by the groom which is now nearing completion. To no recent wedding in this locality attaches such universal interest as to the just culminated because of the conspicuous prominence of the contracting parties and the high esteem in which they are both held by all of the people of the community among whom they have resided for many years.

The bride is the eldest daughter of Mrs. Val Griesy and has lived in the locality almost all her life. For many years she was an exceedingly proficient instructor in the local schools and in that time endeared herself to the children under her supervision as well as to the mothers of Belmond who entrusted their little tots, the idols of their hearts, to her patient care and tender ministrations. She possesses all those qualities of womanhood so much admired by an observing and critical public; a beautiful character, an even temperament, a splendid disposition and a spirit of unselfishness in the service of others. She is in every way fitted to become a most desirable helpmate and is worthy of every affection and consideration at the disposal of a devoted husband.

*election-campaign scene in front of the Griesy family's hardware store, Main Street, Belmond; circa 1920*

The groom is the eldest son of Mr. and Mrs. Fred Luick and is the junior member of the firm of F. Luick and Son, a firm well known throughout this part of the state as the owner and operators of extensive realty interests in this section. C.P. Luick is one of most prominent and respected citizens of Belmond. He has for many years been actively identified with the agricultural and commercial interests of Belmond and vicinity.

*Chester Packard Luick, mid-1890s*

*Chester's father, Fred, sat on the board of the State Bank of Belmond, shown at the far left. Despite his family's material wealth, though, personal happiness seemed to evade Chester P. Luick. He easily could afford, for example, sporty cars—but those same roadsters could be fatal, as seen in a Globe-Gazette death announcement on 9 August 1952: Mrs. Chester P. Luick, 67, who was injured in an automobile accident south of [a town to the north] Klemme Tuesday night in which Sanford L. Overlie of Thompson was killed, died at a hospital here Friday. Her husband, who also was injured in the crash, is reported [to be] getting along favorably at the hospital. [...] The Luicks won much renown last March when they deeded a 400-acre farm to the Belmond Community Hospital, the land being valued at $100,000. It was in this hospital that Mrs. Luick died. [...] Besides her husband, Mrs. Luick leaves two daughters.*

---

New York. Manhattan. Gotham City. The City that Never Sleeps... the Big Apple.

No other city in America is so antithetical, so alien to the agrarian life of my people—who, up until Ashlawn Farms' collapse in 1985, tilled New World soil for 355 years—nor played such a decisive role in our lives. With few exceptions, it was the gateway through which each branch of my extended family entered the fledgling colonies or, later, young federal republic that became the United States. And, on Memorial Day weekend, 2011, I felt keenly aware of my family's special relationship to this global city.

I stayed at 91st and Broadway with Sally and Chuck, yet as my people poured through early New York today's Upper West Side wasn't thought of. In fact, when the Luicks came through in 1833 Greenwich was a sleepy, separate village some distance from what's now Downtown. Further back, two centuries earlier, my Dutch ancestors who'd braved the

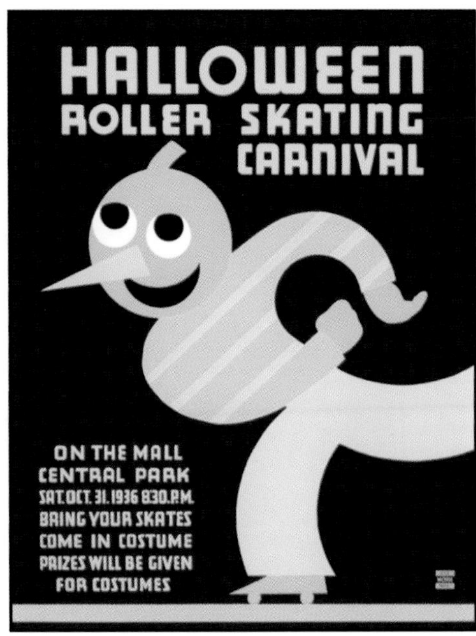


*WPA poster promoting Halloween party, late 1930s*

journey arrived in a Nieuw Amsterdam that ended at Wall Street—and thus the name: The tiny settlement's fortress-like first incarnation as an outpost of the European realm was an enclosed military installation with a fort, a wind mill, a few houses and some gardens.

Beyond a 4-H trip to Chicago and my parents' delayed honeymoon in New York in the mid-'50s, my nuclear family did not take "cultural excursions" to big cities; we avoided them. Unlike in Europe where it is a norm for middle-class families to purposely venture to a given city for an extended stay in order to explore its top tourist attractions as well as the backstreets which house its very soul, we rural Heartlanders shied from facing our little limits in large urban areas. For various reasons, however, New York served as the one exception—and its foreignness for us was exactly what drew us to it.

The first two times I came to Manhattan on my own, as a young adult, the place literally exhausted me: By the time I extracted myself from it and fled via train to Boston or, later, bus to Vermont, I felt emotionally strained and physically drained. The city's endless activity, its 24-seven street scene, its pulsating with everything imaginable—and much more that had been unimaginable for me before I got to know it in New York—overwhelmed my ability to integrate so much that contradicted all I'd ever known or valued. It challenged the persona I thought of as my own; it dared me to see our world anew

The third time I came, however, I was ready to be shocked—and loved it. By then, I'd navigated three years of undergraduate study at what I dismissed as "Iowa Straight" University in quiet, tidy Ames, then lived four years in a commune in loud, tatty Whittier, an inner-city neighborhood flanking downtown Minneapolis. And, I'd launched my graduate studies at Vermont's funky Goddard College. Yes, I came hungry: I wanted to absorb all I could before advancing to my next stage in Life—which soon after my teaching internship began at Friends Academy on Long Island, I found out would be a teaching post with the Peace Corps in post-communist, now-non-existent Czechoslovakia.

This time, though, even if—once again—Gotham was a transit station for someone in my family, it was the first time as far as any of the people I knew knew, that a Luick or Thrams, an Ehrhardt or Falcon, Moorehead or Juhl had ventured to New York enroute to live again in the Old World. As daunting as I found the prospect of emigrating, of leaving behind everything and starting over again with nothing, I saw no other choice. Like my people before me, chopping my own tap root seemed my only option left. Ironically, while Heinrich Luick fled Swabia on the heels of committing a capital offense, I was fleeing Iowa after incurring a moral crime committed by a local heel.

For a fleeting weekend, I'd savor all the Big Apple had to offer me—I'd enjoy my country's capital as much as my distracted self could—then, on Memorial Day Monday, I'd get on a ship and sail away.

*WPA poster promoting opening of the U.S.' first Foreign Trade Zone on Staten Island, New York, 1 February 1937*

———

The "Belmond and vicinity" area referred to in the swooning feature about Chester Packard Luick's and Sarah Martha Griesy's marriage wasn't the only place that "agricultural interests" were key to turn-of-the-century Midwest culture—and to the larger Luick clan. The only son of Heinrich and Katherine (Gerstenmaier) Luick not to make the move from the Big Woods to the endless prairie was John, who stayed behind in Michigan, where he farmed a modest 110 acres while fathering nine children—five of whom he gave the names of his brothers or sister, who were all the way out in Ioway.

*John Luick, 1890s*

John (who sometimes let his name be spelled as "Lewick" on public records ) visited his five siblings in the Hawkeye State repeatedly, yet the geographical distance between him and them meant that while he periodically could orbit around the other Luicks, he could not be a close, consistent part of the dynamic local energy field they comprised in Belmond. When John died, his terse obituary in the *Greenville Independent* on 3 April 1907 seemed to confirm the modest life he had lived compared to that of Henry, David, William, Katherine and Frederick—likely one much different from that he would have had, had he taken the leap and joined them in the rest of his family's frontier adventure. Still,

> Another old pioneer [was] gone. John Luick died at his home in Belding Wednesday morning, March 20, after a painful illness of several months duration, aged 78 years. He was born in Germany. He was an honest, hard working man and had lived in Otisco 62 years. He was the father of 9 children, 4 sons and 5 daughters, all but one of whom survive him and were present at his funeral. He also leaves an aged wife [Louisa, who died in 1924]. Funeral was at his home in Belding Friday, interment in Otisco Cemetery.

———

On Memorial Day Monday I got up too early, got Sally up too late, then somehow got my eight bags into a New York taxi and hurriedly set off for Newark, New Jersey. But, Luickly, the streets were empty.

As the Iranian taxi driver provided a rolling narrative about the cityscapes dashing past outside the window, I held Sally's hand and stared forward. *This is it; there's no turning back: I'm really leaving now.*

After the taxi emerged on the Jersey side of the Holland Tunnel and finally found the docks from which I was to depart, I turned, studied Sally's face and waited for her to say "Don't go; stay"—but, her lips remained silent and still. Lacking a bid to remain, I cracked open the door, paid the driver, then pried my too many bags out of the back of the mini-van. As Sally hugged me, then got back into the vehicle, rode off along the busy dock and then disappeared among the many workers and moving containers, I felt numb and nauseous. Luckily, a crew member recognized me as one of the three passengers booked to board and soon an assortment of Philippine

*container ship like the one on which I crossed the Atlantic, summer 2011* sailors were slinging my eight groaning suitcases over their tanned, muscly backs like so many bags of down feathers or puffed rice. Realizing that my boarding was now complete other than me walking my own body onto the big boat, I lurched into motion and scaled the gangway, no longer allowing myself to wistfully look backwards: I *had* to look forward now.

The Philippine sailor with the widest, warmest smile showed me to the cabin which would be mine. At $1,600—so, a hundred bucks day for food, lodging and passage—it was no steal. Supposedly, my late booking meant the only cabin left was the most expensive one, but desperation can force even the most destitute hand. *At least* I consoled my bruised self, *I have a luxurious space to spend two weeks to begin to heal, holed up in a floating tin can*. As the ship would not set sail for another hour, I unpacked essentials, set up a writing desk beneath a portal window and generally settled in for a long, slow trip.

Lost in my emotional haze, suddenly a bottomless whistle blew and I could feel the *Hanjin Palermo* lurch into motion. With that, we were off—and I was mortified. Still, I made my way to the deck and looked out over the busy waters of coastal New York-New Jersey. Too soon, I watched with a sinking heart as first Lady Liberty, then the piercing skyline of Lower Manhattan, even the mammoth Verrazano Narrows Bridge grew tiny and then, sans ceremony or another mortal to share the occasion, vanished.

With only the cliffs of South Jersey still in view, I retreated to my cabin, fell onto into the oversized bed, closed my eyes and wondered how I'd ever survive a fortnight at sea. For a few minutes, I pictured my European ancestors crammed into windowless steerage, headed to *Amerika*, hoping to survive the weeks-, even months-long crossing. When I remembered that they'd somehow survived on dried, salted and pickled "food" for the duration, I felt ashamed of my own carpeted spoiledness. Unlike them, I most likely wouldn't contract a deadly disease and be buried at sea, a thin corpse wrapped in a sheet, simply slid over the nearest railing to plop into the dark waters below and left to sink into the waiting abyss. I felt humbled for a moment, realizing how bad they'd had it and how good I actually had it.

Then, despite being mindful of my good fortune yet still immobilized by an emotional cocktail of dread spiked with hefty doses of self-pity, sleep mercifully overtook me. For the first time in ages, I fell into a deep slumber as that big hulk of a ship carried my weary body across the ocean, towards *Europa*.

---

While not nearly as monetarily wealthy as his uncle Fred and cousin Chester Luick, Michael Henry Luick clearly possessed riches money could never buy. For one, the mate he chose shared a common life with him for ten days short of six decades. Together, they parented a handful of children who reportedly were close both to their father and mother, as well as each other. And, if texts written about him by others can be trusted, he earned the confidence and esteem of the community his family had founded.

Michael married Sarah Jane (Lathrop) Baker, daughter of Zebadiah and Maria (Thatcher) Lathrop, on 18 October 1864 in Belmond. Sarah was the widow of John Baker, who was killed in a Civil War battle in Tennessee; they had a son, John D. Baker. When she married Michael, he took John as his own but never adopted him, perhaps out of respect for John's father. Michael seemed to have been a kindly man—as reflected in an uncited feature about him, likely from the teens or early 1920s:

*Henry Michael Luick, 1910s*

> Michael Henry Luick, well-known farmer, extensive stock raiser and prominent citizen of Belmond Township, Wright County, Iowa, was born in January 22, 1844. [He] received his education in the public schools of Wright County and in a subscription school conducted by Isadore Fisk, the first school teacher of Wright County. After his school days, Michael H. Luick became a farmer, working with his father until 1864, when he bought forty acres of land near the home place, which he improved with primitive buildings and where he lived as a farmer. He has prospered and is now the owner of seven hundred and eighty acres of well improved land, on which he engages in general agricultural pursuits.

Michael and Sarah later divided up their land, giving a farm to each of the children and keeping one for themselves. In his last years, widowed Michael lived with daughter Mignonette, who never married. Still, as long as he farmed, he remained active—especially in the business and art of animal husbandry.

> Michael Henry Luick makes a specialty of stock raising, feeding each year about seven carloads of cattle and sheep and from one hundred to one hundred and fifty head of hogs. The farm of Michael Henry is one of the most valued and best improved of the county: in all, this progressive farmer has spent about twenty thousand dollars for improvements. [...]

*"A.M. Olson" farm as captioned by Martin Thoe, circa late 1910s; dregs of snowbanks seen on the left*

> Michael Henry Luick and his family are members of the Methodist Episcopal Church, a congregation which Michael has served as steward and trustee. In politics he is an independent Republican. He is a Mason of the Belmond lodge since 1869, and past noble grand of the Independent Order of Odd Fellows.

---

On the last morning that I awoke aboard the *Hanjin Palermo*, as I opened my eyes I remembered *Hey! Today's the day...* so rushed to shower, then join my two co-passengers I'd befriended along the way for a last breakfast together at sea.

When I entered the German captain's and crew's dining room, I found short, plump Marie (a social worker from Quebec who was setting off on a year-long world tour) and tall, lanky Andy (a physicist from Virginia who at that time worked among Cambridge's Stephen Hawking) waiting for me. "We wondered if you'd ever get up" they sang in unison as I ran through the door. "We're just finishing" Andy noted. "Come 'n" Marie offered, "we're 'eaded to za raileen to watch za ship come into za port."

With that, we arrived in the Old World, as if it were just an ordinary day. For me, it was anything but.

A friend, Holm, was waiting for me in Bremerhaven. As we drove towards Bremen, we had much to talk about, but I found it hard to focus on anything other than the presence of a road. And trees. And houses. After two weeks on the ocean, with only the sighting of an occasional school of dolphins or a whale breaching in front of the ship, the most mundane things now seemed rare, precious sights.

We spent the night in the commune of a friend of Holm's, going into the *Altstadt* after we settled in so I could find my land legs and marvel at the beauty of that coastal city carefully rebuilt after The War.

On the next day, we took English-challenged French-speaking Marie along with us to Kassel. There, I was to spend the summer in Villa Locomuna, an urban commune in a massive house—once the 1920s-built, Spanish-baroque showcase of a Jewish margarine manufacturer ousted by the Nazis—where a mutual friend of Holm's and mine lived. I felt expressly grateful, for I had stepped off that container ship with 55 Euros in my pocket. Not wanting to be dependent on the generosity of others any longer than necessary, one of the first things I did after Marketa—a Czech woman who I later discovered had had an affair with Cynthia, a beautiful Jewish woman from Boston with whom I'd taught in disintegrating Czechoslovakia while in the Peace Corps, some two decades earlier—showed me my room was to call that very-British man in *Schwaben* with the job offer. Within minutes of reaching Maurice Peters, we agreed that I'd come to Engelberg ("Angel's Mountain") a month hence for an interview. Although it was not certain that I'd get the position, when I hung up the phone I sensed I would.

As Maurice was returning from Italy with his wife the day I arrived to meet the English-teaching staff, the about-to-retire instructor's colleague, Peg Flora, picked me up from the station in Winterbach. A thin woman with a severe appearance, she limply shook my hand, then we jumped into her car and zipped up the *Berg* to what she informed me along the way was Europe's largest Waldorf schools, size-wise. With her string of fake pearls, tight preppy sweater tied around her narrow neck, preppy slacks and tight preppy shoes, I was unsure what to make of this frail-looking woman who seemed to be sixty.

Any puzzlement over my would-be new colleague evaporated as Peg and I pulled onto the schools' parking lot, for the moment we did I realized I'd been there before! Over Easter break 1982, Eugen Luick had brought green young me for a tour of the school his and Elisabeth's son Wolfgang and, by coincidence, Karl and Ruth Luicks' son Jochen had attended in previous years. Now, 29 years later, that I should find myself about to take a position as a teacher of my native tongue in that very school seemed astonishing—even more so, as I'd randomly submitted a generic cover letter and resume to it, along with some fifty others that I sent to private schools of all kinds across Germany. That this, the sole one that responded positively, should be only sixteen kilometers (ten miles) over the hill that arises behind Esslingen, my father's people's hometown on the Neckar, left me utterly flabbergasted. Algebraically, what were the chances that one Luick out of thousands who lived in faraway America should land a job in a country of eighty million, only a few minutes' drive from where our family had originated? One in...?

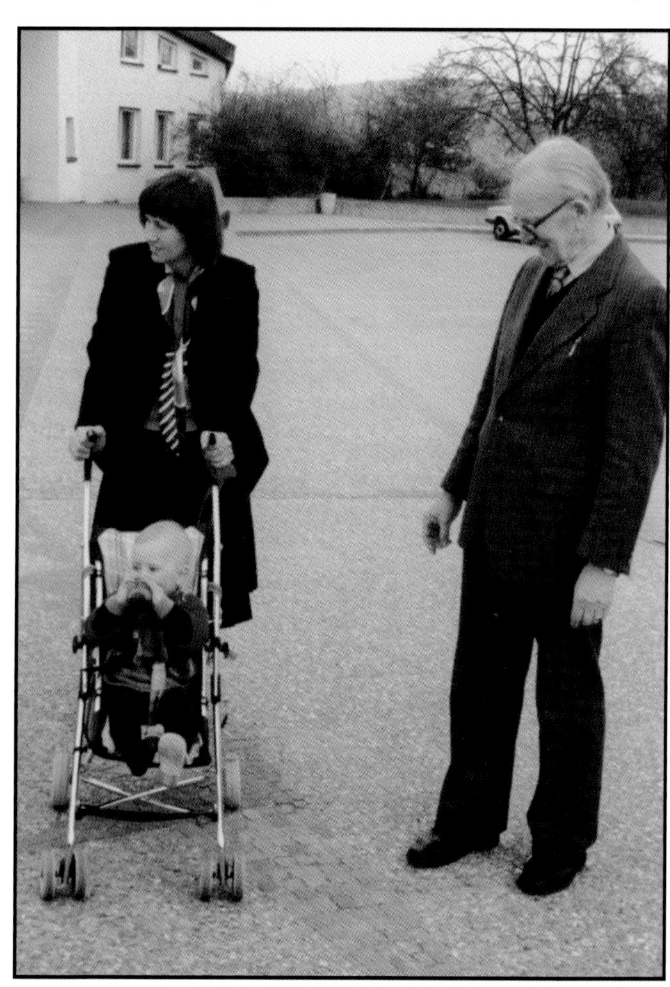

*Saskia Luick, with mother and grandfather, Eugen; April 1982: I had no idea I'd one day teach at the school seen in the back.*

*Had the* Empire Builder *been there then, as planned* I marveled to myself, *I would not be here, now.*

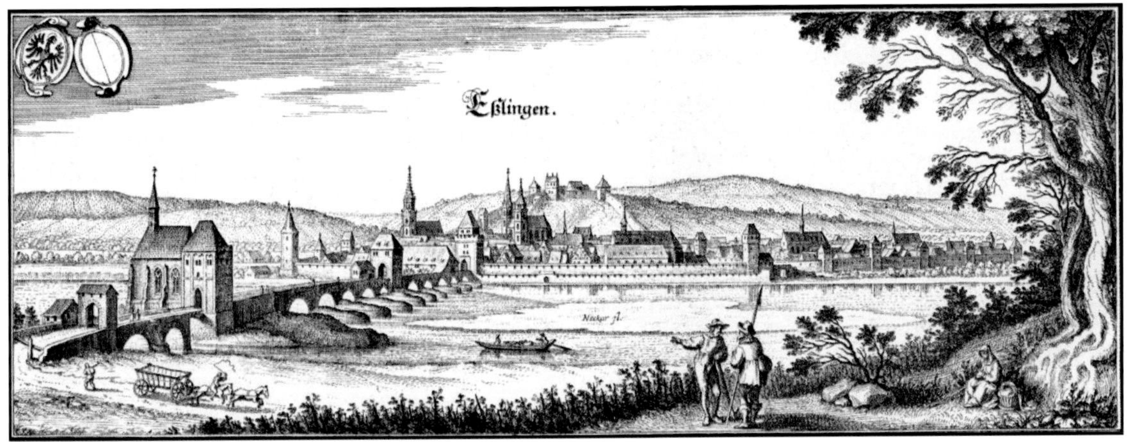


*Esslingen as engraved in the mid-1600s by Matthäus Merians (1595-1650) in his* Topographia Suaviae

---

It seems that the people of North Central Iowa—or at least the region's journalists—never tired of extolling the accomplishments and attributed virtues of the area's earliest settlers. Only months after Wall Street crashed in fall 1929, as the nation faced increasing uncertainty and looked perceptible doom in the eye—maybe, *because* it did so—on 28 February 1930, Mason City's *Globe-Gazette* published yet another tribute to Michael Henry Luick and family. Perhaps sensing hard times were settling upon the country, some local biographer sought inspiration in home-grown tales of hard times of days of yore:

> To M. H. Luick, resident of Wright County, the most noteworthy advancement of the country during his 76 years of life in this community has been the development of communication.
>
> Mr. Luick came to this vicinity in 1858, camping the first night on the edge of Franklin Grove, Sept 8. This part of the state had not been surveyed at that time. Leaving their Washtenaw County, Michigan homes near Ann Arbor, these early pioneers came by rail to Chicago. From there they came by covered wagons to Dubuque, crossing the Mississippi on ferry. Their route took them through Rock Grove to Clear Lake. Two wagons made up the caravan. In the group were Anson Grey and family of six children, Anthony Overacker and family of two, Miss Cramer, sister of Mr. Overacker, and David Luick and his brother Henry, who had a family of four.
>
> In 1852, Henry Luick, the father, with Anthony Overacker, together with David Luick had taken claims where Algona now stands and also at Spirit Lake. Due to trouble between the Sioux and Winnebago tribes, they concluded to throw up their claims, and because of the warnings that had been given them by the Indians, they started to make their way back home. At Franklin Grove near where they camped the first night a year later, they found evidence of civilization and later met a man named Beebe near the [corrected: Iowa] River. They purchased his claim for $10. It consisted of all of the land one could see from the highest tree. Beebe had been frightened by the Indians and decided to get out of the country with his possessions. He had built a small cabin of poles covered with bark. In addition, he had made himself a dug-out. Nearby was a beaver dam at the mouth of the Franklin Grove Creek where it emptied into the Iowa River. Beebe, a trapper, had found plenty of mink, otter, beaver, and other valuable fur.
>
> The next year, 1853, the pioneers came back with their families and proceeded to make this their home. It was a hard battle from then on, their nearest market at that time being Dubuque. Later the railroad came as far as Jesup, then Cedar Falls, but going to market was not a happy journey for there were no bridges between home and market except a beaver dam bridge near Cedar Falls. Trees were found along streams so that it was a trackless trip at best.
>
> In times of blizzards, it was extremely hazardous, for it did not take much for an Iowa wind unhampered by stalk field or wind break to make a real blizzard out of nothing. Necessarily, the trip took many days

with oxen. Usually the homecoming was eagerly awaited by the whole neighborhood for generally there was something for every family from castor oil to provisions.

Early in 1853, hostilities broke out anew between the Sioux and Winnebago Indians. Breastworks were thrown up just northwest of Franklin Grove, and Mr. Luick remembers quite well picking up arrows and other implements of war. The Winnebagoes, assisted by the state troops, pushed the Sioux to the northwest part of the state. In the spring of 1857, this tribe massacred the white settlers near Spirit Lake. The news reached the settlements slowly but in each case so alarmed them that they took steps to protect their lives. The Belmond settlers organized themselves into a military company and erected a mud fort on the west side of the Iowa River, and gathered the women and children into one cabin but the Indians did not arrive. Guards were sent out to the settlement along the Boone River to get the news. Likewise, a group came from the east of Hampton. Mr. Luick relates how frightened he was when he saw them in single file coming over a hill from the east. News spread rapidly in the neighborhood that the Indians were coming in single file. They were agreeably surprised to find them their white neighbors to the east.

On Oct. 18, 1864, Mr. Luick was married to Mrs. Sarah Baker, a young widow whose husband had been killed in the Civil War. To the union have been born three children, Adelbert, Minnie and Jessie, all living. Mr. Luick has been able to add to his stock of knowledge in the school of experience. He boasts that in over 70 years he has never been away from his original home more than four weeks. He has always taken a deep interest in community affairs. He is an Odd Fellow and enjoys the distinction of being a 50-year Mason and the oldest member in point of membership.

---

In late August 2011 I bid a bittersweet farewell to my friends at Villa Locomuna in Kassel. Holm came from the rural commune he lived in, in an old mill near Bodenwerder, and retrieved me and my eight suitcases with a borrowed van. Then, we set off for Engelberg—the main drag of which is "Esslingerstrasse." With that move, I felt I had come home—178 years after the Luicks had left that ancient *Reichsstadt*, that medieval "imperial city" on the Neckar. Problem was my people had known another Esslingen—as had I.

*Photos of modern Esslingen reveal an ancient city nestled in the forward movement of 21st-century Europe.*

Over thirty years I had visited "the other Luicks" at least a dozen times. Each time, I enjoyed being in the timeworn city and its environs. I admired my German relatives' and their neighbors' industriousness, thrift and seriousness. I also, though, experienced Esslingen as a quaint open-air museum, with actors in modern garb who were living a contemporary version of the life the Luicks who relocated to America

Still, despite the encroachment of modern technologies, social trends and political developments that few seem able to steer—let alone fully comprehend—at present, during the year I lived in contemporary *Schwaben* I came to believe that we alive today are blessed with the best Germany the world has ever known. Now spared the excesses of a conceited Kaiser, a hysterical Hitler or an ideologically-hamstrung Honecker, we all gain from a peaceable superpower in the heart of Europe which, while not perfect, is a voice of moderation on a planet consumed by regional disasters and extremist, warring factions. For me, with its lack of real material poverty, its protective social infrastructures that guarantee all residents a decent minimal standard of living, its diversity of political opinions and parties, its colorful cultural scene and its citizens' general satisfaction, despite a tumultuous past the wanting land that once was the home of my people now serves as a global role model for living the Good Life—a role once unquestionably and for so long played by the United States.

*a tower of the former town wall; the "Old City Hall;" exterior & interior views of the two main churches*

---

The glowing public assessments of Michael Henry Luick's person continued for years—for the last time in his obituary, published in the *Belmond Herald* on 4 August 1931. The piece carried the headline:

***County's Oldest Settler Starts on Last Long Trail.***
***M.H. Luick, Sturdy Pioneer, Passed Away Tuesday Afternoon.***

> The community is mourning the passing of another pioneer, the oldest settler left in Wright County, M. H. Luick, who passed away at his home northeast of Belmond about five o'clock Tuesday evening.
>
> Mr. Luick was born near Ann Arbor, Mich., January 22, 1844 and came to Belmond with his parents in 1853. He was nine year old at the time. What a vast change in this country, Mr. Luick has witnessed and could bring to mind! He had known all the hardships of pioneer life. Also, the joys and pleasures and neighborliness of those days, for which we do not seem to have time in the fast age in which we are now living. Mr. Luick told the following story of his first piece of land.
>
> "My wife and I worked for my parents the first year after our marriage for our board and 40 acres of land at a price $10 for an old log barn, and in '65 moved it onto our 40 acres of wild prairie land, thus beginning our first home. My first team I got in this way. When a lad I husked corn for my uncle David Luick, and earned a calf. I later earned $2.00 and bought another calf. These two calves were traded for colt. This colt was traded for a better one and by borrowing a horse from my neighbor, I had my first team. My first field was four acres of grain, two acres of wheat and two acres of oats."
>
> Everyone knew Mr. Luick as a most unselfish, and kindhearted man. His every thought was for others. He was quiet and unpretentious, but his deeds of kindness were many. He was always devoted to his home and family and was never away from home but a few short times. His wife passed away Oct. 8, 1924.

> Mr. Luick had only 20 months of schooling, but he was always an interested student of the topics of the day. He was a man of clear vision and a strong mind, and these he retained to the last day of his life. His health was fairly good up to the beginning of hot weather, when the heat effected his heart, and he began to fail steadily until the end came, Tuesday evening.
>
> Funeral services will be held at the home at two o'clock this afternoon in charge of Rev. S. U. Leinbach.

*Sarah (Lathrop) Baker Luick, 1910s*

Michael Henry Luick's devoted mate, Sarah, however, had garnered much less notice when she died—as seen in the obituary about her life and passing in the *Belmond Herald* on 10 October 1924:

> One of the pioneer settlers of Wright County, Mrs. Sarah J. Luick, wife of M.H. Luick, died Wednesday morning at her home a mile northwest of Belmond. Mrs. Luick was 83 years of age, and death resulted from a gradual decline. If she had lived until Oct 18, she and Mr. Luick would have celebrated their sixtieth marriage anniversary. Mrs. Luick was one of the old pioneers who rode in the covered wagon at the pageant given "Homecoming Day" last August.

---

Eager to share my year of living in my family's historical *Heimat*, our homeland in *Schwaben*, I invited my mother to spend a month with me in spring 2012. Based out of my cozy digs on "Angel Mountain," we toured Southern Germany from Bodensee, at the foot of the Swiss Alps, to Kassel, in North Hessen.

And, exactly thirty years after my first visit to Esslingen, we took part in a Luick-family reunion that I had organized before Mom's arrival by combing Deutsche Telekom's on-line phone book for every Luick in its directory. Fielding a good yield of *"ja"* responses over several exciting evenings of cold calling, on Easter Monday some fifty Luick relatives gathered at Galerie 13, the private gallery run by Eugen Luick's now-aged adult children, Wolfgang and Margrit, and Wolfgang's artist daughter, Saskia. Housed in a big, half-timbered *Haus* built in 1362, on our reunion day that massive building was full of Luick life. The sole non-Germans among a gathering representing about ten percent of all Luicks alive today in Germany, we two souls comprising the Iowa delegation felt particularly pleased to be part of this one-time event.

*Margrit & Michael Luick, Eastertime 1982, and with her niece Saskia & brother Wolfgang Luick, on Easter Monday, 2012; Saskia in her stroller, in the parking lot of the Waldorf school in Engelberg, Eastertime 1982*

As several, till-then-mostly-unknown Luick kin had brought along assorted German *Kuchen* to share, between servings of delicious cakes and generous glasses of bubbly *Sekt* or cups of rich *Kaffee*, those present took turns offering summaries of the resumes of each branch of the Luick tribe, with short vignettes. One by one, representatives of a half-dozen or so divisions of the larger clan gave accounts of events or experiences that had helped mold their end of our extended family into what it is today.

What our Luick relatives shared varied, yet identifiable themes did emerge, as did an assembly of apparent coincidences, of tragedies, absurdities and miracles that deeply colored and forever cast our collective fates. Unexpectedly, I had the sense that our belonging to one, oddly-named family had real, deep value for each of those present, despite any visible or biographical differences—which were many:

Our differing experiences ranged from the amusing and anecdotal, to the inspiring and substantial. Rainer Luick, for one, discovered upon taking possession of his room as a foreign biology graduate student at the University of Michigan in Ann Arbor in 1981-82 that a commercial building next to his bore the name "Luick." He later learned that it once belonged to the Luick Brothers Lumber Company. Given the rarity of our shared surname, he found that expressly intriguing. When I explained to him that "the American Luicks" had first settled in the Big Woods of Southeast Michigan before pushing on, a generation later, to the vast prairies of North Central Iowa, he smiled and nodded as he registered the unlikely yet tangible connections between Luicks in the Old World and those now in the New.

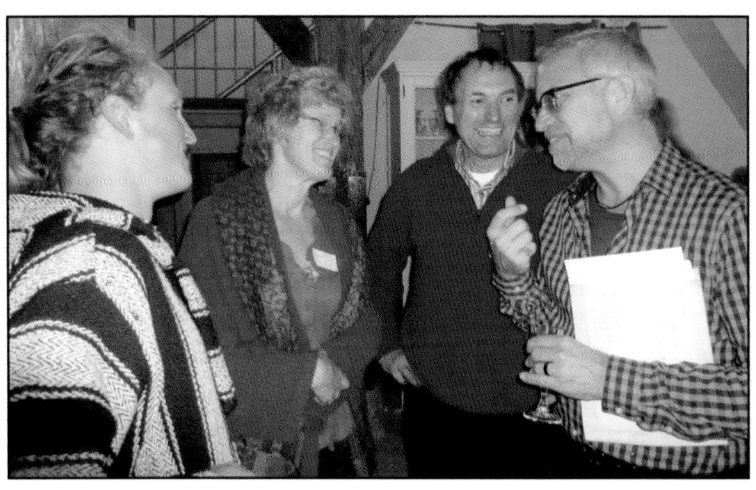

*Joris, mother Sabine Korn, father Rainer Luick & Michael Luick-Thrams*

As a young man living in the West Germany of the 1970s, Rainer had been free to study and to travel wherever he wished. Not all Luicks alive during the Cold War, however, could:

*George Garrigues shot a view of the Wall while on vacation in Berlin in August 1977. On 5 January 1990, two East-German border soldiers inspected a hole in the disappearing wall, near the Reichstag parliament building.*

Through some now-obscure fate, one outlier of the larger Luick diaspora found itself at the end of The War on the Baltic coast. As the Soviet Red Army pushed back Hitler's forces, those Luicks fled west—but, being on foot, pulling their few remaining possessions with them in handcarts, they only got as far as what, after the guns finally fell silent, became the so-called German Democratic Republic, the communist-controlled "East Germany" Aunt Jeandelle had pointed out to me on that dime-store globe Gramma Luick presented me one Christmas. As we listened to the somber tales of the children and grandchildren of those who had suffered the longest from the failed Nazi project once the dust from its destruction had settled, the rest of us shook our heads and *tsk-tsk*ed, but felt grateful that we had been spared that whole, absurd communist experiment. Happily, at least our East-German cousins could report that after the fall of the Berlin Wall they were allowed to travel freely, far and wide—and did.

Other branches of the family also had tales of travel abroad—of emigration to Argentina, of extensive trips across Western Canada or Eastern Europe, and of years-long stints working with AIDS patients in deepest Africa. Perhaps a self-selective group, those present seemed prosperous and well-established in their respective lives. As a group, our relations seemed to be solid, substantial characters. Even though I did not yet know that Jochen's great-grandfather—also named "Karl Luick"—had once marched through the streets of Meißenheim, sword drawn to defend Prussian order against even his drunken sons, I could see that those assembled were strong personalities, with pronounced traits.

*Ja* I editorialized to myself silently, *a whole pack o' 'alpha dogs,' each bearing the last name 'Luick.'* If I think of pioneer-trapper David Luick off on his own, gathering pelts 'til some natives strip and humiliate him; of off-duty cop Jennifer Luick in suburban Milwaukee, pinching some rough's butt on a crowded dancefloor; of Henry Luick instigating a "county-seat war" or stealing a neighbor's wife, twice; or, of my own care-to-the-wind dare-devilry during repeated wanderings over the whole globe the past thirty-five years, I can only conclude *We Luicks like to live intensely, deeply and widely, no matter what the risks.*

*Iris and Jochen, with his now-deceased father Karl and me in April 1982, and in April 2012 posing with Ulla, wife of Karl's cousin, Günther Luick, and with Jochen's sister Ursula (Luick) Bodenstein and their American cousin Michael*

Any lingering influences from worldwide travels or primal DNA strands, though, pale in proportion to the long shadows of war that so deeply defined the experiences of 20th-century descendants of those Luicks who chose not to leave all they had ever known and set off to lands unknown. Either as eager or as unenthusiastic soldiers in Hitler's Wehrmacht, Luick men fought to advance the Nazi project, from the steppes of Russia in the east, to the coasts of Brittany in the west—even as Luick boys from the Midwest shot at or, later, captured their German cousins. Decidedly against the "new order" imposed upon all Germans living in the Third Reich, Eugen Luick—for one—served his nation, even if it had gone astray. He was not, however, the only artistic young Luick male to wear a German uniform in the largest armed conflict the world has ever known. As his daughter Richarda (Luick) Grözinger related her father's story, I found fascinating the existence of a second artistic Luick cousin alive and active in the last century.

*How could it be* I pondered as I heard about the man, *that one family could give rise to two artists, cousins?* Another German cousin, Markus (like me a '62 baby), serves as a lay pastor in his church—as does my brother David, who plays a parallel role in his Minnesota congregation, as do my five nephews and nieces, all of whom have served in pastoral or missionary roles in the U.S. and abroad. *Do Luicks have a propensity, a 'need' to tap art or religion as ways to interpret the world* I mused, *and if so, what does that say about us as a family, a people genetically connected albeit living on separate continents?*

*Otto Luick, with mother Maria Anna (Prim), father Wilhelm, sister Maria and brother Gustav: older sisters Sophie and Anna were edited from this 1910 family pose; self-portrait by artist, with wife Gertrud in background*

Whatever the answer, I saw parallels that I could only interpret as telling:

My great-x4-grandfather, Heinrich Luick, was the son of a *Schneidermeister*, a master tailor. A century later his future, distant cousin Otto Luick was the son of a *Schuhmachermeister*, a master shoemaker. Otto's father, August Wilhelm, wanted his second son to follow in his trade; while Otto's older brother, Gustav, coalesced, Otto would have none of it: He was determined to become an artist—and in 1926 earned a coveted place in the Staatliche Akademie der bildenden Künste Stuttgart.

Around the time Otto entered the German army in 1940, he married a fellow artist, Gertrud Conrad, and began a family: He and his wife eventually had three girls. Between the births of their first and second daughters, the war ended—and aspiring artist Otto Luick found himself a prisoner of war in newly-liberated France, together in a camp with Otto Dix, the renown *Neue Sachlichkeit* painter once decried by the Nazi regime for his grotesque but honest depictions of war's brutality and senselessness.

Once fate demoted Otto from occupier to prisoner, he found himself in a surrealistic setting. He and Dix generated art that reflected what they saw around them: But, even as the fed their souls, they were unable to feed their stomachs. In the end, emaciated and sickly, Otto was reported to have died—an erroneous rumor that first confused, then when countered relieved his anxious, waiting family. The true story of the fate that had befallen him was much more complicated and colorful than a simple death:

> The capitulation on 8 May 1945 was for many German soldiers the beginning of months or even years of imprisonment. My father, too, was taken prisoner, in France.
>
> In 1939, Otto Luick was drafted into the Wehrmacht. At the time, he was 34 years old and had just finished building his house and studio atop the Neckarhalde, just above the Esslinger vineyards. He experienced World War II as a soldier in France. On 20 March the French Army freed all of Alsace; he was imprisoned at the POW camp in Colmar in spring 1945. By 19 April all important towns in Württemberg were occupied and according to reports 1,800 prisoners were taken on 18 April alone. It's well possible, that my father was one of them. In his sketchbook there is an ink drawing of destroyed Pforzheim dated 17 April, while on the next page there is a drawing of the camp in Colmar dated 11 May.
>
> The camp was called *Camp des prisonniers de l'Axe* ("Axis POW Camp"). It can be assumed, that there were around 7000 prisoners in the camp, a *Reservoire*, a transit point. Forty percent of the men were

permanently in the camp because they were sick and weakened, and therefore not able to work. The others were sent to work on farms or used for civil or military missions, such as searching for land mines.

As a camp site the French Military Administration used a spinning and weaving mill on the banks of a stream, the Logelbach, in the vineyards 4km south of Colmar. It was a five-story building, built between 1824-1826 and considered the most beautiful spinning mill in the whole of France because of its special oak interior. There was no heating and the prisoners slept on the floor. The biggest problem, however, was the terrible famine; I quote the camp doctor Dr. Heussen: "We lost 4 to 5 prisoners every day."

Despite these difficult circumstances two remarkable institutions were established in the camp. There was a "room for the painters". Artists among them were my father Otto Luick, Peter Jakob Schober (a painter from Stuttgart), Hermann Berges (a sculptor from Werl), Lajos Cziraki (a Hungarian painter) and 53-year old Otto Dix, who was drafted into the "Volkssturm" in March '45. This group of artists was used for painting jobs, such as large street posters with De Gaulles' portrait for the liberation festivities.

The second institution was an evangelical [Lutheran] and Catholic chapel on the top floor of the camp building, which was looked after by two imprisoned clergymen. Otto Dix painted a triptych with the title *Madonna in front of barbed wire and debris* for the Catholic camp chapel. This Madonna was never put up in the camp chapel, however; it was generally assumed in the camp, that camp commander Rueff took the three-piece painting. Thereupon, Dix painted a second version of his Madonna without the two side pieces of Peter and Paul. This painting was then put up in the chapel.

Dix also made a portrait of my father. This drawing is the preliminary study for a painting called *Portrait of a POW*, which is in possession of the Unterlinden Museum in Colmar.

*Otto Dix' sketch of Otto Luick as a starving prisoner of war; Otto Luick's 1945 painting,* The Steadfast Column

When Otto's youngest daughter, Richarda, had concluded recounting how The War had dictated the course of her father's and, thus, her whole family's resume, Margrit Luick stepped forward and told her father Eugen's story of surviving the bombing of Dresden. As she did, I noticed Rainer's college-age son, Juris, translating for my mother, who sat at the back of the room, absorbing as much as she could of his partial, imperfect summary. Of the bits I heard, it seemed Mom was getting served fare full of "war" every few words, mixed with a sprinkling of "devastation" and "death," topped with a touch of "despair." As I watched her expression fade from a slight smile to sober sadness, I felt keenly aware how fortunate we New-World Luicks had been to be spared the Old's serial slaughters.

At some point, not wanting to distract from Margrit's moving account, I slowly made my w2ay back to Phyllis as unobtrusively as I could to check if all was well with her. Unable to easily ford the last few meters of jumbled laps and legs, I stood still and mouthed the words "Are you OK?" as I pointed as part of my mime. At that, the Iowa farm girl who had grown up on a steady diet of hawk, fed to her by Hitler & Co. and his Allied foes, simply wagged her joyless face. Knowing her longer and better than most mortals, I could "hear" her unarticulated words: *How could all this be? It's all so sad and horrible—and so, so tragic.* Her sentiments reflected my own. *Was all that 'necessary?' Might it have been avoided?*

Having researched a sub-chapter of the wider World War II drama as a dissertation, I'd long before become inured to stories such as she was digesting now—remembrances of how her dead husband's kin had experienced The War from "the other side." As a girl, my mother spent recess with her classmates combing nearby ditches for milkweed silk and collected scrap metal or bomb-bound kitchen fat with which to "whip the Germans." Now, for the first time in her life, she was (re-)living The War through their "enemy" eyes. *It's good for her* I told myself: *It's time Mom learn a bit about what it's like, to not be an American—and the hollowness of the term, 'enemy.'* And, this time she didn't have to "whip the Germans:" She was in a room full of them, doing that to themselves—decades, generations later.

Suddenly—before Mom and I could swap any more telepathy—something Margrit was saying caught my attention. "My father," the retired teacher was explaining, "painted likely the last likeness of Dresden's intact *Frauenkirche*. As he later wrote in his book about his stay in Saxony" Margrit quoted,

> On the 2nd of July 1944, after long months in a military hospital, I reached Dresden as a soldier sent to a replacement unit. There, I encountered this city's incomparable beauty as well as became a witness to her greatest tragedy. My water colors tell it; my pictures report about it.
>
> Dresden thrilled- me from the very first day. I used my rare leisure time to sketch. I can't forget my first leave: I strolled upstream along the bank of the Elbe River, over the flowering meadows, and for the first time I saw the delectable sight of the Augustus Bridge, and the domes and towers on the opposite bank.
>
> I could not get my fill of this view [even though] I did not know yet the names of the buildings. I saw this panorama of rare beauty and harmony as a whole. Now I knew why the much-vaunted "Florence on the Elbe" had presented exaltation and inspiration to so many and such different artists.
>
> Till that day, I had known the city only from books, from old engravings and paintings. I could hardly believe it that after the bitter years in Russia, I had the privilege to live in this wonderful city. Here I could forget and convalesce in body and mind.
>
> [About the] Brühlsche Terrace: At the stone staircase that led down to a street surrounded by picturesque gabled houses, I unpacked my painting supplies. As my first motif I chose the *Frauenkirche*, which had been created so boldly with its stone dome and delicate towers on the sides by *Baumeister* Baehr.
>
> The magic of that summer day made me forget the restraints of military order. Only after the sun set, with its changing colors on the baroque figures, was reminded I of the time; I realized that I had overstayed the time of my leave. I had been a soldier long enough to know what consequences this might have caused.

*Dresden's Frauenkirche ("*Church of our Lady*") as painted by Eugen Luick (left) in early July 1944 and again, post-bombing, in mid-February 1945*

As Margrit finished reading Eugen's words aloud to her mute, reflective audience, I could see even Mom sink deeper and deeper into a heavy silence. I knew this meditation, this guilt-driven self-searching by the off-spring of those who have committed grave wrongs—or, allowed them to happen, unopposed.

Mercifully, Margrit realized our relations were drowning, so turned and bid in her cheeriest English "So, Michael—tell us, now: What about our American cousins; what about *your* Luicks?"

*Klaus and Ursula (Luick) Bodenstein, with Ruth (Luidhardt), Karl, Iris (Glaser) & Jochen Luick and (in front) the Bodensteiner children: Nicolai, Christine & Katherine, after an Easter-egg hunt, 1982; Luick-family Easter Sunday dinner at Ashlawn Farm, 1977, with (l.- r.) David, Doug and Jeandelle* (Luick) Olesen;* head of Doug's wife, Deb, behind Barb's husband, Tom; Lorraine (Luick) Jones with then-boyfriend Chuck Ryan, Dad, Chuck Olesen, Gramma, back of Barb's head, Wayne* & Sheranne* (Luick) Joyns*, Phyllis (Thrams) Luick standing, right; (*names altered)*

As I'd served as emcee most of the time till that moment, by default, I hadn't given thought to what I might say when it was my turn to represent my branch's biography. There'd been no time for that; I had rolling duties. Now, standing there in from of a hundred or so eyes, I froze—a most uncharacteristic response for ham me to experience in front of a group. *What do I tell 'em* I panicked as scenes from my family's American saga flashed through my mind like an out-of-control mental Rolodex. *How much 'truth' do I reveal to people I hardly know, about people no longer here nor able to tell their version of our shared story?* For an instant I looked to Mom, but was unsure if she even realized "we" were "on."

Just then, I recalled Gramma Luick's cruel fib, that "We came from 'Luick,' a village in Germany"—*But, in a way* I smiled, thinking of her and the Mike Luick I'd once been, *maybe she was on to something.* Seeing in front of me people who also had inherited this one-of-a-kind surname, it seemed as if a small village had gathered there that day, awaiting word of those bearing the same rare mark who had set off over a century and a half earlier in search of something they needed more than anything else, but were convinced they could no longer find here. As the crowd looked to me and waited to hear something worthy of the day, I struggled to summarize that driving spiritual hunger into a deserving soundbite.

*Ja, what can I say that will mean anything to these people?* I asked myself. *From the flight of that first family leaving "Luik" in Reformation-torn Flanders for Protestant Schwaben, 'their' people and 'ours' were the same. It's after 1833 that we emigrating Luicks took a different path than our stay-at-home kin.*

At that point, Margrit cocked her head, clearly puzzled. I could "hear" her thinking *So, what's up?*

*But, when exactly did we stop being 'Germans' and become something, some one different from them, from who all our people had been for generations; when did we become 'Americans'—and how?*

"Michael, is everything all right?" Margrit whispered to me as she smiled nervously to the others.

I nodded affirmatively, even while worrying *Will they be able to understand what drove Heinrich an' Katherine to petition Aich's Bürgermeister to leave? What will they think, if I spill the beans 'bout our Luick males' bad tempers—about ol' Heinrich thrashin' that cocky noble to an inch of his aristocratic life, or Don beatin' Dad and Dad beatin' the stock to a hair of theirs, let alone Dave an' me?*

I saw Mom shift in her chair along the thick stone wall in the back of the cavernous medieval room. She didn't know me not perform when I had a chance to take center stage. It confused and worried her.

*Can they imagine what it takes to walk away from everything you've ever known, had, been? Can they envision what it was like to board a ship, the* France, *an' risk going down over the Atlantic? I can, now—too well.* Someone at the table full of empty cake pans coughed. The clock ticked. *Will they really be able to picture the Gotham City of the 1830s; will they know what the Erie Canal was? Or, what about fledging Buffalo or Detroit: What's all that to them? Their people were here, cozy in the heart of Europe.*

As scenes from "my" Luicks' Great American saga continued to play in my mind's eye, I surveyed what I could—or "should"—tell my audience so they might understand what distinguished "us" from "them." Certainly, they'd seen enough Western re-runs on late-night television to know about log cabins and covered wagons, "Injun" attacks and homespun frontier folk, but *What do I say of 'Empire Builders' who oversaw the wholesale rape of a flowering prairie, of land-speculators-turned-bankers?* Just then, I "saw" columns of buffalo and elk fording the ambling Iowa River, two stones' throw from the doorway of the Luicks' lonely cabin on the empty prairie. *Do I dare mention 'Nigger Bridge' and Great-Grandpa George's KKK follies? Will they understand what the Farmers Holiday and NFO meant to us—and why? They'll recognize 'Dillinger' but what will 'W.P.A.' say to them? While we slogged our way through the Great Depression on our own, they had their squawking Adolf, ribboning Germany with* Autobahnen.

At that, I swore I could hear my father's voice somewhere among the crowd. As my eyes darted from one stern Teutonic face to the next, I could hear Luwarren Myrle Luick ask *Why you still so fascinated by these sticks in the mud, Mike?* Remembering the time soon after I returned from a year in Craven, as I recounted some of the things I'd experienced living in North Yorkshire, when Dad protested "What's Europe but big ol' palace gates to keep poor people out?" I struggled to reply to this, his latest query.

*Dad?* I called out into the foggy abyss that had settled between my ears at that moment, *That you?*

*Ya, an' I can tell ya sompthin' else. We Americans, we took care of our own. We didn't turn to thugs like Hitler* Bud scolded. *We worked our way outta that mess without turnin' ta a dictator ta do it.*

GLOBE-GAZETTE Mason City, Iowa Jan. 25, 1966 19

MEAT COMMITTEE — Four of the members of the meat bargaining committee for 1966 of the Cerro Gordo County National Farmers Organization (NFO) look over some figures. The men are (seated) Don Luick (left), Thornton, and Al Staudt, Dougherty, and (standing) LaVerne Lee (left), Fertile, and LeWarren Luick, Mason City.

*article about NFO activities our patriarchs supported*

How I wished it were so, that we—who'd turned our backs on village life, on communal stone sheds to bake our bread or wash our clothes so that the whole community didn't burn down—were the self-ruling democrats I'd believed in my youth and young adulthood us to be. How much easier it'd be to tell our German kin what made us different, perhaps even "better" than themselves, if only we—who'd forsaken the narrow, cobblestone allies of Old Europe to strike out solo to claim homesteads on the wide, open prairie—were the champions of freedom we'd always told ourselves and the world we were.

Looking to Margrit, who I knew had demonstrated vehemently against the U.S.' wars in Vietnam and, later, Iraq, I asked myself *Can these people imagine why we ever sent Lorraine's boy, Danny Jones, off to fight the Viet Cong, or Tyler the Afghanis? What would Fred Luick's helping Sherman leave a swath of destruction through Georgia mean to them, whose entire country lay in shards in May '45? Would they care, that gay Uncle Henry served in France in World War I, against their dandy Kaiser? What is—*

"Michael!" Margrit called out loud enough to jar me out of my trance, "What *is* the matter?"

For the first time freeing myself from an all-consuming, intra-cranial familial film, I blinked and looked around. As I peered into the crowd that filled Galerie 13, I remembered where I was and what those in front of me were expecting of me. Still, I could only stand there before them, dumbstruck. As I surveyed the faces staring at me, I suddenly realized *Oh, they all look* so *'German'—and so,* so *serious.*

*Esslingen, where my long search for my Luick family's roots started—and, thirty years later, finally ended.*

At that moment, I remembered the question that had led me to Esslingen in the first place, three decades earlier: "Why is my family the way it is?" Having just heard more than enough stories to know why the German Luicks are "*so* German" I realized why we American Luicks are the way we are:

"We're the way we are, because of the things we've done and the people we became, doing them."

*Luick-family reunion, circa 1913, including: Fred (with hat) & Alice, Michael (far right) & Sarah, and so many more...*

———

Volume I: *Roots of Darkness*

1) from the *persona*: my disrupted granny

Volume II: *Chasing Restless Roots*

2) about the *populi*: my disappearing people

Volume III: *Tap Roots Betrayed*

3) for the *polis*: my derailed country

**conclusion for the *polis*: my derailed country**

It had been a great month—but Christian and I were ready to return to Germany.

While in the Upper Midwest, we'd seen and done a lot: visited relatives and tourist sights, eaten way too much, done a bit o' shopping, given a few presentations—and now were headed back to Dresden.

*Michael Luick-Thrams, Phyllis (Thrams) Luick and Christian posing as* American Gothic *in Eldon, Iowa; August 2014*

The night before our afternoon flight from Chicago to Frankfurt, we slept at Scattergood School. As usual, last-minute packing left me frantic and grumpy. Plucky Christian, though—carrying his shit shield ever high—went to explore the rural campus while I sank deeper and deeper into order-making despair.

When he returned, I felt gratified by his report that, by coincidence, an exhibit was being displayed in the school library just then about the Scattergood Hostel for European refugees, 1939-'43. And, the major source of its content consisted of my book *Out of Hitler's Reach*. When my German boyfriend told me that, I thought with a smile *Ja, maybe my work as a public historian has some lasting worth after all!*

---

Too early the next morning, we fell out of bed and into our waiting clothes, then stumbled to the already-packed car. Before we reached the gravel road at the end of the school's driveway, Boy Wonder was fast asleep. I didn't care: I had a lot of impressions to mull over before once again—for the zillionth time—leaving behind my beloved Midwest. But, I didn't expect my early-morn reverie to end so soon.

Driving through nearby West Branch, I cast an inspecting eye towards the Herbert Hoover National Historic Site: *Yep, still there* I noted, *and, like Quaker Herbert, still very Republican*. As the motor of the lemon rental car we booked in O'Hare for the month strained to make it up the teeny incline leading to Interstate-80, then relaxed as we coasted over the level freeway bridge, I savored the emerging sunrise.

Waiting for a pokey tractor pulling a flat rack loaded with hay bales to pass, I did not see the old man waiting for a ride at the top of the freeway ramp until I'd crossed the opposing lane and was accelerating to descend into traffic. Realizing the moment when I spied the ancient figure standing just off the pavement that I knew him, I swerved onto the gravel and screeched to a stop. Christian didn't move a hair or make a sound as our unexpected passenger slowly got into the back and shut the door.

*I-80 east of Iowa City, with spectacular skyscape looming on the horizon*

Already re-accelerating, I peered into the rearview mirror and effused breathily, so as not to awaken Christian, "Why, Uncle Ike! Where *you've* been all these years! We've *so* needed your steady hand."

"Well, it always does an old heart good to hear the young folks might have use of him now or again."

"We need your moderation and words of wisdom or warning" I assured him, "more than ever."

"Glad somebody does" I heard Uncle say under his breath as in the rearview mirror I saw him smile. "Say, what brings you here? I didn't expect to see you this grand morning—and certainly not so early."

"My friend and I" I explained, tilting my head towards the snoozing German in the front seat, "we're just finishing a month's tour of America's Heartland. Now, we're headed to our flight back to Europe."

"Oh, that sounds very fine" Uncle affirmed. "And tell me, how was your month's stay among us?"

"Mixed" I answered without thinking.

"Why is that?" Uncle wanted to know. "Didn't you like it here?"

"To the contrary, I love my Midwest" I assured him, "but maybe too much."

"How can one love his homeland 'too much'?" the native Kansan with an Iowan wife wondered.

"'Cause it pains me to see it so grossly mismanaged and run into the ground by an invisible junta."

"*Ah-h-h*, yes—*those* bad boys again" Uncle *tsk-tsk*ed as I watched him turn and gaze out the window.

"Don't take it too hard, Unc" I told him. "You *did* try to warn us. It's just that—"

"—that nobody wanted to listen then" he finished my thought. "Now look at the mess we're in!"

"That we surely are" I agreed. "Ya know, this isn't the country I grew up in—and it's certainly not the one you grew up in, nor one that my people strove for over almost four centuries."

"'Your' people?" he echoed. "Who were 'your' people?"

"Oh, no one special—jus' a buncha farmers an' cowhands, sheep shearers an' ditch diggers, bus drivers an' cafeteria cooks; soldiers, fiddlers, soda jerks an' all the rest needed ta make a nation run."

"You didn't mention 'bankers' or 'lawyers,' son."

"Yeah, well—that was Chester P.'s line. My side of the Luick clan was the landless lot, the drifters."

"The 'Luicks'? Who were the 'Luicks'?"

"They were stereotypical pioneers—trail blazers, trappers, land speculators, empire builders—but true 'pioneers,' too: They went where there were no people like themselves and forged a new culture." I checked my speed quickly, as in the past tasty, rousing talk had cost me hefty speeding fines. "Ya know, we need such bright lights again today, 'cause our nation's lost its way. We've gone astray, haven't we?"

*Uncle Ike had a playful side that few knew outside his family and circle of friends. I saw it in my rearview mirror.*

Instead of answering my rhetorical with a verbal, the retired general-cum-statesman's eyes lit up as he pointed at me tellingly in the mirror. I nodded—and drove on. For a few miles, we rode in silence.

When we finally fell back into flowing conversation, we agreed "America's in trouble—deep trouble." As a hobbyist historian, my chatty passenger also sought a historical parallel as a base for comparison.

We quickly found a mutually compelling one, as Uncle had spent time in Germany in the '40s and knew the Old Germany. Despite too many Germans having colluded with naughtiness, while others openly dabbled in outright evil, he admired much about the culture. Like me a German-American with Mennonite ancestors, he respected the Teutonic ability to rise, ever again, from disasters, which for that beleaguered *Volk* never seemed far away. He even replicated their super-highway system—invented not by the Nazis, but by *Weimarer Republik* democrats—for use stateside. And, he showed no moral qualms recycling tainted Nazi scientists when it served our republic's purported postwar national purposes.

Given his outdated contact with the country and my currently living there, just as the car passed the exit for West Liberty, Uncle asked me for my impressions of contemporary Germany—my being a "resident outside observer," looking in for 35 years. Surrounded by endless fields, it felt odd to think about a world so far away from the American Heartland, a country that had become my second home.

"You know, it's been a fascinating ride. For the first decade, there were two Germanys, not one. My movements mostly were in the West then, although I did visit Berlin and the odd East in summer of '85. I saw the consequences of two diametrically opposed systems, being practiced by peoples who earlier had been one. It was a fantastic social experiment" I grinned, "like a big lab with 80 million Guinea pigs."

"Humans always establish some sort of 'system' to get what they need most" Uncle Ike chimed in.

"*Ja*, even chimps in the jungle have a pecking order, a division of roles that move all forward. The earliest humans also created systems, ways of procuring their needs, thus securing the group's survival."

"The problem is" the gent in the back continued, "even the most equalitarian systems get co-opted by this or that dominant figure. The most insidious is always a clique, a cabal of the power-hungry who steer the whole from the sidelines but hold the reins tight. That's what I tried to warn America, but—"

"—but we weren't ready to hear the truth. Perhaps we are, now" I ventured.

I checked Ike's reaction to my wishful thinking. He only shook his head and peered out the window.

"The stakes were lower when we all lived in animal-hide tents or grass huts, and hunted with stone-tipped spears. Now, though" I reflected "human settlements have grown so large, so complex and—"

"—and our weapons so deadly, so impersonally ruthless and destructive."

"But, it's not just our systems of getting food, water and shelter, or of keeping the neighbors out of our granaries and beds. Almost all the systems we moderns have cobbled together over the last decades are failing" I protested—so loud that Christian finally stirred, only to swiftly slip back into slumber again.

"They are?" the aged man responded, which surprised me, as I thought my conclusion to be a given.

"Sure—but where to begin? For one, we dismantled the family-run farming system we had in place as recently as a generation ago, but now the mostly processed 'food' the nation consumes in over-sized portions not only doesn't sustain health, but it actively leads to disease. We are a small portion of the global population, but use a major share of its energy and don't use that energy very efficiently. We're addicted to petroleum as much as we are to high-fructose corn syrup—so we're even willing to poison our precious land and shatter its substrata to bits in a last-ditch effort to suck every drop o' gas outta a choking planet." Uncle nodded his head, then waited to hear more as I shifted from an inventory of the tangible to the social. "America's banking system is rigged to serve the bankers, not the borrowers, who *lose* money on their savings—their nearly-zilch interest calculated against inflation—but woe to those who wish to borrow a loan: The interest will milk ya." I adjusted the visor, as the sun began to pour into the car and cast an illuminating light throughout. "Employees enjoy few protections and, in turn, offer ever less loyalty. Our 'justice' system too often yields injustice, our penal system pushes to punish more than to reform or reintegrate, and our military system fails to keep terrorism from spreading—in fact, it seems to fan it. If that's not bad enough, we spend billions on public education and yearly introduce touted reforms, yet our kids' average scores steadily lag behind other developed nations'."

"Yes, I see" the wizened man behind me conceded. "But, what do you—"

"And" I barreled on, "the system of delivering post-secondary education not only too often produces middling results, but increasingly is a realm accessible only to the children of the rich or to those willing to oblige themselves to modern serfdom—to lifelong debt management. 'Public' universities have to a large degree become owned indirectly by corporations, which pay for cooked research by non-tenured profs held on a leash, afraid to displease the givers of their research grants. Besides privatizing education, we've awarded fat contracts to mega-companies to outfit our army, incarcerate our criminals and park our care-needing seniors in front of nursing-home televisions. Sure, we now have compulsory health insurance—written by insurance companies and so problematic that its failure is built-in. And, our 'mental-health' system? We need an effective one more than ever, but instead of adequate mental-health facilities we get ever more acts of wanton shootings, of sadistic crimes beyond all moral limits." Ike's eyes grew larger and larger, more and more distraught the more social problems I aired. "And, how should we find solutions to all these dilemmas when the media—which once informed and facilitated public discussion—has devolved into a market of cheap distractions rather than a forum for real discourse? We used to see the press as a keystone of democracy; now, it's jus' a bedrock of advertising." As I swung my head sadly, my pulse raced, fed by a cocktail of sorrow spiked with rageful indignation.

At that, Uncle Ike bit his lip. "If all that you say is true, how does the nation limp on? It's a disaster!"

"In the aggregate, we *are* talking about a systemic failure, the inability of numerous subsystems to provide for the best-possible well-being of the people." I breathed for a moment, then challenged a man far my elder "Do you realize that in America today, everything the people *need*—food, shelter, energy, education, healthcare—is increasingly prohibitively expensive, while all the 'electives' like junk food and lesser electronics, plastic clothes or pressboard furniture are too cheap to pay to repair? *Why* is that? What sort of system is that and how's it supposed to satisfy basic human needs with dignity, over time?"

"None of this sounds good. It's truly dire" Uncle finally was able to break in, "but what do you—"

"And, the sickest system of them all is the country's political one" I thundered, this time too loudly:

"Hey, hoo ist dat in da beck seat?" Christian asked sleepily, one eye still closed as he stretched.

"*Guten morgen*" Uncle greeted the awakening lump in the front. "I'm a former American pres—"

"—precious friend of Grandpa and Grandma Thrams" I interrupted, not wanting to go there.

"Oh, dat's nice" my only-half-conscious boyfriend casually replied. Then, Christian turned to me and pleaded quietly "*Pupsi, ich muss mal...*"

"*Ja, OK*" I caved in, by chance about to reach a roadside rest. "We'll stop here—but just a moment."

As soon as the car skidded to a stop, Christian's door flew open and he ran off to the nearest hidden corner. I helped Uncle out of the back and offered "Wouldn't you rather sit up front now? You'd—"

"—have to compete with me for it" a disembodied voice challenged. Both Uncle and I looked around but saw nothing. Then, as if out of nowhere, a young buck walked out from behind a nearby semi. He strode up to us with noticeable confidence and an extended hand—which I shook, but Uncle refused.

*Christian never tired of exploring something that doesn't exist in over-populated Germany: wide, open prairies.*

Noticing that Christian by now was off examining an adjacent prairie-restoration patch and out of ear shot of the two men's curt exchange, I wondered what I'd done to deserve this: with little choice but to chauffeur the old guard beloved by my mother's people, in the same car as an upstart who the stoic sage despised but my father's family had adored. Cousin Jack *was* a gem, but one had to like such rocks.

"OK" grinning Jack rallied us as Christian bounded back to the car, "let's head 'em out!" He held the front passenger door open and, bowing, with a sweeping arm bade Uncle to sit up front. Of course, Ike didn't: Seeing this, Jack smiled broadly, winked at Christian and me, then hopped in the back next to Ike.

As he scooted in next to me, Christian searched my face for an explanation, noticeably perplexed. I pretended to smile, shrugged meekly, then turned on the engine, backed up and sped off.

"So, what waar yaa gents discussing so intently when I found yaa?" Jack wanted to know.

As Uncle began to sputter some objection, I offered "We were reviewing America's political woes."

"That should be entertaining" I watched Jack mumble to himself. "How long'd yaa say the d*r-r-r*ive ta Chicaaga is, still?" he asked loudly, with a Baasten accent that made me smile for its out-of-place-ness. I glanced into the mirror: Even the slice of Jack's face I could see conveyed a cool, cocky self-assurance.

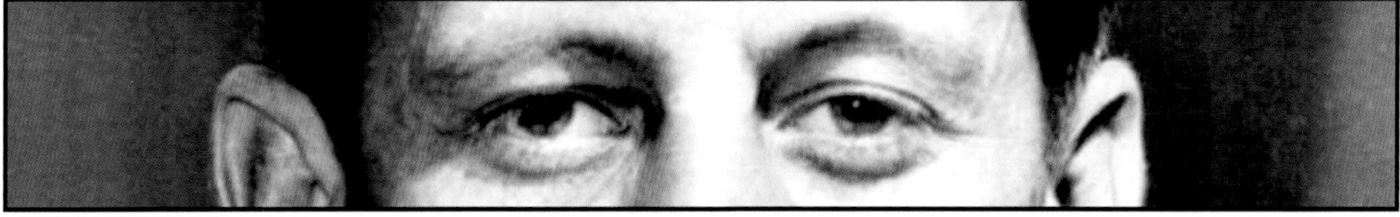

*I wanted to like Cousin Jack, but sensed an edge about the man—even in the slice of him I spied in the car's mirror.*

"Once, we were the light of the world" I jumped back into my previous, postponed discourse, "the glowing hope for Europeans fettered by local tyrants or regional dynasties. Two and a half centuries ago, *we* were 'modern;' *we* comprised the world's political avant-garde—but now, just look at our misery in Washington, that den of corporate whores who cultivate a culture of deadlock to reach cynical ends."

"Do you mean to imply that the deadlock isn't organic, but orchestrated?" Uncle questioned as, just then, the car crossed I-80's bridge over the broad Mississippi River and we left peaceable Iowa behind.

"Of course! Think about it: Who gains by the evaporation of an effective government? It ain't the ordinary folks—people like mine or [I pointed out the window to the nearest drivers] any of theirs. It's all hollow theater, a big scam to appear like genuine 'political process' but it's far from real. It's staged, choreographed and impression-managed from beginning to end—and we swallow it as legit fare daily."

"We have now in this great country of aars" Cousin Jack piped up sarcastically from the back, "the 'best democracy money can buy'—an' none of yaa have the bucks ta so much as even rent an iota of it."

Playing Good Cop to Jack's Bad, I looked up into the mirror and argued our common cause. "They all came here, Uncle—France's de Tocqueville and Dickens from England (twice) to tour, Schurz from Germany to stay—fed up with calcified Old World powers, lookin' for fresh political air in the New." Then, I guided the car over spaghetti-like ramps and we merged into traffic on I-88: Chicago awaited us!

*Charles Dickens, Mary Lease and de Tocqueville all enriched America.*

"After the British failed to contain what they called an 'insurgence' in thirteen of their seventeen North American colonies" Jack pointed out, "they dismissed aar struggle as a mere 'Waa for Independence,' but establishing the first new republics since the Romans' really was a 'revolution.' Besides that of self-contained Swiss cantons, the world then didn't have groups of people exaacising self-government."

"But now" I scoffed, "it's other countries that are perfecting participatory government, not us. Our political system, with its sham parties and career politicians, is a paper tiger. We say we rule ourselves democratically, but the real power holders never attend public forums. No" I wagged my chin, "we've morphed into a system that refuses to change an' that we seem afraid to tinker with. We've become so stiff in how we share power in this country; we hide behind empty husks. Even our currency has hardly changed in 150 years! The younger republics that came later, they gained from our trailblazing, but they didn't stay camped in some agrarian mindset of the late 1700s. They continued to experiment, to make mistakes, resume and improve. And, we? We perpetuate our system solely out of habit, not rationality."

"Know why Americans vote on Tuesday?" Cousin Jack teased our aloof uncle. Ike shook his head to the negative. "Once harvest was ovaa by early November but winter hadn't yet set in, the farmers could come inta town to vote—but a Monday wouldn't work, because they'd have to hook up the buggy and set off on Sunday, the workless Sabbath, and as Wednesday was maarket day, only Tuesday remained available. Today" Jack noted, "almost every democracy but aars holds elections on a Sunday, so that people don't have to vote opposite their work. Yaa'd think we could update aar voting culture a bit—"

"—or finally abolish that absurd, anti-democratic Electoral College" I bandwagoned, "put in place by reactionary Federalists like Madison and Hamilton as a bulwark against the 'tyrannical masses.' Those are the same guys who made voting contingent upon landownership—by white males over 21. Such provisions in our antiquated system came out of the same era that held blacks are '3/5$^{th}$s a man.'"

"Whatever happened to Thom Jefferson's admonition" Jack queried as we passed a sign for the turnoff to Prophetstown, Illinois, "that 'a little rebellion now and then is a good thing'—"

*As far as the eye can see, a sea of corn where tropical seas once lapped along shores that dinosaurs saw.*

"—or Mary Lease's plea to Kansas farmers" I interrupted, "to 'raise less corn and more hell'? Our system's become antiquated, corrupt to its core and irreformable—an' most of us jus' sit an' stare at it."

"We have these two big parties that, togethaa, have existed for more than 350 years, but how do they serve us now?" Jack barked at Ike in the back. "Do they do more good or ill? I'll tell yaa: They've become monoliths, elite-appointed gatekeepers that dole out licenses to vie for power! The Democratic Party is the oldest political party in the world today, and even used to be *fused* with the Republicans! They claim to be opposites, but if yaa want to look for real opposition, don't examine them too closely." As we flew across the prairie, bound for the big-shouldered Windy City, big winds blew in the back. "Why do we keep these dinosaurs around that no longer serve our people? Where's any sense in that?"

Instead of answering his impertinent junior seat mate, the senior man froze for a moment to think. When, after a much-watched silence, he finally spoke in measured tones, Uncle Ike said "Each of you might be right in some particular regards—but what do you propose we do about this jumbled mess?"

My eyes met Cousin Jack's in the mirror the moment we both realized that we'd finally convinced our cautious, conservative compatriot, yet neither of us said a word. Of course I had something to say, but I waited per chance what he could offer might be more edifying than anything I could.

My family had had big hopes for Cousin Jack. He left us when I wasn't even a year old, yet we kept a thin orange photobook about his truncated career in our bookcase, otherwise dedicated to children's tales, religious tracts, atlases and dictionaries. Inside its creased covers were yellowed, musty articles that Dad or his folks had clipped out of the *Globe-Gazette*, while the photos chronicled his young life up to its tragic end. They included shirtless shots of him with sunglasses, in sun-soaked boats during The War, and portraits with his patrician family or, later, photogenic wife. Yes, our Jack could do no wrong.

Still, he had to explain himself. "I repeat" Ike huffed, "what do you propose we do about this mess?"

"So, yaa grant that we *do* have a problem, do yaa?" Jack grilled as we all passed Sterling, Illinois.

"Yes, of course we have a problem! Anyone who loves this country knows that it's not what we once had or hoped for. America's not a land of promise anymore—but what would you have us do about it?"

"I can tell you what I *wouldn't* have us do" I interjected. "I wouldn't keep doing what we've always done, 'cause if we do, we'll always get what we always got. Look" I argued, "before industrialization there were no big parties. Mass movements only arose as we had mass production, swelling cities and bloating bureaucracies. Such parties once served a purpose: In Europe, they offered about the only hope of countering the power of the aristocrats and their attendant oligarchs—but, that world is gone."

"That's right" Jack chipped in. "As of the mid-1800s, *everything* became big: big factories, big machines and ships, big unions, big churches and universities, big armies, big waas, big—"

*"Uncle Sam" by Thomas Nast, 1877*

"—everything" I jumped in. "But, now, big isn't better: It's in the way of finding mid-sized solutions to local problems that truly make a difference. Lumbering institutions or offices can't move fast enough, nimble enough to address the climatic, technological, economic, demographic or other shifts that are altering our world every day, ever faster. We need to walk away from those top-heavy institutions that don't solve our problems, but rather perpetuate them. We need to divest ourselves from the illusion that they can—or even wish to—rescue us, and instead to focus all our energies, to use all our resources to create new bodies, innovative organizations that reflect the novel ways of living we will have to forge if we're going to deviate from the express lane to Doomsday we currently seem to be stuck on."

"I understand yaar reflex towards caution, Ike" Jack conceded, "but by their nature, all the bodies we have created ovaa many decades, ovaa centuries when other conditions reigned, aar programmed to sustain themselves, whether or not they aar any longer appropriate or able to respond to what's going on around them. As they sense they aar losing their grip, their survival instinct is to hunker down, to burrow in even if the world would be better served by something new, which better reflects the times."

"Look at the Luicks" I bid, "how they—"

"Who were they, again?" befuddled Uncle asked.

"My people: You know, the 'farmers an' cowhands, sheep shearers, ditch diggers, bus drivers'—"

"—'cooks, soldiers, fiddlers, soda jerks' and all the rest we need to make the nation run" Ike echoed.

"Anyway, what I wanted to say was: Look at the Luicks. They really *did* accomplish great feats; they seized virgin prairie and laid out a town, set up churches an' schools an' various levels of governance. They formed felt-boot orchestras an' glee clubs, quilting bees and PTAs. And, some of them, at least, became incredibly rich in the process—with a handful of those cycling some of the wealth we extracted from so much fertile land back into the community."

*American ditch diggers: my people—and yours*

Jack cocked an eyebrow, obviously wondering where I was headed.

"But, once they'd accomplished all those impressive feats, we who followed rested on our laurels. The pioneers' obituaries waxed endlessly about my people's reported virtues and heroism, our almost super-human qualities, but by Great-Great-Grampa Louis' time our achievements didn't cut the grade anymore. By his generation 'good enough' sufficed, so while other Luicks built banks, or set and reached other goals, my branch slipped from the larger clan's level and sank into affable mediocrity and under-achievement. It's a pattern as old as human civilization."

When I abruptly stopped painting my parable, it took a moment before the two in the back reacted.

Finally, Ike asked "Are you implying that America is suffering from a parallel dynamic of paralyzing self-satisfaction? Are you trying to say we aren't living up to our potential, as a people or as a nation?"

"Well, while we were busy enjoying our postwar power and affluence half a century after The War ended, the Germans were retooling and regrouping, 'til today they're a world leader and we're [I paused as I peered into the mirror] not so much. And" I bolted onward, "look at China. In the seventeen days I spent there two years ago, it seemed China's stolen not only America's playbook, but even our brand: I literally heard speeches and read articles touting 'The Chinese Dream.' We no longer have a monopoly on rags-to-riches stories, and social mobility—rising from poverty to a middleclass standard of living—is actually easier to achieve in South America than it is in the American South. How can *that* be?"

"Do you really think the answer lies in studying the fates of a buncha farmers and ditch diggers?"

"What else do yaa think he's saying, Ike?" Jack retorted. "He's dissecting his very-American family as a microcosm of the macrocosm, so we can see in it laarjaar trends—the fate of a nation, in one family."

"I find that a bit of a stretch" Uncle protested.

"Do yaa have a better idea how to locate which false turn we took—where we went wrong, when?"

As Jack and Ike took positions, Christian played with his ring, wondering how to join a conversation that was too complex, too fast to run with. Usually, the tables were turned: Back in Dresden I often felt elbowed out by the natives but now, back in Iowa, my indelible Americanness prodded me to speak out.

*The fertile prairies of Iowa have fed my people—and likely yours—for over a century and a half.*

"We've been here 400 years" I noted. "We left hungry, beat-up Europe lookin' for fertile land—and found it, but with 'savages' already living on it. Once we'd pushed 'em aside, we did the American thing and wrestled 'civilization' out of 'wilderness.'" Noticing the speedometer shooting skyward, I let my foot relax a bit off the gas pedal and refocused. "We've seen it all—the nation's booms an' busts, its wars, its power struggles, its recurring waves of anti-Indian, -black, -Asian, -gay or any other anti- sentiments. We've invested too much to abandon the whole project now that the going's gotten tougher than ever."

"How else do yaa want us to understand *where* we aar today" Jack asked Ike, "what we're grappling with as a nation, if we can't better grasp where we've been as families and *how* we got where we aar?"

*On 8 June 1972 South Vietnamese forces accidentally dropped napalm (a jellylike gasoline bomb) on their own troops and civilians—includiung 9-year-old Kim Phuc. As she and other terrified children fled the inferno along with foot soldiers down Route 1 near Trang Bang, Nick Ut of the Associated Press snapped a photo that became iconic for war's brutal destruction and absurdity. It sobered me so when I saw it as a boy—also 9 at the time—just as it still does, now. Today, Kim Phuc speaks against war's cruelty and travels the globe on behalf of peace and reconciliation.*

"Is that what your family-history research trip just now has been about, boy?" Uncle probed.

"Not only 'just now' but it has been for over 35 years." I waved at Christian, who was dozing again. "Ever since we saw Mark Nagel off to Nam, I wanted to know who were, how we ended up on a farm in Iowa, and how we were different from those people in some village named 'Luick' back in Germany—or from those kids trotting down that road in Southeast Asia, shrieking in terror as their flesh burned from our bombs."

With that Uncle Ike sunk his chin into his chest, rocked his head and muttered "The kid's obsessed."

"What I found along the way wasn't just how the Luicks and Thrams ended up at Ashlawn Farm, but how *everyone* around us ended up where they were. The stories of my classmates' people were virtually the same as those of 'my' people. It's just that few of them knew or even seemed to care how 'we' arose." I swallowed hard, then continued: "We should have cared: Our grandfathers sat on draft boards that sent our brothers and cousins to do grave wrongs in distant jungles. Dad and our uncles said we had to 'bomb the Cong inta the stone age' to protect our Iowa homeland, but I always wondered how the Cong could ever reach us, so far away. I trusted them, that it was for good and just reasons that we sent Terry back after every Christmas leave—after I'd worn his sailor's cap 'round the house for hours or, soused, he'd helped me assemble the war toys I got. And, when Miss Reader kept us first graders in during recess to sing secret songs..." My voice breaking up, I took a deep breath and fought to press on. "We and our people" I finally mustered, "were part of something big, much bigger than we could see or even imagine. We were making history, even as our parents and all the rest tried so hard to ignore it."

"If I'd only known what I'd helped set in motion" Jack murmured in the back, barely audible up front.

"Don't forget" I pointed out, "Hitler never drove a single train to Auschwitz. He didn't have to: He had millions of willing executioners—locomotive engineers, station masters, poison-gas chemists, camp guards, girls in thousands of villages sewing uniforms—to do the work for him. There were those who wanted to 'make Germany great again,' professional soldiers like cousin Karl's officer father, as well as those who had no time for Nazism—cousin Eugen off somewhere with his easel and sticky brushes. Still, the German farmers, ditch diggers and cooks carried out their banal roles as part of a big, dark project."

Jack, in his own film, lamented quietly "We've never really owed up to the things we did in Vietnam."

"Nor the people we became, doing them" I editorialized brusquely, given Jack's self-absorption had waylaid my point. "It's not just what we did to Vietnam" I reminded, "but what Vietnam did to us. Now, sadly, you can add to the list: 'What we did to Iraq' and 'What Iraq did to us.' Who knows, who's next."

*This land's my land; this land's your land: It's shaped what we've been, who we are and how we will live.*

"Yeah" Jack whispered, "just like Americaa—this place [he said, looking out over the endless fields], the very land itself: We came here and became something new, thraagh the things we did here—"

"—and the people we became, doing them" I finished the sentence for him. "History never stands still, of course. Already tardy coming to terms what we did to Vietnam and what it did to us, we haven't even begun to wade into the moral morass of how attacking Iraq a decade ago—a sovereign state, a people who had done us no ill nor had the ability to do so—has changed us forever as a people. All those unprocessed traumas, the senselessness and disillusionment, the wounds—they're all still there."

"Is so much muck-raking really necessary?" Uncle Ike challenged. "The past has passed" he declared.

"*Ah-h-h*" Jack played philosophical poker, "but has it? Don't we make the waarld anew every day, based on a map we carried ovaa from the day before?"

"If an extended family is a community in miniature and a country consists of myriad communities in aggregate, then I'd say based on my family's experience we are only as sick as our secrets. The shadows of the parents *do* visit the children and their children, until they're cast into the Light, seen and named."

Jack sat up and grabbed the back of my seat, unintentionally shaking it—and me—as he excitedly carried the rhetorical torch. "And if we want this country to move faarwaard, we need to awaken from our collective sleepwalking, look reality in the eye and start to deal with what's in front of us."

"And. Just. What. Ex-act-ly" Uncle Ike sounded out in beats as he pounded one fist into his other palm, his voice cavernous, monotone and demanding, "Is. In. Front. Of. Us?"

"How about ecological disaster, social degeneration, moral decay or spiritual death?" I listed off fast.

"So, based on what became of your family over four hundred years" Ike induced from behind me, "you are weaving a trajectory for the whole nation—"

"Wait" I broke him off, "that sounds a bit megalomaniac. Let's just say 'for the Midwest,' shall we?"

"—for the American Heartland?"

"*Ja*" I answered glibly, "that's about the sum of it."

In the mirror I could see that while Uncle disliked the whole idea, Jack smiled slyly, watching Ike sulk.

"There's one factor central to the equation, though, gents." Neither asked what, so I confided "There was something dark, something terribly wrong in my father's family's house. Try as we might, neither my clever cousin Barbara nor I could figure out what it was—until, that is, we found the strength to confront the unconscionable, the whole ugly collection of family slip ups that led to our fall. What we found lurking in the shadows wasn't very pretty, but it did explain a lot of what had vexed us till then."

Again, neither man uttered a word, yet I could see on their reflective faces they were lost in thought.

"For one thing, we Luicks coasted on the vapors of previous generations' fading achievements of yore, and the indulgent self-image we sustained kept us from being honest, let alone critical. Criticism was not welcome—especially the in-house variety: That was 'treason.' So, too, with the U.S., I have the feeling that we over-estimate ourselves, what we've accomplished in the past or do today. Criticism is often seen as disloyalty, so a censored group-think reigns that reinforces our smuggest assumptions about ourselves. What we need, though—urgently—is a frank and honest national self-inventory."

I saw Jack shrug. "How should Americans be 'fraank and honest' when so many of our citizens—"

"—of all political stripes—" Ike interjected.

"—are so blinded by ideology that they can't see a thing for what it is, in itself, but only as it suppaarts their view of how, at a given moment, they think the world works? Even in Ike's and my day" I saw Jack wag his head, "we never approached the level of rabid ideology that taints this country at present. It's like the citizenry has maarphed into opposing aarmies of ideological staarmtroopers."

"Those philosophical chasms are cultivated" I contended, "by those who stand to gain the most from a fractured populace. 'Divide an' conquer' worked already for the ancient Romans in the territories they occupied, and the Europeans used the same mechanism two millennia later as they brutally ruled colonies around the globe. Naturally, politicians and pundits of both parties use the same ol' trick now."

*1872 Thomas Nast cartoon: "Let us clasp hands over the bloody chasm."*

"Democracy only works" Jack spouted, "when consensus arises and common cause binds divergent people togethaa. By haarping on social matters that can't or shouldn't be resolved through legislation—like teenage pregnancy or the private lives of homosexuals—scheming elites keep people's focus on what's going on the bedroom rather than in the boardroom, where the nation's business *really* unfolds 'in the dark.'"

"Well" Ike sputtered back, "we never talked about such things in *my* day!"

"Welcome to the 'cult'raal revolution,' Ike" Jack quipped. "It's *all* fair game, if it's game for the unfair. By publicly obsessing about mattaars belonging to the private raalm, the electorate lets itself be steered in the directions that the Great and Powaarful Wizaards behind the curtain want to drive them. Instead of discussions about how to fairly share aar nat'raal resaarces or the fruit of aar work, the string pullers offaa unproductive distractions like wearing flag pins or fan endless debates ovaa prayer in schools."

Ironically, at exactly that point in our animated conversation, the packed, sagging car we shared zipped past Dixon, the ol' "Gipper's" hometown in Central Illinois.

*Ronald Reagan (youngest in 1916 portrait, with "Dutch" haircut) grew up in the heart of America with his father Jack, mother Nelle (Wilson) and brother Neil. A year and a day older than my paternal grandfather, "Ronnie" posed for the photo on the right in 1922. By coincidence, his future wife—born ten years after him, in New York in 1921, as "Anne Frances Robbins"—moved to Chicago at eight with her mother and adoptive father, where she lived the rest of her youth, until 1939. By that point, her future husband, in Hollywood, had played in 19 films.*

"This moral posturing's so phony" I complained. "In private, Ronald Reagan worried that svelte, ballet-dancing son Ronnie might be gay, and didn't publicly say the word 'AIDS' till after 5,000 Americans had died from that plague—but Hollywood's been fulla gays since Day One: Of course, he and Nan had gay friends! So did George Bush, senior, and Barbara—to the point of standing up with lesbian friends as they married! Laura Bush and Cindy McCain aren't gay-bashing bigots, but their men shot spears for years. And, what about the Cheneys? Lynne feigned indignation when John Kerry mentioned daughter Mary's being a lesbian, calling his reference 'tawdry,' yet Mary and her partner Heather Poe have two children—so? And, sister Liz—who called to congratulate the two when they married—acts as if she hates 'them.'

This whole Republican pretense of being anti-gay is mostly hot air, yet it's fueled a *Kulturkampf* that's served the party for years. And, to supporters, it gave a green light for people like my siblings to disdain folks like me for decades. The Republicans didn't create homophobia, but they happily use it as a political tool. It's the inauthenticity of it all that bothers me most: on one hand, embracing queers ya know, with the other slapping the face of millions who ya don't. Such disingenuousness poisons both the do-er and the done-to: We *all* lose."

"It's no surprise" Jack lamented out loud," that powaar brokers package their pawns any numbaa of ways—even ugly or immoral ones—but the wretched thing is, that so many Americans let themselves be so easily manipulated." Jack fumed "Don't they even suspect that maybe they're being used?"

"Barbara's and my siblings" I noted, "turned to fundamentalist religion to cope with the shadows that had touched us all, but the black-or-white worldview they embraced didn't allow for nuances. The world's more complex, far richer than they imagined. The stiff 'answers' they embraced didn't allow for dissent, the possibility that rationales different than theirs might have validity. It's been this conceptual split, these divisions into ideological camps that have kept Americans artificially separated for too long."

"It's *yaar* paarty's friends" Jack goaded Ike, "who milk diff'raances to sustain the 'stalemate' they need to rule in the vaacuum left by an absence of genuine, open exchange about faactual infaarmation."

Curious how Ike would respond to such juvenile taunting, I watched the old man in the mirror for a moment. When he said nothing, I scolded his one-time partisan foe with "Now justa minute, Jack. The problem of alleged ideological deadlock isn't one sided: Your buddies are to blame, too—but that's also beside the point, which is: The country's become ungovernable, the situation is unbearable. What we have now is not what drew our people to cross an ocean or a continent in search of a better life. The train wreck we have today is not why they went to war or slaved away in fields. Those who came before us believed in something lofty and inspiring—but this present mess is lowly and depressing. The state of the nation's become a disgrace and an embarrassment: I feel ashamed when I have to answer for it. If we wanna be true to previous generations of Americans, we need to turn out the money changers. We need to strike the set and start over, to resettle America. We need pioneers, individuals and families–of whatever sort that might mean—to create new ways of living in environments in sore need of change."

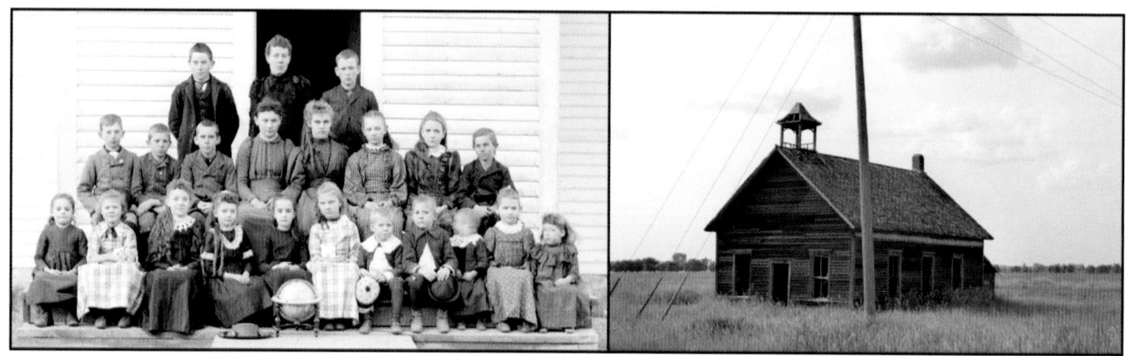

*rural Belmond-area pupils with their teacher, circa 1890: Christian photographed a one-room schoolhouse, too.*

"You're right" Uncle Ike said my way as I looked his and saw him sit up in his seat, "we could do much better than this. I know, because I watched us do so in the not-so-distant past. We used to make things in America" he said softly as he cast an eye at a passing factory, "we used to do things, to tinker and invent, to build and invest. Now, though" he clucked in disgust, "we've become a country of lonely consumers led by bean counters, by niggling, tight-fisted politicians floating the lowest, most base ideas past the few who can still stomach our elections. But, I knew a different United States of America" he said ever louder and faster, "one with ideas as big as our wide open skies. We flourished not when we were fighting over pennies in public coffers, but finding the dollars to grease the wheels of those who wanted to innovate, to move things, to attract thousands who eagerly waited to follow their lead."

By that point, otherwise cocky Jack's jaw had dropped and I, too, marveled at the spunk that rose to the surface when Ike overcame his knee-jerk caution and tapped his compassion for a strayed nation. *My stars* I thought to myself, *the old gent still has some fire in his belly after all!* Then, Ike waxed on:

"America's best hours were moments of generosity: The Homestead Act bestowed public lands to those who proved they could build a life on the prairie; the Land-Grant Acts funded what became some of the finest universities in the world; the W.P.A. employed millions of breadwinners struggling to pay for a meal or a bed—right through to the G.I. Bill that handed eight million men who had fought for our country a ticket to a better life, but one for which they and their families had to work to make it theirs."

By now, Christian had woken from what for a few hours had been an undisturbable slumber. Having missed most of the barbed tête–à–tête between my family's beloved uncle and its impressive cousin, my East-German-born boyfriend gained consciousness as the sagacious old man in the back for once truly held forth—and inspired us all. Even politically cynical Christian—who was only eleven when the Berlin Wall fell—felt moved by the idea of what America had once been or perhaps could become again.

"America did not become so great a nation in such a short time, however" Ike advised, "by going it alone. Every road in this country was once an Indian hunting trail or it followed a pioneers' wagon train, a stagecoach line, a canal tow path or an early toll road. Every farm was once a meadow or woods. Every town once wasn't. Everything we see in America today was built not alone, but by small groups of citizens banding together to realize shared dreams." As Christian nodded, the retired general continued:

*ceremonial ground-breaking for Belmond's first purpose-built public library; Main St., June 1916: The lot bears flowers in such an array and abundance that one wonders if it were virgin prairie.*

"We built our schools, our houses of worship, our libraries and parks not only *with* each other, but also *for* each other. Do not think" Uncle Ike cautioned, "that we always liked each other or, somehow, were selfless lesser saints. We were in some ways more diverse than you who have followed, but we overlooked what today would have kept us apart—and out of that unity, a consensus, we built common structures and finished shared projects that served us all." Then, with that, Uncle Ike paused a moment.

For the first time since Cousin Jack invited himself to join our jaunt to Chicago, no one replied to what a speaker said: We all just listened as, for the first time, Ike opened up and spoke from his heart.

"Earlier generations of Americans planted millions of trees around their newly-won farms or fledglings settlements, to mark the first cemeteries or schoolyards. Few, however, expected to live to see most of those trees reach full bloom. Still, we strove and sacrificed, we dreamt and built and created a world that we knew, at some point, we'd have to surrender—but always with the hope, indeed the assumption, that the world we'd created was better than the one we'd found and, in turn, would provide the footing for a better world for those who were to follow. Now, though..." his voice trailed off.

Not used to hearing public, let alone political oratory of such stature anymore, I felt stunned. Jack and Christian didn't say anything soon, either—but, finally, I felt I must. "You know, Uncle, my research bears out everything you've said. Taking a longer view, over four centuries, I'd say that we Americans have changed; we've turned out differently from who we once thought we were or ever wanted to be."

Slowly thawing, Jack asked caustically "And what was it, do yaa think, that we 'evaa wanted to be?'"

Just then, I got lost in genealogical reverie, for at that moment we drove over the interchange where I-88 and I-39 cross, where I-39 leads south past Pawpaw, Peru and El Paso to Normal, Illinois, or north to Rockford and what's now its suburb of Cherry Valley. There, stuck in my own Very-American Moment, I could not help but think of lil' Georgie Moorehead, a bright-eyed boy tainted by his Irish father's Catholic connections and marked by his English mother's thatch-roofed commoner background. I "saw" the Moorehead-Kews milling about in that green hamlet on the Civil-War-era frontier, only to again start seeing a scene move in reverse afore my mind's eye, through time and space, as George's now-childless young immigrant parents rode wagons, boats, trains backwards to New York—where the Kews backed onto the *Guy Mannering*, which then re-hoisted its sails and slipped out to sea, backwards to Liverpool.

As I heard Jack repeat "So, what do yaa think, that we 'evaa wanted to be?'" I jerked back to life.

"Oh, it's easy" I blurted. "Our ancestors who boarded those boats back in Europe didn't think they were goin' for a short joy ride. Believe me, leaving behind everything you've ever known, possessed or thought you were is one of the hardest things a person could ever do. It's no flip act: Only people who have pressing, concrete reasons for doing so emigrate. Except for slaves brought from Africa or natives who were already here—and their ancestors had migrated, too, from Asia, following food on the hoof—all of our ancestors came to the New World hoping to better their lot. For most, that meant amassing the trappings of a middle-class lifestyle, if not more. So, from the get-go, plenty and comfort were two of our guiding goals. Europeans could realize in the New World standards of living undreamed of back home—and that, early on. Already by the time of the Revolution" I related, using my free hand to punctuate images my words were painting, "we 'colonials' were taller, more robust and healthier than our British cousins. We had more access to better food, cleaner water and air, lots of space, sunshine—"

Jack leaned forward to interrupt with a whisper "What does this have to do with my question, pal?"

*Abraham Maslow (1 April 1908 - 8 June 1970) analyzed levels of getting needs met in the course of a human life.*

"Ever heard of Maslow's Hierarchy of Needs?"

"Sure" Jack shrugged. When I scrutinized him in the rearview mirror, he punted "Well, maybe, but—"

"'But' nothin'! Maslow's theory revolutionized modern psychology" I stated huffily. "He was the son of Russian-Jewish immigrants who'd fled Tsarist pogroms and settled in New York. Later, as a psych prof at Brandeis, he created a theory, a hierarchy of needs upon which he said psychological health depended. The most base have to do with physical—or as he called them, 'physiological'—needs, then become less materialistic and more intangible, focused on emotional needs. In the end, at the top of his scale, he spoke about spiritual needs, which he put in very-'60s terms as 'self-actualization.' At the time he published them, critics questioned his classifications, yet today Maslow's one of the ten most cited psychologists of the 20th century."

"I. Had. Ask-ed" Jack exaggerated each word to show his displeasure, "Just. What. Ex-act-ly. Does—"

"Later in life—the man died in '70 at only 62, from a heart attack, while jogging in California—Maslow critiqued some of the tenets of his own theories, including his vision of self-actualization. Having already suffered at least one heart attack, he knew his time was limited, which shifted his perspective. Having long maintained 'What a man can be, he must be,' his take on a self-actualized life matured, too. He then held that the self can only find actualization through giving itself to some higher goal outside and beyond one's self—through engaging in spiritually-based altruism."

"But, *what*" Jack interrupted again, ending with a shout, "does all that to do with *anything*?"

"Think about it: By and large, when our immigrant ancestors arrived, they set about getting 'physiological' or primary needs met first—food, clothing, housing, sexual expression—and *then* 'safety' needs, conditions that create security and, in turn, opportunity: a stable job, legal protections, savings, education and so on. Whole waves of immigrants came to this country and started to build new lives from the bottom up. That general progression, though, was often disrupted by what was going on here, before the newcomers had landed: economic downturns, political developments, war, social unrest and the like. If the immigrants themselves arrived with stomachs empty but 'baggage' full of trauma—Jews fleeing Eastern European pogroms, Southern Italians escaping abject poverty, Germans dodging war—they arrived with pre-existing hurdles to moving beyond the second stage of Maslow's need scale."

"So?" Jack still waited to see a connection to the rest of our rolling conversation of the past hours.

"The immigrants' offspring, our parents and grandparents, in turn had to survive two world wars, and sandwiched between them the biggest, longest economic collapse this country's ever known—"

"Up till now" Jack interjected.

"—so the majority of those earlier generations in America remained in a mode of guarding against scarcity, of forced thrift, delayed gratification and frantically laying up provisions during fat times—"

"Which is what most Americans did over the last half of the 20th century" Jack noted as he began to grasp where I was headed with my history mini-buffet, garnished with a pinch of pop psychology.

"—like by ordering super-sized portions even when their tummies were smaller than their eager eyes." I turned to Uncle Ike, who'd become as still as he had been before his unexpected speech. "The problem is, the kids of those people you said were so good at banding together and starting or building up things, who wanted to secure plentiful comfort—as soon as they could, their offspring got drunk on material goodies during their own pursuit of happiness. If their immediate ancestors couldn't, then by golly the next generations swore to realize the lowest, most basic levels of the American Dream. In short" I paused as a semi-truck full of big-box-store junk cut in front of me, "be careful what you wish for: You might really get it—like a wall-to-wall comfort that numbs the soul, not liberates it."

"So, yaa're saying that Americaans wanted to make lots of money, to realize a big material dream?"

"*Ouch,* Jack" I feigned, "ya got me!" As I saw Christian giggle from the corner of my eye, I continued:

"My mother grew up wearing old sugar sacks, Grandpa and Grandma Thrams were so penniless during the Depression, but as a teen she grew up amidst the biggest boom the country had ever known. That protracted postwar prosperity is what Deb, David and I grew up to expect, too—not to mention Deb's three sons and David's two daughters. Even though our parents became autonomous adults in an age of material plenty and domestic political stability, into their older age they exercised a residual thrift and fiscal caution that we kids never understood and their grandchildren—my nephews and nieces—find downright 'weird.' Now, despite having slogged for over half a decade through the

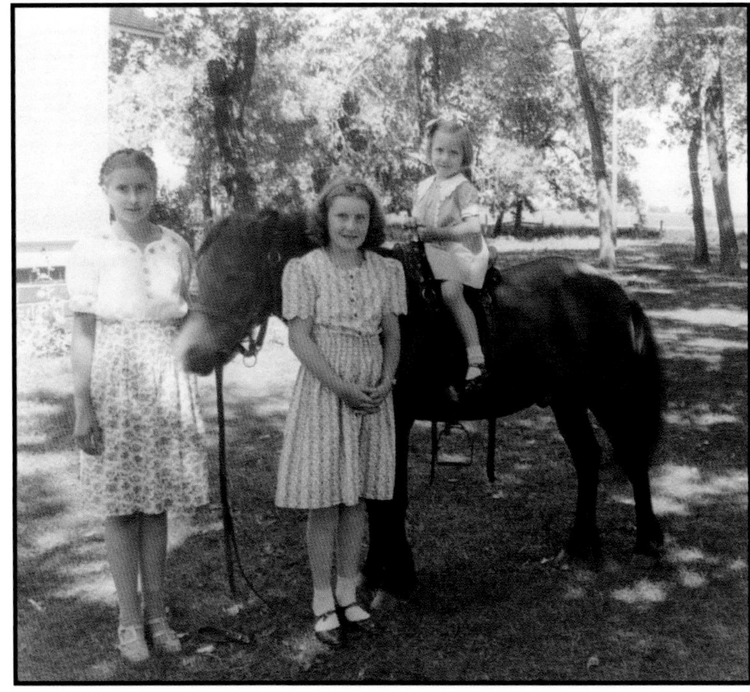

*my aunts Irene Wilma and Dorothy Elaine playing with their kid sister, my mother Phyllis Ann Thrams, on Rex the pony, at Ashlawn Farm; circa 1939*

Great Recession, there are two, three generations of Americans who have known great abundance, who are the products of relative peace and tranquility. Compared to many other countries, even our 'poor' are hardly that."

"Vat ist da problem vit dat?" Christian wondered out loud.

"Our parents and grandparents had reason to move about in a world dominated by getting primary, perhaps secondary needs met—think of the landless Juhls who endured Copenhagen's slums before sailing for 'the moon.' But, the Baby Boomers and onwards who refuse to move into the emotional or even spiritual rungs of the needs-hierarchy scale that Maslow identified remain unnecessarily fixated on the most basic levels of the human experience, of what it means to be fully alive on an plentiful planet. If America's to move forward as a nation" I reasoned, "we have to move upward as individuals, as families, friends and neighbors. We need to wean ourselves, to chase 'having' less and embrace 'being' more. For so long our national obsession has been to collect the most toys possible, but our over-affluence is killing us—and our world. Now that the Chinese, Indians, Latin Americans and even some Africans have made serious down payments on mimicking us, the stakes are too high. The Earth could just manage to carry us, but it cannot carry billions of Earthlings living out the American Way of Life. We gotta change, set new standards, 'cause if we don't none of our families are gonna make it long-term."

"How should we pull *that* off" Jack wanted to know, "and in the shaart time yaa seem to envision?"

"Over the past decades, certainly at least the last 35 years, we've moved farther and farther from each other in this country; we've lost each other and time-tested ties to the communities in which our people have lived. We've cut ourselves from our nation's tap root, that main artery which bound us to one another and to the land that sustained us so willingly, for so long. In our postwar frenzy to get rich—or at least well-padded—we've forgotten deeper, older values that kept us upright despite all that ever happened to us. Now adrift, with most of us seem stuck in some material orgy, obsessed by what's in front of us rather than what's ahead of us, as a nation we are lost."

Once again, Uncle Ike could be heard as he stirred in the back. In the mirror, I could spy some movement but couldn't tell what it was. Then, he recited "Where there is no vision, the people perish."

"So, there have been European settlers in what's now the United States for almost 400 years, right?"

"Correct" Christian nodded, pleased to be able to answer at least one American-history question.

"And when did we and our Allies win the war against the Axis?"

"1945" Christian sang out, visibly enjoying finally being able to contribute to the conversation.

"So, from about 400 years of the American Experience, let's say the first 350 were mostly about setting up the place—sinking roots, establishing institutions, experimenting with democratic structures."

The Verdict of the People *(1854-55), by George Caleb Bingham*

Jack carried on my line of logic with "So, we've been a superpowaa for less than a century, enjoying such widespread mataarial well-being for most of aar people for about the last half-century. So—"

"So" I stole the ball back, "measured against lengths of times spent primarily engaging in one or the other primary activities—providing for the common wealth verses fighting for a piece of one's own—Americans' much longer legacy is that of exploring, experimenting, and of creating, building an external world to reflect what most mirrors our internal one.

Our atomized existence as just consumers is new."

"*That* is our nation's 'tap root'" Uncle Ike proclaimed from behind, "not petty pursuits over pennies. We are our best when we dream" he said, sitting up, "when we lead. I have felt time again" he reflected, looking out over the heart of America, "we know how to be pioneers, how to go where there was no one like us and plant a seed—but now we seem lost, not knowing what to lead ourselves to."

I cringed, thinking of the recent string of films touting interstellar "settlers" who eject from a burned-up Earth just in time to catapult beyond our galaxy to some new, unknown "frontier." *All the energy people put into such fantasies* I thought to myself, *when we should be trying to resettle this planet, which we know can support life, abundantly, rather than to settle some supposed one, which we don't.*

"Without a sense of direction, people drift. We cannot" Ike prophesized, "long sustain that."

"That's what Maslow meant about hierarchical scales" I chimed as I re-emerged from my thoughts. "His concept of 'self-actualization' constitutes an evolution, a progression from lower levels of human existence to higher ones, where more of our neglected potentials can be cultivated, by more people."

"If the nation is in as dire a situation as you suggest" Ike asked, "is this any time to ponder reaching for 'enlightenment?' Aren't there more practical considerations than meditating on spiritual aims?"

"To the contrary" I countered. "We in this country have been preoccupied so long by so little, with material goods and passing pleasures, but securing them hasn't been enough: They neither make us happy nor provide lasting meaning in life. Finding new, more altruistic goals or redefining old values to encompass more compassionate projects are the only means I can think of turning this country around. If we carry on along current trajectories, then we can expect one big, long bloodbath where we all lose."

"Those young men who go into kindaargaartens in Connecticut or crowded cinemas in Coloraado, then shoot dozens of kids—if they aren't lost, then I don't know..." Jack mourned soulfully to himself.

"But those are symptoms, not causes" I rebutted. "And, they are only tips of the iceberg. We've given rise in this country to so much original research, to such bold, innovative thinking over the past couple centuries, yet our young seem to know about and gain so little from it. Maslow's categories of the requisites for 'psychological health' have become generally accepted, even mainstream, yet so much of the population seems hypnotized by what they can accumulate verses what they could experience."

I found it rich when silver-spooned Cousin Jack commented "Getting filthy rich is an old Americaan tradition," then Uncle Ike added "I had no idea, when I brought the Germans' *Autobahnen* home with me that they'd feed the emptying out of our cities and the filling in of our great open spaces."

"We're at a crossroads, gents: We need to decide, what's it going to be? Is the country going to go down in any ugly gunfight as a few try to hoard the best of what remains of an ever-shrinking pie, or are we gonna cook up some new dishes to pass around?"

"You expect a lot of us" Jack warned, to which I noticed in the mirror Ike rock his head in agreement. "You're asking the American people to change, to alter not just how we've been living, but thinking."

"Uncle, do we have a choice?"

"But are we capable of it?" Jack wondered.

"We will be if we truly try" I promised. "Look, of anyone, you two should know what this country's capable of—you, who led millions of young men and women off to war, then broke up dictatorships around the globe. Or you, Jack" I cajoled, "who asked 'Ask not' of Americans so movingly that even I, four decades later, answered your call and served our country in post-communist Czechoslovakia."

"But, that was different" Jack shirked. "The country was different—*we* were a different people then."

Staring into the mirror, I demanded "Were we *so* different? Were we *more* 'worthy' of saving then?"

"And, Hitler" Ike excused absently, "he provided a clear and defeatable target. Now, though, where do we start—who's the 'enemy' and what's the strategy, for which 'battlefield?' I only know that—"

"Watch out!" Christian shrieked as the car drifted onto the shoulder of the road. "*Bist du verückt*!?"

"No, I'm not 'crazy'" I bit back, "but I am stunned to hear two former leaders jus' throw the towel." I glanced back at the men: "What's happened to us? Who've we become? I don't recognize us anymore."

"We had a definable opponent then; we knew what we had to do and had an idea, how to do it."

"What was the cartoon *au courant* then, Ike? 'We've met the enemy and he is us'—or some such?"

Silence. I looked at Christian, who shrugged. I sat up straight and scrutinized the backseat via the mirror until I spotted each of the two men, mutely hugging their respective corners of the back seat.

"Was it something I said?"

*classic Sad Sack (mid-1940s) and Pogo (1971) cartoons that both reflected and defined an era*

"Well" Jack offered meekly, "I think yaa'r mixing up 'Sad Sack,' a popular cartoon figure from The War, with 'Pogo.'" Jack looked to Ike, who knitted his brows, then turned away. "It's like this" Jack said softly: "We waarn't here for Eaarth Day 1970, when that 'enemy' quote first came out in a cartoon."

"Oh, really" Christian asked, "vhere verr you? On vacation?" When neither man responded, he fished "Avay on biz'nez?" Still no response. "On a shoppink trip—a berry, berry long shoppink trip, maybe?"

I knew the answer, but didn't wish to break the spell. So, I abruptly accelerated and announced "Oh, look—there's a rest stop comin' up: Let's pull over for a break!" Seeing that my decoy worked, I sped on.

It was near DeKalb that we left the Ronald Reagan Memorial Highway long enough to make what I wanted to be a pit stop, but Christian insisted become a "sit-down strike." So, we found a booth and sat.

Once we'd bought a drink—only super-sized cups were available—and settled in, Ike asked again "How do you propose that the American people change, to alter how we live and how we think?"

Sucking on my straw, I looked at the cafeteria teeming with compatriots buzzing about, chasing busy lives, and asked instead "At what point do you think our ancestors stopped being German or English, Dutch or Danish or anything else they started out as? When did they—when did 'we'—become 'us'?"

While Jack and Ike didn't even attempt an answer, Christian offered "Vhen dey got off da boat?"

"When you got off that jet a month ago at O'Hare, did you become an 'American'?" I challenged.

"*Nein*, of course not" my cute pharmaceutical-rep boyfriend pushed back. "It's not dat simple."

At that, I offered the following comparisons:

The British established five comparable colonies—those that eventually became the United States, Canada, Australia, New Zealand and South Africa. The settlement and subsequent social development of each varied greatly, yet in addition to being largely English-speaking and dominated by Anglo-Protestant worldviews and values, they retained traits common to "New World" cultures generally, including Latin-lingual dominated ones such as those in Quebec (French), Brazil (Portuguese) and most of the rest of

(Spanish-speaking) South America. Of the five Anglo societies, the U.S. became the least British the earliest, with the greatest cultural diversity at the time of independence.

"Vhy do you dink dat ist?" Christian speculated "Because of da size?"

"Good guess" I granted, "but at two-and-a-half million people in 1776, spread thinly along over fifteen-hundred miles of mostly roadless Eastern coastline, we weren't populous enough to be distinct based only on size. No" I expounded, "we began doing more 'American' things, more frequently, sooner, than our cousins in what became Canada and, in any case, Oceania and southern Africa."

*early "dude" as captured by Martin Thoe, circa 1910*

"*Huh-h-h*? Vhat are 'American' dings?" Christian asked as he swirled the ice in his near-empty cup.

"Well, look at the Luicks" I offered. "Ol' Heinrich was 36 when he thrashed that naughty noble, scooped up his brothers an' all their wives an' kids an' high-tailed it for Rotterdam. When he and his family then set foot on the *France*, in Le Havre, there's no way that the Luicks thought that what would greet them on the other side would even remotely resemble *Schwaben*. They had to have assumed that once they got to a new world—which they presumed would be a better one for them than the one they were fleeing—that they'd have to at least learn another language, if not adopt other trappings of a complete life: a new occupation, other ways of dress and behavior, different food and drink, perhaps membership in a new religious faith, certainly political affiliations unlike they'd ever had or even known." I paused, then added "The act of emigration implies a certain degree of willingness to surrender the person you have been in order to evolve into someone you are not yet, but think that you would like to become. And, by doing so, the life you will have, the world you will build, will be better than is now your lot."

Seeing Jack look at his worn classic of a wristwatch and even Ike faintly drum his thumb and fingers on the table, I accelerated my story, giving the rest more in outline form than as a full account:

"As it turned out, Heinrich, Katherine and even his second wife, Dorothea, seemed to have lived in a German bubble the rest of their lives, there in '*Klein Deutschland*' in Washtenaw County. As soon as they could, they likely found the ingredients to cook mostly Swabian dishes, sought out other Swabians with whom to sing German songs, eventually subscribed to German-language newspapers—but we know they attended German-language church services, enrolled William in a Lutheran seminary and even had their gravestones engraved with German lettering and words. Even in Michigan, then, they did mainly 'German' things, although Heinrich—a farmer and carpenter—surely had contact with Anglos."

"Vas dat diff'rent in Iowa?" Christian astutely wondered as he, too, began to shift in his seat.

"Totally. Henry Junior was 31 when the one-time surveyor returned with his brother, David, and then they fetched their families. 'Beebe' isn't a Germanic name, nor were those of Belmond's other 'first families'—the Overackers, Grays, Dumonds, Jennisons, Culters, Rowens an' all the rest. No, out on the Iowa prairies the Luicks weren't able to sustain doing the 'German' things they'd maintained back in the

Big Woods of Michigan but, rather, now, a generation later and over 600 miles further in-land, they *had* to do mainly 'American' things—things their ancestors *never* had done in old *Deutschland*, like—"

"*Ja*, like vas?" Christian grilled.

"—oh, like interact with Indians, live on cornbread and buffalo meat, dance to frontier fiddle favorites, instigate county-seat wars, convince a railroad to come through their town"—I took a deep breath, then continued my list with—"pan for gold, put down a slaveholders' rebellion, survive locust plagues, join the Ku Klux Klan, fight a Kaiser, split the atom—need I go on?" I asked, to which Christian replied sweetly "*Nein, Danke*."

"Our friends in Canada ate cornbread and buffalo meat, too" Jack contested my theory. "And?"

"But, becoming 'Canadian' took them much longer than it took us to become 'American.' They held on to the Union Jack until I was two, in 1965, and they still have ol' Queen Liz as their head of state. In comparison to our cousins in Oceania, though, the Canadians are downright sovereign: The Aussies still wrestle over whether or not to become a republic rather than a monarchy, but those people just can't find it in themselves to stand on their own. Oh, and they, with their Kiwi neighbors, are still avid cricket and bowls fans, while we North American Anglos invented baseball, basketball and the like ions ago."

Suddenly, our cousin from New England took to his feet and exclaimed "Yaars is a most intaaresting treatise, but I have othaa souls to needle." As his eyes followed an exotic looking young couple with blond dreadlocks, wearing yoga pants and beads, he added "but tell me, quick: If what yaa say is true, about as of what point a person becomes 'Americaan,' what's that got to do with aar mess today?"

"We Americans of European descent—most of us anyway—have only been 'American' for a couple generations, even though our earlier ancestors were this or that ethnicity for hundreds, thousands of years back in the Old World. If anyone 'should' know how to become someone, some *thing* new, it should be us! Our families have undergone this process; it's in our subconscious makeup, in our genes."

At that, tall, lean Jack stepped away from our crowded table and, turning, quoted "My fellow New Englandaar, Henraay David Thaareau, once said 'In the long run, men hit only what they aim at. Therefaar, they had bettaar aim at something high.' So, my fellow Americaans—" and, with that, Cousin Jack disappeared in the direction of the busy, sultry parking lot, apparently in search of more modern dropouts to inspire. As the breeze from his evaporating fast tickled our faces, we three stared at his trail.

Quietly, one by one, we remaining fellow travelers rose, floated out the door and into the steaming car. This time, Christian and I insisted that old Ike drop his stiff frame into the front seat, which he finally did. Only after we'd rejoined the whizzing traffic did Ike speak: "So, how do you propose—"

"Isn't it obvious, Uncle?" I brushed his repetitive question off, once again. "The people who our people became, after they left Europe and replanted our families here, reflected their times, a horse-and-buggy world that was. Problem is, the things we later 'Americans' strove for, we've mostly

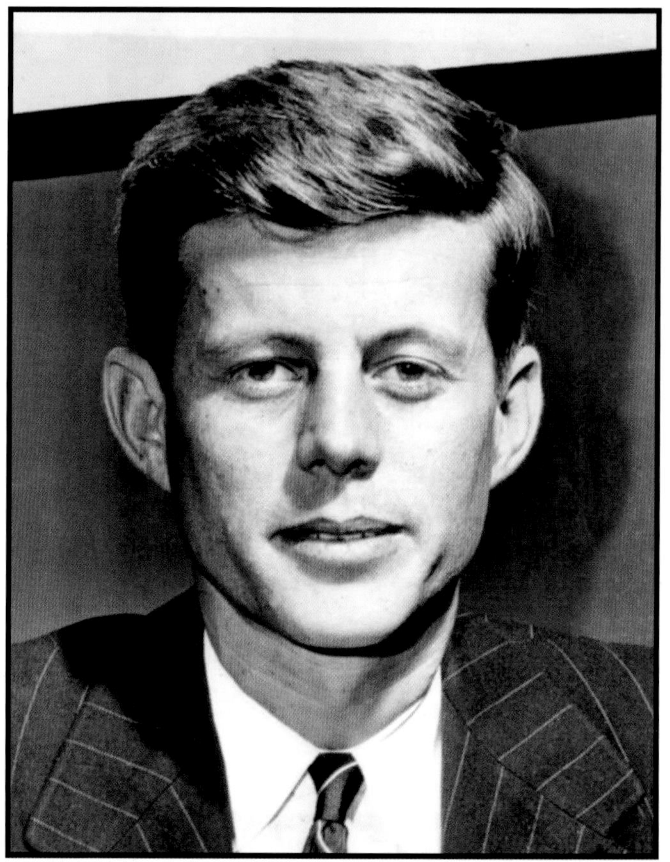

*Cousin Jack was a cool and compelling, but also cunning man.*

attained, but now find that same plush comfort is killing us. Still, most of us seem loathe to separate ourselves from exactly that which has become more destructive than constructive. Too many of us are willing to sacrifice the future of our planet—of our children and their children—in the name of sustaining a set of systems that not only are not functioning optimally, but that few of us believe in or even want around. We're so addicted to our comfort that we can't, we don't wanna see another way."

For the too-many-eth time, Ike asked "What do you propose we do about the problems we face?"

"Why do you always ask *me*? Why do *I* need to know? Isn't that part of the problem? We've all become so accustomed to being served, to consuming what someone else has started or built, but we've forgotten how to solve problems ourselves—or, we've lost the will to do so." Startled by my reaction, Ike stared at me for a moment. "I'm sure Barack Obama's a clever man, an interesting fellow—a great beer mate for an evening: May riveting conversations *never* end! But, isn't he also the product of some hidden kingmakers—the same who churned out Jimmy Carter, Ronald Reagan, Junior Bush—"

"And, me, too" Ike mouthed under his breath.

"What's that, Uncle?" I tested what I'd already assumed. "What'd ya say?" I drilled as I drove slower to fit the suburban "Chicagoland" traffic snarls I could see coming ahead.

"I was a Mennonite farmboy from Kansas, then a West Point cadet-cum-general. I'd never held office—but do you think that gave any of them pause? No, I think they liked me even more due to that."

"Gave any of who pause, Ike? Who were 'they' every time?"

"Yes, well, who do you think?" he shot back, looking at this lap. "The same ones who put Ulysses Grant in the White House after the Civil War, a century earlier. The same ones who brought Woodrow Wilson out of the lecture halls of Princeton, and Harry Truman out from behind his haberdashery cases—the same ones who always sit at the top, but behind a curtain, pulling the strings. The thing is, they always expect something back; they always want to be paid for the favor of having made you the most powerful person on the planet—at least for a while, till they find and roll out the next marionette."

"Oh, I see" was all I could muster for a moment. Christian looked at me, waiting for a cue.

"It's all just a show, you know" Ike said. "The real power holders aren't those they shove out front."

After a few moments, I opined "Despite our ardent hopes, we've seen that Obama's not his own man. Oh, I don't mean to imply he's 'evil' or even sinister—he can't be that bad: He and Michelle send their two girls to a Quaker school, after all—but he didn't fund running for office with bake sales! Clearly, he belongs to the handlers who bankrolled the most expensive campaigns in the history of the world. The banks, the—"

"—the oil and the insurance companies, the armaments manufacturers, the—"

"—computer and internet firms, the lawyers' guilds, the—" I continued until Ike interrupted me.

"Every interest imaginable except that of the American people" Uncle Ike sighed.

"I drank the Kool-Aid, too, Uncle. I saw Barack speak live four, five times, in Iowa and in the Twin Cities. I heard Michelle talk" I counted, as I pulled out to pass a lumbering bus, "a time or two, too."

"Did you?" Christian marvel. "Vhat vas dat like, to be dere vit dem?"

"Of course, it was intoxicating. The audiences were always charged, the energy electric, the moment singular—but it always came to an end, we always left and emerged out into the sobering light of day."

"Did you vote for Obama? I mean, how vas dat—da feeling, to be part of so a moment in 'istory?"

"Sure, I arrived at the polling station half an hour before it opened—an' found a line already over a block long. Tears came to my eyes as I stood and wondered 'Is this the same country I grew up in?' Me, great-grandson of a KKK activist!" I breathed. "Who wasn't inspired by the significance of that day? Even Mom and Aunt Dorothy, lifelong Republicans, voted for the man, along with ever-Democrat Aunt Irene. No matter how history remembers his administration, Barack Obama has blazed a trail long overdue."

"What changed, then?" Ike asked as he turned and looked me straight in the eye. "The majority of the voting electorate chose to put a Negro in the White House—and this time in the Oval Office, not the butler's pantry. It was supposed be a turning point in American history—"

"And it *was*—but it wasn't enough."

"What would have been 'enough?'" Ike demanded. "The people chose, the republic endured."

"But that's just it—this *form* of 'republic' endured, a form forged in the day of sailing ships and whale-oil lamps, a form no longer commensurate to the culture we live in. How can over 300 million people look to *one* man or *one* woman to institute 'change we could believe in?' What we've seen the past half-decade has been the worst bastard child of waiting for a messiah, crossed with consumerist entitlement: 'I traded in my vote for you; you won; now *you* gotta deliver change.' How should that ever work? That's what's wrong with this country: We know how to consume, but have forgotten how to create, how to converse with each other, reach consensus, to cooperate to reach common goals, and—"

"—*that* is the tap root that needs to be sunk again" Ike declared, to which Christian nodded, smiling. Seeing my boyfriend's shining face, he cautioned "But don't think it'll be easy. Jack was right: We have two parties that have been bought and sealed up tight. You won't penetrate them very easily or soon."

*Harper's Weekly cartoon of 7 November 1874, with the caption: "An Ass, having put on the Lion's skin, roamed about in the Forest, and amused himself by frightening all the foolish Animals he met with in his Wanderings"—Shakespeare of Bacon; by Thomas Nast*

"OK" I spouted off the cuff, "then we won't—and we shouldn't even try." Both men peered at me, perplexed. "If we can't beat 'em, then let's walk away. It's as simple as that! Trying to muster the forces to take them over—even if we resist being corrupted by the same greed virus that has infected almost every knight with a lance who's charged them before—will only consume inordinate amounts of time and energy, neither of which we can afford wasting on the outdated or irrelevant. So, instead of trying to move two massive parties, let's throw a thousand, or even hundreds of thousands, of mini-parties." I slammed the steering with my right hand and shouted "That's *it*! We'll divest from dinosaurs that think they're lions and simply let them die out for lack of new blood. Once they're extinct, we won't even miss 'em!"

By this point, both Christian's eyes that I could see in the rearview and Ikes's betrayed incredulity.

"The timid or benighted can put their heads in sand if they want" I warned, "but if we're to stop doing what we've always done, then we gotta start doing things we've never done before. We gotta stop propping up Midwest party hacks with our 'lesser of two evils' ballots just as urgently as we gotta stop propping up Middle East oil sheiks with our gas dollars, *if* we want to withdraw from the madness."

"*Bravo*" Ike literally applauded for a few seconds from the front side seat, but then stopped abruptly. "There's one thing, however, for which you, in all your oratory, have forgotten to account" he noted.

Now having to keep my eyes on the increasing number of kamikaze Chicagoland drivers, I couldn't look at Ike but motioned to him with one hand, palm up. "Lay it on me, Uncle: What might that be?"

"If I understand you correctly, young man, you wish to convince your compatriots to move away from representative democracy and ease—"

"—make that 'jump,' actually."

"—jump into participatory democracy. Is that correct?"

"Well, we do live in an era of digital hookups, instant messaging and the like—not of town criers and hand-printed broadsheets, like when this experiment in self-governance all started."

"So, you desire that your fellow Americans take more responsibility for how the country is run."

“We left the crowns of Europe behind for a reason, you know. Why should we have told the king of Württemberg where to get off, just to carry the yoke of some self-selected dark knights in Washington? We were serfs in the Old World, but we’re supposed to be ‘citizens’ in the New—aren’t we?”

“As I was saying—”

“—and as I was saying, I don’t feel safe living in a populace that let’s others call the shots, where we all become drudges or guns for hire. I want to live in a land of equals again, where we all have a say.”

“That’s all fine and good, but there are some in this great land of ours who don’t want that.”

“Are you talking about ‘them’ again, Uncle?”

“Indeed.”

“*Hum-m-m*” I fretted, “I see what you mean. Those are the ‘they’ you keep referring to—right?” Ike’s balding head bobbed to the affirmative. “Are they also—”

“Yes, the same ones that I mentioned the night before I handed over the reins to young Jack.”

“Oh” I exhaled, dumbly. “I guess we do have a challenge ahead of us, huh?”

”You see” Uncle Ike began to explain as he inched forward on his seat, “we have a shadow that hangs over this country—maybe always has—but in the last half-century has taken on a hunger for power and a tenacity that likes things just the way they are, with the people distracted by hollow theater and circus rather than busied with genuine exchange and consensus. As long as the people continue to tolerate it, though—”

*Even on sunny days, dark clouds hang over the American landscape.*

“—it’ll continue?”

“Exactly.”

“Well, I guess we gotta roll up our sleeves and get to work, *huh-h-h*? ‘The only way out is through!’”

“If you remember my farewell address, I spoke about the soul of the nation, about how it was endangered by unseen, uncontrollable forces” Ike recalled. “Now, those forces have the upper hand.”

“We really are speaking about the ‘soul of America,’ aren’t we?” Ike nodded slowly but firmly. “Either ‘we the people’ live for the moment, enabling obscured figures to steer the country, to get rich selling us junk food and junk bonds, junk mortgages and junk values, or we decide we’ve had enough and will not endure our self-prostitutionalization any longer. These questions are central to self-governance.”

Christian asked Ike “Vill de people be able to see vhy dey vill gain from taking part in de process?”

“We are not discussing here solely the self-respect of our people, but of their self-preservation. Yes, Americans should reclaim our country out of principle, but it need not be only an abstract act: There are pragmatic reasons to seize the fate of America and restore it to sanity, stability and sustainability.”

Christian and I waited—the hockey-puck traffic conditions all around us kept me distracted, anyway—but when Ike didn’t continue, the fresh-faced German boy asked “*Und* vhat are dey?”

“The well-being of all we care about—our families, friends, homes, neighborhoods, the very survival of everything we value. I don’t understand it” I *tsk-tsk*ed as we watched a motorcyclist roar alongside us, then swerve between two trucks and disappear on the other side. “We Americans take so many steps for ‘security:” we buy insurances of all kinds, we install alarms and cameras, we have an emergency plan for almost any contingency, some with cellars stocked for Armageddon—and increasing numbers carry guns shopping or to school. Yet concerning the most basic things—the quality of the air we breathe, the food we eat, the weather raging outside our doors—we shrug our shoulders, neglect the problems year after year as conditions deteriorate, and wait for some miracle to take place.”

"Amerika's goink to need a 'miracle' if it's to turn avround planetary vetter trends" Christian fretted.

"True self-governance" Ike interjected, "necessitates two capabilities among our people. One is the ability to take responsibility for one's own being—the ability first to see a need, then to seize the commensurate opportunities to involve oneself in stilling that need, to secure one's own well-being."

"So" I induced, "to lobby on behalf of one's best interest, to set about getting one's material and emotional needs met adequately at present or, even better, on an on-going basis?" Ike nodded a *Yes*.

"Und de udder avility?" Christian prodded the old man up front.

"The other is measured, respectful self-assertion, to make clear to others what one is willing to do, or not, and what one is willing to tolerate, or not."

*"Oh-h-h"* I moaned, "we're not doin' so hot on that score." Ike glanced at me, searchingly. "We're almost to O'Hare now, Uncle, and ironically we're back to the base comparison where we started when you got in the car—Germany. When Cousin Jack was listing all the institutions that have gotten 'big' in the past two hundred years, I realized that along with everything else, big media only arose in the past century or so, too. The Nazis, for one, learned early on how to use it skillfully for their own purposes—"

"Did dey ever" Christian chimed in.

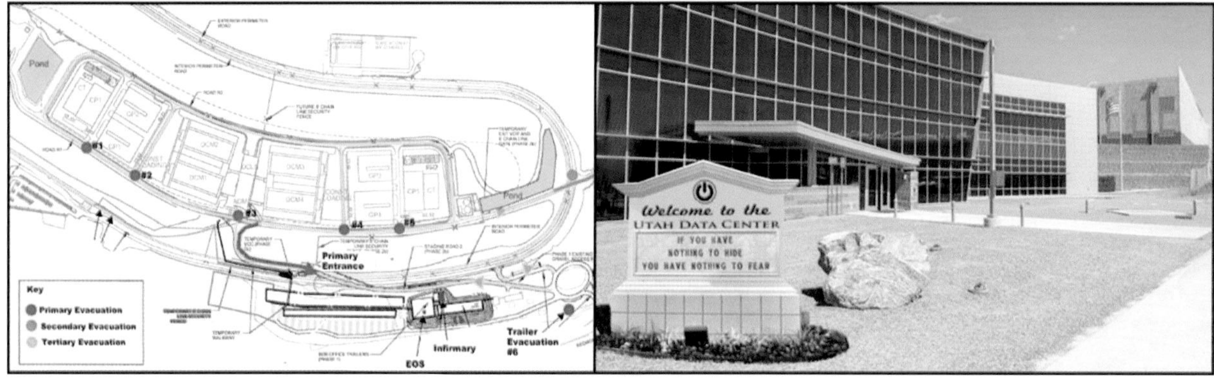


*interior and exterior designs for NSA's Utah Data Center at Camp William near Bluffdale, completed 2014*

"—as did the clique that replaced them in the East, the communists. It's a modern problem" I bemoaned, "that won't go away: Jus' look at the NSA's mega-spying Utah Data Center! We tolerate government agencies that have perfected surveillance to intricate levels like the Gestapo and Stasi in a thousand years never could have dreamt of. What are they doing with all that endless information?"

"Their motto" recited Ike, who oddly seemed to know everything about everything, "claims that 'If you have nothing to hide, you have nothing to fear'—"

"But vat person vill decide dat?" Christian begged to discuss. "Vhich peoples are dey *und*—"

"Who elected them?" I interrupted in turn. "If 'they' decide you do have something to hide, are 'they' going to call an investigation? If so, who will be allowed to appear with you, if anyone—and, later, who may even know that an investigation has taken place? Damn" I scowled, "this whole thing stinks."

At that, no one said anything for a few moments, as we'd reached a debilitating low point.

Then, Christian smiled broadly as he blurted out "If it stinks, it must be cheese!"

Unable to turn my head from traffic jam thickening ahead of us, I could only glance at him in the mirror and shrug. *What the...* I thought to myself, yet found enough grace to merely ask "Excuse me?"

*"Ja*, in Germany, da most delicious cheese *ist* ready only vhen it stinks. *Und, der Wein ist* ready also only after it has—" he grappled to find the right work, "vhen it has..."

"'Aged'" I offered, "like oil paintings or plaster of Paris. Are you saying that all fine things take time?"

*"Ja*, Germany hat many hard times, so many dark dings happened to people. Ve hat so long, so much var, so much fights und sick people vit bad power. Our cities vere destroyed, our money vithout value. But today, our cuntree *ist gut*; we are doink vell *und* ve have a *gut* future for us. If ve hat not hat da—"

"—if you had not had the dark, you wouldn't have been able to see the Light: Is that what you want to say?" From the corner of my eye, I saw Uncle Ike nod, approvingly, as if he, too, had just understood something present all the time, but which none of us had not been able to see so clearly. "These shared moments, these national experiences—they're all like compost" I extrapolated, "or like all that tall grass over ten thousand years that fell every fall, decaying and making a deep bed of rich prairie soil. Or—"

"—or like slavery, or early urban sweatshops, recurrent wars against the Indians, the long hate of the Irish and all things Catholic, or the rantings of that rabid Joe McCarthy" Uncle Ike added. "Yes, America has had dark spells, too—but always overcame them, somehow taking what was learned forward to help master the next hurdle. Today's challenges are great—but such trials can also breed greatness."

*Martin Thoe once again captured America incarnate.*

"But, Uncle" I protested, "was America ever so rudderless like at present? I have my serious doubts."

"There have been periods of drift before, even if less essential than this one. But as your Teutonic friend so poignantly testified" Ike pointed to Christian, "Germany—the ancestral home of so many of us Americans—has struggled for its very existence, repetitively, for most of the past two thousand years. We are a young nation, no longer the economic engine nor the land of unlimited possibilities we once were. Just as the Germans had to learn to overcome their collective lowest angels, so must we learn to vanquish our own. It will take time, but every nation weathers such storms. Question is, to what end?"

"If there's no real change after an era of furor, no good was served" I ventured, "but, if something of genuine substance endures at the end, then perhaps all that went lost along the way was not in vain."

"It's up to America" Ike warned, "whether the trials ahead will forge a new national resolve, or fray it further. In the past, the country pulled together in the face of external threats; how it will respond to internal ones, to our blind spots, self-imposed limits, fears or greed is unwritten. As we are as a people, so will we be as a nation. Over the past decades, we've not lived up to our own ideals, let alone others'."

"As the boy said, the Germany of today is the envy of the world—which was not the case for at least half a century following the Nazi debacle. But the Germans have tried on so many different systems, so many contrasting ways of organizing a society. At times their societal hammering about has had brutal consequences, but they now know firsthand the fruits of hate and war, of dictatorship or violent force." I looked over my shoulder for a fleeting moment, then said to Christian as I drove off the freeway and on to the access road to the car-rental realm just outside O'Hare Airport, "Who would have ever thought?"

"Ve nebber dreamt ve vould someday be free—but it has happened *und wir lieben es*, we love it."

At that moment, Uncle Ike leaned over and tapped me on my lower arm, glued to the steering wheel. "Just pull over here, young man" he ordered. "I'll get out and find my own way from now on."

"But, Uncle" I began to protest as I pulled over under a well-lighted underpass, "how—"

"Do not worry for me, America" he cut me off. "You have too much to do, cleaning up your mess, to fret about a onetime leader. I had my day; I took my chance: Now it's up to you to have yours: Take it!"

With that, the old man flung open the car door and then, like a vapor, vanished into the August air.

As Christian sprung into the front and closed the door behind him, I smiled as I spied in the rearview mirror ol' Ike grin broadly, then flash us a victory sign as I pulled away from the curb.

As of that moment, Christian and I fell into a mindless routine I knew too well: return rental car, shuttle to the right terminal, endure endless security lines, slam down a bottle of spring water, scurry to our boarding gate. All the while, though, my mind was anything but empty: Rather, it was preoccupied.

*Uncle Ike was an affable, empathetic man —out of the public eye.*

I had flown to Europe from this very airport, for the first time, in June 1980, as an Iowa farmboy on a church-youth tour of the Old World, where I had no idea I'd one day live. Now, I was leaving the New yet again, for the umpteenth time, with Christian, born behind a now-vanished Iron Curtain. As we took out our tickets and waited to pass the the last control, I looked around—and out a big floor-to-ceiling window, over the flat, Midwestern horizon. I smiled, thinking of ol' "Mad Bobcat" Henry Luick and his frontiersman-trapper-in-the-making brother David crossing the same plains, by foot, headed for Iowa, where, a little more than a century later, I'd become "me."

"Sir" the young woman called out, "are you ready—can I *please* see your passport and ticket?"

For a second, my mind returned to boarding, to numbly coalescing with my removal from the region I so love, but then turned to peer—for now, for a last time—out over the American Heartland.

*My father, Bud Luick, holding my sister Debra; Jack & my aunt Eleanor (Thrams) Hunt; my mother's aunt and uncle Bernice (Reid) & Williard Thrams; Phyllis (Thrams) Luick; my aunt Irene (Thrams) & Thurman Floyd, my grandfather, Elmer Thrams; (front row) Marcia & Terry Hunt; twins Steven & Cindy Floyd; late summer 1955 at Ashlawn Farm*

For a moment, I was not sure if the dry-throated sentimentality already settling upon me had to do with missing my family and friends, or a country we once inhabited but no longer recognize as our own.

"Sir" the shrill voice repeated, "are you ready—or do you *need* something to board the plane?"

"A 'need'" I echoed, "I'm not sure if it's a 'need'—but I sure do *want* our country back some day!"

With that, I scaled the boarding bridge to the jet plane waiting to return me to Germany—for now.

———

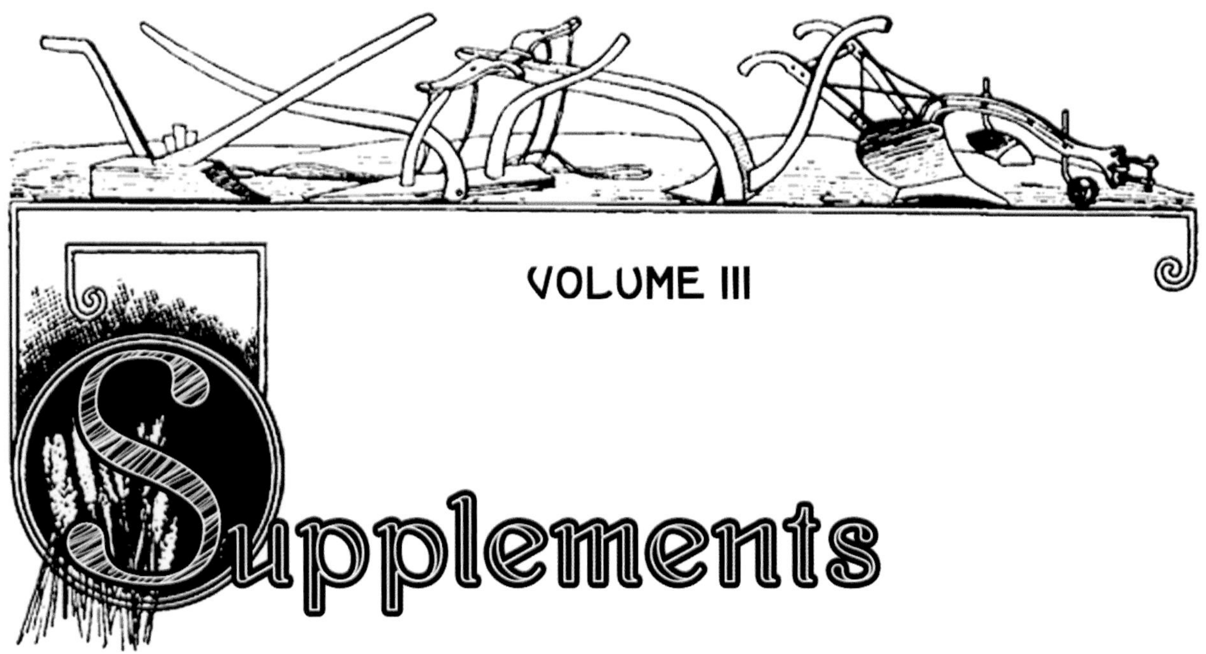


**President Dwight Eisenhower's farewell address**

*— adapted from Wikipedia, "the free encyclopedia;" accessed 14 July 2015:*

Eisenhower's farewell address (referred to as "Eisenhower's farewell address to the nation") was the final public speech of he gave as President of the United States, delivered in a televised broadcast on 17 January 1961. Best known for advocating that the nation guard against the potential influence of the military–industrial complex, a term he is credited with coining, the speech also expressed concerns about planning for the future and the dangers of massive spending, especially deficit spending, the prospect of the domination of science through Federal funding and, conversely, the domination of science-based public policy by what he called a "scientific-technological elite."

Eisenhower served as a president for two full terms (eight years), and thereby was the first U.S. president to be term-limited from seeking re-election again. He had overseen a period of considerable economic expansion, even as the Cold War deepened. Three of his national budgets had balanced, but spending pressures mounted. The recent presidential election had resulted in the election of John F. Kennedy, and the oldest American president in a century was about to hand the reins of power to the youngest elected president.

**The speech:**

As early as 1959, Eisenhower began working with his brother Milton and speechwriters, including the President's chief speechwriter Malcolm Moos, to develop his final statement as he left public life. It went through at least 21 drafts. The speech was "a solemn moment in a decidedly unsolemn time," warning a nation "giddy with prosperity, infatuated with youth and glamour, and aiming increasingly for the easy life."

> As we peer into society's future, we – you and I, and our government – must avoid the impulse to live only for today, plundering, for our own ease and convenience, the precious resources of tomorrow. We cannot mortgage the material assets of our grandchildren without asking the loss also of their political and spiritual heritage. We want democracy to survive for all generations to come, not to become the insolvent phantom of tomorrow.

The only general to be elected president in the 20th century, he famously warned the nation about the potentially corrupting influence of the "military-industrial complex". This is frequently characterized as a criticism of the arms industry. He in fact declared such an industry to be necessary. His concern was of its potential for corruption:

> Until the latest of our world conflicts, the United States had no armaments industry. American makers of plowshares could, with time and as required, make swords as well. But we can no longer risk emergency improvisation of national defense. We have been compelled to create a permanent armaments industry of vast proportions. Added to this, three and a half million men and women are directly engaged in the defense establishment. We annually spend on military security alone more than the net income of all United States corporations.
>
> Now this conjunction of an immense military establishment and a large arms industry is new in the American experience. The total influence — economic, political, even spiritual — is felt in every city, every Statehouse, every office of the Federal government. We recognize the imperative need for this development. Yet, we must not fail to comprehend its grave implications. Our toil, resources, and livelihood are all involved. So is the very structure of our society.
>
> In the councils of government, we must guard against the acquisition of unwarranted influence, whether sought or unsought, by the military-industrial complex. The potential for the disastrous rise of misplaced power exists and will persist. We must never let the weight of this combination endanger our liberties or democratic processes. We should take nothing for granted. Only an alert and knowledgeable citizenry can compel the proper meshing of the huge industrial and military machinery of defense with our peaceful methods and goals, so that security and liberty may prosper together.

He also expressed his concomitant concern for corruption of the scientific process as part of this centralization of funding in the Federal government:

> Akin to, and largely responsible for the sweeping changes in our industrial-military posture, has been the technological revolution during recent decades.
>
> In this revolution, research has become central, it also becomes more formalized, complex, and costly. A steadily increasing share is conducted for, by, or at the direction of, the Federal government. [...]
>
> The prospect of domination of the nation's scholars by Federal employment, project allocation, and the power of money is ever present and is gravely to be regarded.
>
> Yet in holding scientific discovery in respect, as we should, we must also be alert to the equal and opposite danger that public policy could itself become the captive of a scientific-technological elite.

**Legacy:**

Although it was much broader, Eisenhower's speech is remembered primarily for its reference to the military-industrial complex. The phrase gained acceptance during the Vietnam era and 21st-century commentators have expressed the opinion that a number of the fears raised in his speech have come true.

*button from 1952 Eisenhower presidential campaign*

———

**President John Kennedy's 1963 American University commencement address**

— *adapted from http://www.jfklibrary.org/Asset-Viewer/BWC7I4C9QUmLG9J6I8oy8w.aspx:*

The ceremonies, held at the John M. Reeves Athletic Center in Washington, D.C., began earlier than expected, so network cameras missed the first half of the President's prefatory remarks. In his speech, Kennedy asked the graduates to re-examine their attitudes towards peace, the Soviet Union and the Cold War, famously remarking, "If we cannot end now our differences, at least we can make the world safe for diversity." He also announced that he, Soviet Premier Nikita Khrushchev and British Prime Minister Harold Macmillan had agreed to hold discussions concerning a comprehensive nuclear test ban treaty. Finally, he explained that the United States would not conduct atmospheric nuclear tests on the condition that other countries uphold this same promise. Some historians have argued that this speech put Kennedy at odds with the so-called military-industrial complex warned about by his predecessor, Dwight Eisenhower—and therefore spelled his demise in Dallas later that same year.

> I have [...] chosen this time and this place to discuss a topic on which ignorance too often abounds and the truth is too rarely perceived—yet it is the most important topic on earth: world peace.
>
> What kind of peace do I mean? What kind of peace do we seek? Not a Pax Americana enforced on the world by American weapons of war. Not the peace of the grave or the security of the slave. I am talking about genuine peace, the kind of peace that makes life on earth worth living, the kind that enables men and nations to grow and to hope and to build a better life for their children—not merely peace for Americans but peace for all men and women—not merely peace in our time but peace for all time.
>
> I speak of peace because of the new face of war. Total war makes no sense in an age when great powers can maintain large and relatively invulnerable nuclear forces and refuse to surrender without resort to those forces. It makes no sense in an age when a single nuclear weapon contains almost ten times the explosive force delivered by all the allied air forces in the Second World War. It makes no sense in an age when the deadly poisons produced by a nuclear exchange would be carried by wind and water and soil and seed to the far corners of the globe and to generations yet unborn.
>
> Today the expenditure of billions of dollars every year on weapons acquired for the purpose of making sure we never need to use them is essential to keeping the peace. But surely the acquisition of such idle stockpiles—which can only destroy and never create—is not the only, much less the most efficient, means of assuring peace.
>
> I speak of peace, therefore, as the necessary rational end of rational men. I realize that the pursuit of peace is not as dramatic as the pursuit of war—and frequently the words of the pursuer fall on deaf ears. But we have no more urgent task.
>
> Some say that it is useless to speak of world peace or world law or world disarmament—and that it will be useless until the leaders of the Soviet Union adopt a more enlightened attitude. I hope they do. I believe we can help them do it. But I also believe that we must reexamine our own attitude—as individuals and as a Nation—for our attitude is as essential as theirs. And every graduate of this school, every thoughtful citizen who despairs of war and wishes to bring peace, should begin by looking inward—by examining his own attitude toward the possibilities of peace, toward the Soviet Union, toward the course of the cold war and toward freedom and peace here at home.
>
> First: Let us examine our attitude toward peace itself. Too many of us think it is impossible. Too many think it unreal. But that is a dangerous, defeatist belief. It leads to the conclusion that war is inevitable—that mankind is doomed—that we are gripped by forces we cannot control.
>
> We need not accept that view. Our problems are manmade—therefore, they can be solved by man. And man can be as big as he wants. No problem of human destiny is beyond human beings. Man's reason and spirit have often solved the seemingly unsolvable—and we believe they can do it again.
>
> I am not referring to the absolute, infinite concept of peace and good will of which some fantasies and fanatics dream. I do not deny the value of hopes and dreams but we merely invite discouragement and incredulity by making that our only and immediate goal.

Let us focus instead on a more practical, more attainable peace— based not on a sudden revolution in human nature but on a gradual evolution in human institutions—on a series of concrete actions and effective agreements which are in the interest of all concerned. There is no single, simple key to this peace—no grand or magic formula to be adopted by one or two powers. Genuine peace must be the product of many nations, the sum of many acts. It must be dynamic, not static, changing to meet the challenge of each new generation. For peace is a process—a way of solving problems.

With such a peace, there will still be quarrels and conflicting interests, as there are within families and nations. World peace, like community peace, does not require that each man love his neighbor—it requires only that they live together in mutual tolerance, submitting their disputes to a just and peaceful settlement. And history teaches us that enmities between nations, as between individuals, do not last forever. However fixed our likes and dislikes may seem, the tide of time and events will often bring surprising changes in the relations between nations and neighbors.

So let us persevere. Peace need not be impracticable, and war need not be inevitable. By defining our goal more clearly, by making it seem more manageable and less remote, we can help all peoples to see it, to draw hope from it, and to move irresistibly toward it.

[...]

*Former President Dwight Eisenhower and then-current President John Kennedy met to confer with military advisors in Camp David, Maryland, on 22 April 1961. Despite their fine speeches, both men remained hostages held by... [?]*

**disclaimer:**

Growing up on that farm on the Iowa prairie, my brother and I shared the same parents, grandparents, cousins, etc. We toiled with the same sweat-streaked neighbors during harvests. We sat at the same initial-etched desks at Clear Lake High, listening to the same teachers and, on Sundays, sat on the same stiff pews at our people's Methodist church, enduring the same dry sermons. We wore many of the same clothes, but because David is five years older I often snuck into school clad half a decade behind the times. Despite our common childhood culture, however, we became wildly different people. Were he to tell our shared familial tale David, for one, would write a markedly different account. And, it's good so.

This book, then, is my subjective investigation of why our family is the way it is. As any detailed story requires a central character or theme to hold it together, I and my decades-long searching serve as the literary glue of this telling of a story belonging to dozens. I apologize here if my siblings and cousins find their experiences omitted or different from mine: Blame "literary necessity" if you must, but trust that no conscious malice was intended.

Although written about a specific family tree that germinated in Europe, then was transplanted into New World soil almost four hundred years ago, I offer this as a case study for reflection on and edification for *all* families, *everywhere*. My research into this specific lineage began back in the late 1970s, when as a teen touched by the American Bicentennial my hunger to know my own roots led me to interview more than fifty relatives, family friends, former farmhands, etc. It found even earlier form, however, in the genealogical siftings of (to name just three) sweet Nelda (Ehrhardt) Talman, crazy cousin Cloe Jenison and devoted Albert Lee Luick—and, prior to that, in late-19th-century chronicles about then-recent pioneers compiled by amateur, market-driven "historians."

My research continued over the intervening decades, then resumed with a flourish during the first five months of 2014 as I wrote the first draft of this tome about my father's house. Internet-accessible data channeled via instant electronic connectivity uncovered both a quantity and rawness of records unknown to this budding family raconteur forty years ago. I reconnected with photo-endowed Gary Luick and met smart, astoundingly productive third-cousin Tony on-line through this project and know the latter only through emails and phone calls. Together, we've amassed so much and such disparate material that the planned combined-lineage book by necessity broke into three separate-but-intertwined stories. At times, the vastness and variety of the traces we found of who my people had been over four centuries overwhelmed my ability to integrate them into one coherent account. Most factual mistakes are mine; all are unintentional. Any misguided interpretations of findings are non-malevolent; any false conclusions arise from sincere attempts to understand both visible as well as masked dynamics.

## acknowledgments:

**primary sources:**
**[alive during 2014-15 research]**

Anthony Luick
Barbara (Jones) Noonan
Craig Sale
David Luick
Debra (Luick) [Wass] Junker
Dennis Olesen
Don Jacobsen
Gary Luick
Iris (Glaser) Luick
Jan (Jacobsen) Gobeli
Janet (Gullickson) Dahlby
"Jeandelle (Luick) Olesen"*
Jeanette (Jones) Bram
Jennifer Allen
Joan (Pruisner) Troe
Jochen Luick
Lois [Luick] (Juhl) Kraemer
Margrit (Luick) Gregorius
Marie (Neuberger) Miller
Mary (Luick) Shaw
Michael Thrams
Paul Juhl
Peggy (Jones) Lettow
Phyllis (Thrams) Luick
Rainer Luick
Richard Rhode
Richarda (Luick) Grözinger
Sebastian Fattorini
"Sheranne (Luick) Joyns"*
Steve Luick
Steve Gardner
Sue (Jacobsen) Meints
Tim Jenison
Tim Jennison
Virgil True, Jr.

* names altered out of respect for privacy

***[deceased since 1970-'80s research]***

*Albert Luick*
*Bertha (Hadsall) Juhl*
*Carl Hansen*
*Charlotte (Juhl) Luick*
*Cloe Jenison*
*Cleo (Juhl) Gullickson*
*Eric Kew*
*Ernest Campbell*
*Ethel (Luick) Tuttle*
*Gerald Allen*
*George Luick*
*Hans Jacobsen*
*Jean (Luick) Jackson*
*Lorraine (Luick) Jones*
*Luwarren "Bud" Luick*
*Marion (Luick) Smith*
*Mattie (Luick) Farmer*
*Maude (Fuller) Moorehead*
*Olga (Hansen)[Christensen] Luick*
*Roger Jennison*
*Velma (Luick) Jacobsen*
*Winnie Campbell*

***secondary sources:***
***[researchers authors or editors]***

*Alan Nothnagle*
*Belinda Sidabutar*
*Ceile Hartleib*
*Christian Mämecke*
*Dale Herter*
*Dianne (Ziskin) Siegel*
*Florentina Purwokinanti*
*Issa Dabain*
*Issam Dabass*
*Jörg Seiler*
*Kai Mämecke*
*Kerstin Bellmann*
*Pat (Larsen) Schultz*
*Rafat Beirat*
*Stephan Krause*
*Sue (Rattay) Hicks*
*Terry Stollsteimer*
*Ulrike Bürgel*

***[other sources of support]***

*Christian Willno*
*Holm Wehmeyer*
*Karin Kohler*
*Sally Curtiss Campbell*
*Thomas Mulford*

***readers***

*Aisha Ahmad*
*Annelee (Soelch) Woodstrom*
*Becky Sturm*
*Doug Alderfer*
*Eberhard Fuhr*
*Elizabeth (Dorsey) Hatle*
*Georg Schiefer*
*Helen Gunderson*
*Jayne Traendly*
*JoAnn Burgess*
*Karen (Lloyd) Luick*
*Konstanze Fabian*
*Leighton Siegel*
*Linda Luick*
*Michael Gehrig*
*Patrick Valentine*
*Rick Plewa*
*Roy Woodstrom*
*Salomea Genin*
*Sherry (Pancoast) Hutchison*
*Stefan Crawcour*
*Stefan Ritter*
*Warren Jones*


---

## footnotes and sources of images

Due to printing-costs considerations, the footnotes and image registry planned for inclusion here are, instead, available elsewhere, gratis. Copies of them will be posted for the foreseeable future at www.roots.TRACES.org as well as will be offered as reposits to the state historical societies of: Illinois, Indiana, Iowa, Kansas, Michigan, Minnesota, Missouri, Nebraska, North Dakota, Ohio, South Dakota, ansd Wisconsin.